ATLANTIC COMM. COLLEGE

UP FROM WASHINGTON

UP FROM WASHINGTON
William Pickens and the Negro Struggle for Equality, 1900–1954

Sheldon Avery

Newark: University of Delaware Press
London and Toronto: Associated University Presses

© 1989 by Associated University Presses, Inc.

All rights reserved. Authorization to photocopy items for internal or personal use, or the internal or personal use of specific clients, is granted by the copyright owner, provided that a base fee of $10.00, plus eight cents per page, per copy is paid directly to the Copyright Clearance Center, 27 Congress Street, Salem, Massachusetts 01970. [0-87413-361-0/89 $10.00 + 8¢ pp, pc.]

Associated University Presses
440 Forsgate Drive
Cranbury, NJ 08512

Associated University Presses
25 Sicilian Avenue
London WC1A 2QH, England

Associated University Presses
P.O. Box 488, Port Credit
Mississauga, Ontario
Canada L5G 4M2

The paper used in this publication meets the requirements of the American National Standard for Permanence of Paper for Printed Library Materials Z39.48-1984.

Library of Congress Cataloging-in-Publication Data

Avery, Sheldon, 1936–
 Up from Washington : William Pickens and the Negro struggle for equality, 1900–1954 / Sheldon Avery.
  p.   cm.
 Bibliography: p.
 Includes index.
 ISBN 0-87413-361-0 (alk. paper)
 1. Pickens, William, 1881–1954. 2. Afro-Americans—Bibliography.
3. Civil rights workers—United States—Biography. 4. Afro
-Americans—Civil rights. 5. Afro-Americans—History—1877–1964.
6. United States—Race relations. 7. Civil rights movements—United States—History—20th century. 8. National Association for the Advancement of Colored People—History. I. Title.
E185.97.P593A95 1989
973'.0496073024—dc19
[B]   88-40467
                                                                                                  CIP

PRINTED IN THE UNITED STATES OF AMERICA

To Evelyn, Peter, Daniel,
and the memory of
Celia Avrutzky and Jack Gross

CONTENTS

Preface		9
1	Up from Washington, 1881–1914	15
2	"The New Negro," 1914–1919	35
3	The Field Secretary and "The Emperor of Africa," 1919–1927	51
4	The Reluctant Republican, 1920–1928	75
5	The NAACP Comes of Age, 1920–1931	89
6	Pickens, the Communists, and the Scottsboro Boys, 1926–1933	112
7	New Deal or "Old" Deal? 1933–1940	135
8	A War on Two Fronts, 1934–1942	159
9	The Last Battle, 1943–1954	181
Notes		200
Works Cited		233
Index		241

PREFACE

Gunnar Myrdal, in his major 1944 study, *An American Dilemma: The Negro Problem and Modern Democracy*, wrote, "Negroes can never, in any period, hope to attain more in the short-term power bargain than the most benevolent white groups are prepared to give them." Because of their powerlessness to effect racial change without white support, Myrdal added, "Negroes seem to be held in a state of eternal preparedness for a great number of contradictory opinions—ready to accept one type or another depending on how they are driven by pressures or where they see an opportunity." Myrdal was writing about the race as a whole, but his thesis was valid also in describing the attitudes, actions, and programs of the race's leaders, especially those militant black activists who were committed to the goals of racial equality and social integration and who, until recently, had to follow the difficult course between militancy and accommodation, between principled protest and expediential compromise, between those changes demanded by their people and those that whites would accept. Therefore, the life of a nonradical black activist, or "race man," more than of any other reformer, was filled with paradoxes, frustrations, disappointments, and personal sacrifices, sometimes including that of life itself.

Throughout its history the black leadership of the National Association for the Advancement of Colored People (NAACP), has consisted of a group of race men who generally achieved a balance between agitation and conciliation. This study is a political biography of William Pickens (1881–1954) who, along with W. E. B. Du Bois, James Weldon Johnson, and Walter White, helped make the NAACP the Negro's most effective civil rights organization.

Pickens was an important race leader between 1915 and 1945, a period that has not received adequate attention from historians of black America. He was a product of the rural South and, although he was a Phi Beta Kappa graduate from Yale (class of 1904), he had an unsophisticated but effective rhetorical style, which made him, between the first and second world wars, one of the most popular black orators in America. As field secretary and, later, director of branches of the NAACP (1920–40) and, finally, as director of the interracial section of the Treasury Department's Savings Bonds Division (1941–50), Pickens came into more direct contact with the Negro masses than any other black leader of his time. He was also, from 1919 to 1940, a prolific and provocative contributing editor of the Associated Negro Press (ANP), which was the nation's leading Negro news-distributing service. In his weekly articles, which appeared in more than one hundred black newspapers across the country, he chronicled and commented on most of the events that Negroes were concerned about.

He serves well as a model to test Myrdal's thesis because Pickens, in a long and active career as a race man, often found himself caught between conflicting approaches to the race problem. As the title of this study suggests, Pickens, in joining the NAACP in 1909, broke with the leading black accommodationist, Booker T. Washington. But as NAACP field secretary, he often clashed with the Association's leadership on important issues, such as the Garvey movement, the Communist challenge, the New Deal and, finally, the Negro's proper response to World War II. Pickens was often the center of controversy, in part because he was an impulsive, dynamic, and, at times, self-serving man, but also because of the perils and frustrations that were part of the daily life of a race man, and because of the resultant tensions and rivalries that existed within the black protest movement. A subsidiary theme of this study is the internal discord and deep personal animosities that existed inside the NAACP between 1920 and 1940 and that threatened to undermine the organization's effectiveness.

Two major sources for this study are the NAACP Papers, at the Library of Congress, and the William Pickens Papers, which, at the author's request, Pickens's daughter, Harriet Ida Pickens, deposited at the Schomburg Collection of the New York Public Library. The Pickens Papers include his personal correspondence with leading figures, both white and black, in the civil rights and other reform movements, material related to the work of the NAACP, and original manuscripts of Pickens's speeches, newspaper columns, and magazine articles. They cover the years 1914–54 but are most comprehensive for the period between the first and second world wars.

Whatever value this study has was inspired by William Pickens, who lived the life and saved its record; John Hope Franklin, who taught me to love history and seek objectivity in writing it;

Kenneth Porter, who proved by example that whites could write fairly about blacks; Tom Govan, who, along with Drs. Franklin and Porter, insisted that black history be written within the framework of American history; and my wife, Evelyn, who read every word, commented wisely on every chapter, and made the whole enterprise worthwhile.

UP FROM WASHINGTON

1
UP FROM WASHINGTON, 1881–1914

> It was a dangerous road he had to travel between the white and the black races, both of them sensitive and suspicious of any new movement along the color line. The leader of a minority people in such a situation is like a tight-rope walker, with very interested observers and resentful and threatening voices on both sides of him. It is a great tribute to his skill when he does not fall to his destruction on one side or the other.
> —William Pickens on Booker T. Washington, 1934

Booker T. Washington, the principal of Tuskegee Institute in Alabama, was, in the decades from 1895 to 1915, the most influential Negro in America. Living at a time historian Rayford Logan has called "the nadir" of the free Negro's status in American society, Washington was willing to accept temporary second-class citizenship and social segregation for his race if, in exchange, they could enjoy greater educational and economic opportunities. As an outspoken advocate for vocational education, laissez-faire capitalism, Christian morality, and middle-class values, Washington had wooed and won the support of wealthy white men, such as Andrew Carnegie and John D. Rockefeller, thus securing for himself the key to the Negro's philanthropic treasure chest. President Theodore Roosevelt invited him to dine at the White House and recognized him as the dispenser of Negro political patronage. By skillful management of these economic and political levers, Washington became the most powerful black man in American history. Some blacks, generally called "radicals," criticized Washington's accommodationist approach to the race question, but most Negro leaders recognized his great power and influence and refrained from publicly challenging his leadership. However, by 1910, many black leaders were forced to choose between Washington and the radicals. William Pickens, an instructor at Alabama's Negro Talladega College, joined with the radicals and, in so doing, launched his career as a black activist.

Booker T. Washington was always looking for intelligent, articulate, and right-thinking young blacks to join his staff at Tuskegee. In 1903 he detected a potential recruit in William Pickens, a southern-born Negro student at Yale University and the first of his race to win the coveted Ten Eyck Prize for oratory. Washington sent the twenty-one-year-old junior majoring in foreign languages, a congratulatory letter, to which Pickens replied: "Thank you for your favor. . . . Yes, by hard work I outstripped my 37 competitors. I am glad to be able to do some little thing that will help us."[1]

Pickens's prize-winning address, "Misrule in Hayti," a discussion of the history and problems of the only black republic in the Western Hemisphere at the time, was essentially an accommodationist tract, supporting the prevalent attitude among whites that blacks were incapable of self-government. "Down to the present day," Pickens had said,

> there has been nothing constant and uniform in Hayti save revolution and decline. . . . We will not be so severe in our judgment or so sweeping in our conclusion as to call it a demonstration of the incapacity of the *negro* race for self-government; but it is complete historical proof of the inability of any *uncivilized* race for maintaining a civil community with no outside constraining force. . . . The savage and the child to rise to higher things must feel the power of a stronger hand.

The American Negro, in Pickens's view, was "centuries ahead of his Haytian brother," because of the "special blessing" of white, Christian civilizing influences. "As the case stands now," young Pickens concluded, "the intervention of some outside power [into Hayti] is imperative. . . . The subjugation of the island by . . . America would be an act of kindness."[2]

A decade later Pickens, more mature and independent, renounced the views expressed in "Misrule in Hayti," but in 1903, because of this address, he was drawn into the conflict between Washington, the chief black accommodationist, and William Monroe Trotter, the Tuskegeean's leading critic. Trotter, militant editor of Boston's Negro weekly, *The Guardian*,[3] accused Pickens of being "the first Negro ever to have won . . . oratorical honors at Yale by surrendering his self-respect, sacrificing his pride, emasculating his manhood, and throwing down his race."[4] Trotter saw in Pickens's address the "slavish servile and sycophantic" approach to race relations of Washington and his followers. He belittled Pickens's achievement, pointing out that other blacks had won distinction at Yale, and added, "This uncouth and provincial Pickens is the first Negro at Yale who blindly accepted the white man's estimate of the Negro."[5] It was "Anglo-Saxon policy" Trotter insisted, "to single out and honor as a genius the Negro who wallows in the mud and mire of American prejudice."[6]

Trotter, who had difficulty maintaining a sense of proportion on the race issue, even made a racial slur about Pickens's appearance. "A glance at this Negro freak," Trotter wrote, "with his enormous lips, huge mouth, and monkey grin, . . . makes one wonder that Pickens does not go further in his race attack."[7]

Trotter's editorial barrage against the young student reflected his passionate disapproval of Washington. He knew little about Pickens, but, because of the accommodationist tone of the Ten Eyck address, he suspected him of being a "Bookerite," and vented his anger on the alleged disciple. Two months later, the Boston *Guardian* editor had an opportunity to confront Washington himself. On the evening of 30 July Washington appeared before an audience of two thousand "of the better class of Boston's colored residents" at the First African Methodist Episcopal Zion Church. Trotter, his sister Maud, and several other anti-Bookerites were in the audience prepared to embarrass Washington with questions from the floor. Before Washington could even begin his address, Granville Martin, a Trotter supporter, began shouting questions at the Tuskegeean. Policemen were brought in, and as they were removing Martin, fights broke out in the audience. One man was stabbed, cayenne pepper was tossed upon the platform, and a number of spectators broke for the exits. During the melee Trotter rose and shouted some questions at Washington, but in the confusion he could not be heard. After Trotter and his sister were removed from the hall and arrested, order was restored and Washington delivered his speech. In the aftermath of the "Boston Riot," as it came to be known, Trotter and Martin were tried and convicted of disturbing the peace and were both sentenced to thirty days in the House of Correction.[8]

Washington wanted Trotter and his coeditor on the Boston *Guardian*, George Washington Forbes, punished further for their part in the Boston incident, as well as for their consistently virulent opposition to his leadership.[9] The Tuskegeean knew of Trotter's editorial attack on Pickens and asked Wilford H. Smith, a Negro lawyer from New York, to persuade Pickens to bring libel charges against the *Guardian* editors. "By all means Trotter and Forbes must be muzzled," Smith replied, "and at once. Just as early as possible I shall go to New Haven [to see Pickens] and exert my best endeavors to bring it about."[10]

Smith was able to convince Pickens to bring suit against Trotter and Forbes. After a warrant was issued and a trial date was set, however, Pickens hesitated to follow through with the prosecution. He knew that he was a pawn in a power struggle between groups representing two divergent approaches to the race question. He also learned that Trotter and Forbes planned to retaliate by having him arrested on a fabricated charge—leaving Massachusetts while owing a civil debt—and he did not relish the prospect of appearing in court as a defendant.[11] Furthermore, W. E. B. Du Bois, the eminent Atlanta University scholar who was moving toward an alliance with Trotter against Washington, wrote to Pickens's former mentor, G. W. Andrews, the white president of Talladega College, asking him to get Pickens to drop the libel suit. Du Bois informed Andrews that Pickens was being used as a "cat's paw" by Washington against Trotter and Forbes. Andrews replied that he thought Pickens would drop the charge if the Boston *Guardian* printed an apology.[12]

Forbes, fearing conviction, overruled Trotter, who was still in prison, and published, in the *Guardian*, an apology dictated to him by Pickens's lawyer. As a face-saving device, Forbes claimed that the retraction came only after Pickens had repudiated his remarks on Haitian misrule. Pickens, relieved that he was no longer caught in a crossfire between Washington and Trotter, accepted the qualified retraction and dropped the charges.[13] Had he pressed the suit he might have permanently alienated the radicals, as Washington's critics came to be known. On the other hand, he knew Washington would be disappointed that Trotter and Forbes had escaped prosecution. He wrote to the Tuskegeean, reassuring him that he had accepted the apology without recanting anything.

> I see that the good gentlemen are very skillful at assigning beautiful and innocent reasons for having to swallow their own scandal. Men who have to resort to such hypocrisies should accuse no one of inconsistency or make-believe. I sincerely hope that they are yet capable of learning from the experience.[14]

Had Pickens, in 1903, been forced to fully commit himself either to Washington or the radicals, he probably would have supported the Tuskegeean. He knew Washington could help an ambitious and talented young black man get ahead, and that opposing the Negro leader might destroy his career before it even began. For example, at the same time that Pickens was pressing charges against Trotter and Forbes, he had been engaged in extensive negotiations with Washington for a teaching position at Tuskegee.[15] But Pickens also accepted many of the tenets of Washington's race philosophy: the importance of hard work and self-discipline, the emphasis on economic progress, the need to work with the better class of white people, and the acceptance of an accommodating and gradualist approach to improved race relations. Furthermore, young Pickens strongly identified with Washington's personal struggle to raise himself from humble origins to a place of prominence.

Although Pickens, unlike Washington, had been spared the humiliation of having been a slave, both his parents were among those freed by the Emancipation Proclamation. Born on 5 January 1881, "according to the recollection" of his parents, in Anderson County, South Carolina, William was the sixth of ten children and the first son. His maternal grandfather, who probably died a slave, was half-Cherokee Indian; his maternal grandmother was "a characteristic little African," who lived for forty years with a broken back, the legacy of her years in bondage. Pickens's mother, Fannie, was a "brown" woman; his father, Jacob, was "dark-skinned, dark-and-woolly haired."[16] William himself was quite black, with a high forehead, protruding brow, flat nose, and thick lips.[17]

His father, in many ways a remarkable man, greatly influenced young Pickens's development. Jacob Pickens, of average height, but of powerful build, escaped being brutalized into passivity by the poverty and racial exploitation that were part of everyday life in Anderson County. He preferred tending bar and managing a local white hotel in Pendleton to tenant farming, the occupation of most blacks in the area, because, although wages were small, they were "paid promptly, and there was no binding debt." Furthermore, his children could get better schooling, since "the landowner would not tolerate a tenant who put his children in school in the farming season."[18] Jacob was a faithful Baptist and superintendent of the village Sunday school. He also served as the "henchman" of Ben Dacus, a white leader of one of the rival political factions that dominated Pendleton. As Dacus's man, he often had to prove his prowess as a fighter.[19]

When hard times hit Anderson County, a planter's agent induced Pickens's father to sign up as a tenant-farmer and to take the family to Arkansas. The move, made in 1888, proved to be disastrous. After the first year's settlement of accounts with the planter, Jacob was deeper in debt than on the day the family first arrived. "And who could deny it?" William Pickens later wrote. "The white man did all the reckoning. The Negro did all the work." As a young man, Pickens often remembered hearing a rhyme popular among the black tenant-farmers and sharecroppers of Arkansas's "bottom lands."

> A nought's a nought, a figger's a figger
> All for de white man—none for de nigger.[20]

After a second year of "debt slavery," the enterprising elder Pickens found a landowner in Little Rock, Arkansas, willing to advance enough money to enable him to rent a small farm and cover moving expenses. Upon his return, the family packed their few belongings and, during the night, escaped from their trap of unrewarded toil.[21]

The Pickenses settled in Argenta, across the river from Little Rock. The children were kept out of school for a year to help pay off the debt, but the following year, 1891, ten-year-old William resumed his studies, "not to miss another day for the next seven years." Young Pickens relied on his excellent memory to get to the top of his class. "I learned my lessons verbatim every day," he wrote, "so that I could repeat them, just as they were written, with as much ease as I can say the Lord's Prayer."[22]

When Fannie Pickens died at age forty in 1894, Jacob was hard pressed to keep the family together. William helped out by working for forty cents a day before and after school as a "skiff ferry man," crossing the Arkansas River between Argenta and Little Rock. He remembered years later how a friend of the family repeatedly criticized his father for allowing his able-bodied son to attend classes while the father worked overtime to make ends meet. Although the extra money William might have brought in was sorely needed, Jacob Pickens never seriously considered keeping his son from school.[23]

Since Argenta did not have a black high school, William, with the endorsement of his principal and forty dollars saved from his labors, applied for admission to the Negro high school in Little Rock. When he easily passed an oral examination administered by the Little Rock principal, William was ecstatic. "What a critical moment was passed; what a vista was opened for me! Three more years of schooling were assured.[24]

Young Pickens continued to excel in school and was chosen to deliver the valedictory for his graduating class of 1899—the eighteen-year-old's first experience in public speaking. He also passed the state teacher's examination, but, determined to continue his education, won his father's approval to pass over the opportunity to earn forty or fifty dollars a month. A black Congregationalist minister in Little Rock had heard Pickens deliver the valedictory and suggested that the young orator apply to his alma mater, Talladega College. When Pickens wrote to the Alabama school, the clergyman added his personal recommendation.[25]

The response from G. W. Andrews, Talladega's white president, reached Pickens in the Arkansas wilderness, where he and his father were construction workers on the "Choctaw" railroad. "Your frank and interesting letter has been received," Andrews wrote. "I cannot say definitely now, but write to say you can have hope." With nothing more than that "hope" and fifty dollars saved from his job, Pickens trekked the five hundred miles from Little Rock to Talladega, Alabama, and presented himself to an astonished and impressed Mr. Andrews. After testing the candidate's scanning of Virgil's *Aeneid*, Andrews enrolled him in the sophomore class.[26]

Talladega College was a product of post–Civil War philanthropy. What had been a school for white boys, built by slave labor in 1852, was converted, in 1867, by the Congregationalist American Missionary Association (AMA), into a Negro college.[27] Typical of AMA schools, Talladega's white president and predominantly white faculty were primarily concerned with training young blacks to be good Christians and to use their talents to help uplift the race. Many of the school's graduates became either congregationalist ministers or teachers.

Pickens studied the traditional liberal arts curriculum and majored in foreign languages. He also discovered a new church—the Congregational—with which he could identify. Ten years later he wrote:

> I believed in God and the Church, and had always been a most faithful worshipper, but I could not dream dreams and see visions. Without dreams and visions no one was allowed to join the average Negro church of the past. . . . At last I had found a church which did not require that I visit hell . . . and make a narrow, hair-raising escape.[28]

During his first year at Talladega, Pickens won an oratorical contest and was sent with four student singers and a white teacher, J. M. P. Metcalf (who later became president of the college) on a fund-raising tour of several border and northern states. The nineteen-year-old student was deeply impressed by his first experience out of the deep South and he considered his prize-winning speech "the doorway" to his future.[29]

In the summer of 1900, Pickens made the second of several trips north, speaking before AMA meetings in Tennessee, Kentucky, Ohio, New York, Massachusetts, and Connecticut.[30] At each gathering the young orator delivered his prize-winning speech, "Negro Evolution," which was designed to please conservative white Christians concerned with Negro uplift, and that expressed the same kind of accommodationist sentiment as the Ten Eyck address he would deliver three years later at Yale. Pickens said:

> Ever since the days of Egyptian civilization, one of the most fruitful quarters of God's sunlit earth has been peopled by a race void of the right conception of a common faith or an eternal life. It was from such a condition of life that Providence caused many thousands to be transported to a land where, in immediate contiguity with civilization, three centuries would develop more Christian character than a millennium of missionary work could effect in their native jungles.

Since, under slavery, the transported African's mind was allowed to develop to a certain level and no further—"to approach . . . so near to God and no nearer"—one might think that man, for a time, had surmounted the divine plan." "Not so!" reasoned young Pickens. "When we consider the preponderance of dross that needed to be burned from this metal, the ages of bad influences that needed to be purged out of this savage blood, we are compelled to bow our heads in humble recognition of the great wisdom of God."

Having delivered this rationalization for southern slavery, Pickens went on to suggest that Providence then turned to the nonslaveholding North to complete the civilizing process. He praised the AMA as a "providential accident, which helped complete the work begun by northern arms." Among blacks, he added, "the word Northland is synonymous with freedom and justice, and Yankee means philanthropy.". . . There is a large element, principally southern, that favors the limiting of the Negro's education to manual training. . . . But to these the American Missionary Association schools are offering that conclusive argument which Philip presented Nathaniel—'Come and see.'"[31]

"Negro Evolution" can be interpreted in several ways. It may represent the sincere thoughts of a young black Christian, grateful to white philanthropy and anxious to please his benefactors. Pickens may have rationalized away slavery, so that his audience, relieved of a sense of collective guilt, would make generous contributions to the institution that produced such a fine young man. Finally, his contrast between North and South, and between vocational and higher education, may reflect an ambivalence, an uneasiness, with the accommodationist approach, an unwillingness to leave the race question entirely in God's, or the South's hands. It is not surprising that a nineteen-year-old black college student, especially one with Pickens's experiences in the North, would have, and express, ambivalent feelings about his race's destiny. It must be remembered, too, that Pickens was making a public address and it is always difficult to divine an orator's convictions from his rhetoric.

"Negro Evolution" and its author were everywhere well received. When Pickens and the other touring students from Talladega visited ex-President Benjamin Harrison's summer camp, several guests were surprised that Negroes could perform and deport themselves so well. The young orator was impressed with the goodwill of his white northern patrons, but he noted, nevertheless, they "had a very inadequate idea of the real capacity of the American Negro." The tour netted one thousand dollars for Talladega.[32]

The AMA invited Pickens to speak, in October 1900, at its annual meeting in Springfield, Massachusetts. On the train to Springfield he met Booker T. Washington for the first time. The Tuskegeean, who was also to address the AMA meeting, graciously shared his Pullman compartment with Pickens and treated him "with such kindly consideration that I was asked by passengers if I was not Mr. Washington's son."[33]

On another of his northern ventures Pickens visited Yale University. He was enthralled by the New Haven school. "I had seen Yale," he wrote ten years later, "and had actually looked upon its elms, its ivies, its outer walks. From that day the audacious idea began to take me that I must push my educational battles into its gates."[34]

Because of his excellent academic record at Talladega and the numerous contacts he made with prominent whites on his northern trips, Pickens had little trouble getting into Yale. Dean Henry P. Wright equated his three years at Talladega to two at Yale, and admitted him, in the fall of 1902, into the junior class.[35]

One of less than a dozen black students at Yale, Pickens seems to have made the transition smoothly. He had few friends among his classmates but many well-wishers. Several prominent whites, who heard about Pickens from friends in the AMA, sent him cash gifts. After the Christmas examinations he was classified an A student, which exempted him from paying tuition, and, when he won the Ten Eyck Prize, he was able to give up a part-time job in the YMCA kitchen. He performed so well in his major field, foreign languages, and in his other studies, that, in his senior year, he was accepted into Phi Beta Kappa. Pickens thought that he was the first of his race admitted into the Yale chapter of Phi Beta Kappa, but at least one other black, Edward Alexander Bouchet of the class of 1874, had been so honored.[36] Nevertheless, it was a great personal triumph for Pickens.

With graduation approaching, Pickens made plans for his future. A young Phi Beta Kappa graduate from Yale, normally, would have had a broad range of career opportunities to choose from. If he were poor, some of those options would be closed to him; but if he were poor and black, he had a very limited choice, indeed. Pickens briefly considered an offer from a New York speaker's bureau to make a three-year lecture tour of the United States and Europe. A Negro with a sound education, a "New England" accent, and a gift for oratory was a novelty that many on both sides of the Atlantic would pay to see. His decision to decline "show-lecturing" was based on two factors. The Negro poet, Paul Lawrence Dunbar, whom Pickens had met in Chicago, strongly advised against such a world tour. Dunbar had previously accepted such an arrangement and found the experience distasteful and degrading. Moreover, the offer conflicted with the young graduate's sense of mission. Acutely aware that he was a privileged member of his race, Pickens believed the Negro "of brains and character must not only feel responsible for his individual conduct, but must have interests amounting almost to a sense of responsibility for the rest of his race."[37]

Since he had little interest in the ministry or business, Pickens turned to one of the few remaining careers open to an educated Negro—teaching. In January 1904 Washington offered him a position at Tuskegee. "While the renumeration is not very large," he wrote, "I think you will find it a good beginning and there will be other considerations that may make up somewhat for the smallness of the pay."[38] Pickens knew the advantages of working with Washington, but he was pressed by the AMA to return to Talladega. "It does seem," Dean Wright of Yale had written, "as if [the AMA] had a right to hope for some aid from you in doing the more advanced work which the Society has wisely instituted."[39] Having chosen to return to Talladega, Pickens wrote Washington, "While my whole preference was for Tuskegee, I have decided that there is a greater need at my own college."[40]

Whether at Talladega or Tuskegee, Pickens had decided on a teaching career, in part, from necessity, but also because of his strong identification with his race. "The work of education," he later wrote, "seemed to offer a greater field of usefulness to a Negro than any other profession. . . . Back to the south was my inclination. That section of the country is big in the destiny of the American Negro, and therefore with the future of the Negro race in the whole world."[41]

When Pickens returned to Talladega in 1904, he still seemed very much under the influence of Washington's approach to race relations. In an article for an AMA journal he wrote:

> Ask him [President Andrews of Talladega] if there has been progress in the condition of the Negroes, and he will relate the vice, the poverty and the ignorance of 1874, and then point to the hundreds of young men and women, many of them children of alumni, with such neatness of dress and alertness of mind as would gladden any Christian heart and give hope to any race. Ask if there has been progress in the good will of the whites, and he will relate how that thirty years ago the private homes of Talladega teachers must be guarded and patrolled like military posts, and then refer to the fact that the whites of the present day make special contributions to the institution, while their pastors and professional men accept invitations to lecture, address and advise the Negro students. Reasoning thus on the facts of the past, he claims the right to expect just as much of the same sort of progress and change within the next thirty years.[42]

Despite these sanguine phrases about Talladega, the young instructor harbored some doubts about Washington's program. Although Pickens recognized the Tuskegeean's accomplishments and influence, especially with white leaders, he began to question Washington's emphasis on vocational education as well as the Negro leader's unwillingness to tolerate other blacks' points of view. Pickens hesitated to express these reservations because he was still relatively young, inexperienced, and unsure of his position, both at Talladega and within the Negro leadership. Nevertheless, when Du Bois called upon black intellectuals to speak out against all forms of racial discrimination, Pickens supported his "Niagara Movement."[43]

In mid-July 1905, twenty-nine black leaders, including Pickens, met in Fort Erie, Ontario, near the Canadian side of Niagara Falls, to formulate a program aimed at implementing the rights granted to Negroes by the Reconstruction amendments. The platform of this Niagara Movement demanded rights that Washington thought unattainable for several generations—manhood suffrage, abolition of all caste distinctions, and recognition of the principle of "human brotherhood."

Pickens considered the Niagara Movement "the first national movement of colored people with a primary regard for their equal citizenship."[44] Although the Niagarans generally refrained from direct attack on the Tuskegeean, their demands for "an unfettered and unsubsidized press," for greater opportunities in higher education, and for constant and militant protest against all forms of racial discrimination, challenged Washingtonian practices.[45]

Pickens, like many other blacks who endorsed the goals of the Niagara Movement, hoped it would not be necessary to sever relations with the Tuskegeean. J. M. Murphy, editor of the Baltimore *Afro-American-Ledger*, best expressed the view of those who worked with Du Bois, but would not reject the work of Washington. "Dr. Washington stands for every principle enunciated by the Niagara Movement," Murphy wrote, "only he wisely leaves the leadership along certain lines to those better qualified than himself. . . ."[46] "Both [approaches] need emphasis," he added, "and certainly we ought to be able to do it without seeking to belittle the most illustrious member of the Negro race in the World." Murphy appreciated Washington's precarious position and understood why he was "exceedingly careful in his public utterances" on suffrage and civil rights. "While we ourselves feel perfectly at liberty to be more radical than Dr. Washington," Murphy wrote, "we doubt whether, if we had passed up to the position held by him, we would be less cautious in such utterances than himself."[47]

It was soon apparent, however, that Washington would not tolerate a movement that rivaled his leadership, challenged his tenets, and, as he saw it, threatened to undermine the progress made by the race since the Civil War. He used his considerable influence with black editors to have the press either ignore or criticize the movement; he sent spies to report on Niagaran meetings and also counseled influential whites to withhold funds from the militant organization.[48] By his opposition to the Niagara Movement, Washington forced a number of Negroes to choose between himself and Du Bois's group. His heavy-handed attempts to crush the opposition may have angered independent-minded blacks like Pickens, who would have preferred to work with both camps. Years later Pickens recalled supporting the movement because it brought together "the few liberal-minded Negro men who, in that perilous time, dared to have thoughts of their own . . . and who were foolhardy enough to run the risk of the great crime of being called 'radicals.' "[49] The Niagara Movement, as a separate organization, accomplished none of its goals, but it provided a forum for those who felt constrained by Washington's leadership or impatient with his accommodationist approach, but who were unwilling or unable to oppose him. Once the Tuskegeean was openly attacked, it became increasingly easier to do so, especially after 1905, when his power began to wane.

Despite isolated attacks by radicals such as Trotter and Du Bois, the Tuskegeean's power remained undiminished until that protest was broadened and amplified by the formation of the Niagara Movement. The following year, 1906, two events—the Atlanta "riot" and the Brownsville "affray"—raised doubts among blacks concerning the wisdom of Washington's approach. In Atlanta, contrary to Washington's assumptions, white mobs attacked not only Negro "riff-raff," but prominent black residents who had worked for years for racial harmony. After an alleged battle between Negro soldiers and white residents of Brownsville, Texas, President Theodore Roosevelt, with whom Washington was closely identified, dishonorably discharged, without benefit of trial, all the members of three Negro companies of the Twenty-fifth Regiment. Furthermore, it became increasingly apparent that southern blacks were rapidly losing whatever political and social rights they had left without any appreciable gains in economic opportunities.[50]

Between the establishment of the Niagara Movement in 1905 and the Atlanta riot of 1906, Pickens moved gradually into the anti-Bookerite camp. He did not become a Niagaran (no blacks in Washington's home state of Alabama officially joined the movement), but Pickens wrote a number of articles for the pro-Niagara *Voice of the Negro* during this period. The *Voice*, a black monthly journal edited by J. Max Barber, lasted only four years (1904–7), but it was "easily the most outstanding Negro magazine of the period."[51]

Pickens, in his *Voice* articles, never attacked Washington by name, but made veiled critical references to the Tuskegeean by using such code words as "level-headed" Negro and race "leader." For example, in April 1905, several months before the Niagarans' first meeting, Pickens wrote with obvious sarcasm:[52]

> Has not every "wise" white man and every "level-headed" Negro in the land declared that no black man should darken the threshold of higher learning until the whole race has some wealth and high type of character? It does not occur to them that it is equally reasonable to say: Nobody shall touch water till the majority can swim and none should see ice till all can skate.

By January 1906 Pickens was sounding like a Niagaran. "Every intelligent Negro in the country," he wrote in the *Voice*, "who is worthy of American citizenship, has, as one of the main objects of his existence, the attainment by himself and his race 'equal manhood rights' with every other race in this republic;—Equality, industrial, social and political. . . ."[53]

Four months before the Atlanta riot, Pickens's philosophical identification with the Niagara Movement was complete. He analyzed for the *Voice* the position of the Washingtonians and the Niagarans on four major issues: economics, politics, education, and social equality. These were the questions "affecting the very highest and deepest interest of the Negro race in America, questions which every intelligent and self-respecting Negro should weigh in his own mind. And he must choose."[54]

On economics, one camp (the Washingtonians, but not named by Pickens) argues, "Seek ye first the almighty dollar, and after its acquisition all things will be added thereunto." The other camp (the Niagarans) respond, "The dollar is of little avail in the absence of civil and political rights." On politics, the Washingtonians according to Pickens, say: "Take no thought of the ballot. There is nothing in America so useless as voting. Become wise and rich first and that meaningless privilege—citizenship—will follow as the shadow the substance." The Niagarans reply; "The ballot is your most powerful auxiliary in the fight for education and wealth." On education, the Washingtonians argue: "Learn to work (i.e., with your hands) and be useful for the present. Men plowed before they wrote poetry." Pickens has the Tuskegeean's critics answer: "Learn everything; true independence for the race can result only from diversified attainment. . . . What glory is there in being merely the pack-animals of civilization?" Finally, on social equality, the Washingtonians advise: "Quietly accept the imposition of inferiority. It is a lie, but just treat it as the truth for the sake of peace." A Niagaran responds: "I ask for nothing more or less than the liberty to associate with any free man who wishes to associate with me.... Color has absolutely no virtue for me, and however much I am outnumbered, I will not retreat one inch from that principle."55

After presenting both sides of the argument, Pickens made his personal choice clear. "It is the worst kind of folly," he wrote, "for the Negro race to think of resigning its political destinies to the good graces of Time, Fate and the white man. The very things which they tell you to get first and then vote are the very things which to get and hold requires the ballot."56

As a case in point, Pickens compared Negro and white public education in the South. Without the ballot blacks could not expect equal educational opportunities. Throughout the South black teachers earned less than whites and had larger classes; black children had a shorter school year and attended physically inferior schools. Without a political voice, Pickens argued, blacks were powerless to rectify these inequalities. "I wonder," Pickens concluded, "if those Negro 'leaders' and white 'friends' who about ten years ago began vigorously preaching to the race the harmless and pacific results of giving up the ballot, are not now thoroughly ashamed of themselves and their gospel."57

Pickens eventually challenged Washington at what many considered the Tuskegeean's strongest point—his emphasis on vocational education. Pickens felt vocational training was "probably" necessary "for a race economically situated as the Negro race is in this country," but such training should follow, and not be a substitute for, a good grade school education. As a product of liberal arts training at Talladega and Yale, he insisted that "a man should be a man before he is a piece in the world's machinery."58 Furthermore, he considered much of what was passing as vocational and industrial education in Negro schools to be a sham. "It is sometimes simply a game," he argued, "between the superintendent trying to graft another system on the already meager system of academic instruction, and the colored principal trying to satisfy the white superintendent without really doing the thing supposed." "The helpless Negro pupil" was thus denied a proper education of any kind.59

Although he saw a need for vocational education, Pickens shared the Niagarans' concern for quality higher education for all Negroes who could benefit from it. His first direct confrontation with Washington, in the summer of 1908, resulted from his commitment to the concept of "the Talented Tenth." During numerous fund-raising speeches for Talladega, he compared the quality of education at his own school with that of Tuskegee

Institute, with Washington's school always on the short end. Several informants told the Tuskegeean that Pickens was saying, "Tuskegee teaches girls to wash clothes; Talladega teaches them to think."[60] Bypassing Pickens and the president of Talladega, Washington wrote directly to James W. Cooper, corresponding secretary of the AMA. "There is entirely too much work in the South for Talladega, Tuskegee and all the other schools . . . to do for any of us who are in earnest to make these belittling comparisons. . . ."[61] He went on to suggest that Cooper call to Pickens's attention "the folly of this thing." Cooper promptly replied: "I would assure you that we will do all in our power to prevent a repetition of the offense. . . . We believe in Tuskegee as you do in Fisk and we will stand by one another in this common work for uplifting the race."[62]

Pickens apparently dropped the vexatious comparison, but continued to retain close ties with Washington's opponents. Although the Niagara Movement had become, by 1909, little more than a paper organization, the National Negro Committee (NCC) a new vehicle for militant protest, emerged to replace it. The NNC was run by a Committee of Forty, which included several former Niagarans, such as Du Bois, Reverend J. Milton Waldron of Washington, and J. Max Barber. The new organization also retained much of the Niagara program.[63]

"We denounce," began the platform of the National Negro Committee, "the ever-growing oppression of our 10,000,000 colored fellow citizens as the greatest menace that threatens the country. . . . As first and immediate steps toward remedying these national wrongs," the Committee demanded:

> 1. That the Constitution be strictly enforced and the civil rights guaranteed under the Fourteenth Amendment be secured impartially to all.
> 2. That there be equal educational opportunities for all and in all the States, and that public school expenditure be the same for the Negro and white child.
> 3. That in accordance with the Fifteenth Amendment the right of the Negro to the ballot on the same terms as other citizens be recognized in every part of the country.[64]

One major difference between the NCC and Niagara Movement was the inclusion of a number of prominent whites among the new organization's leadership. The Committee of Forty included, among others, New York *Evening Post* editor, Oswald Garrison Villard; Professor John Dewey; the Reverend John Haynes

Holmes; the social worker Mary White Ovington; the journalist William English Walling; and the Boston attorney Moorfield Storey.[65] Without these and other influential whites as active members, the NNC might not have survived longer than the Niagara Movement.

In 1910 the Committee of Forty changed the organization's name from the National Negro Committee, to the National Association for the Advancement of Colored People (NAACP).[66] It also established a Committee of One Hundred, which would be responsible for fund-raising drives, and from whose members the executive committee would be drawn. On 7 June Pickens was one of fourteen elected to the Committee of One Hundred.[67]

Since Washington was no less hostile to the NAACP than he had been toward the Niagara Movement, Pickens found it increasingly difficult to avoid a complete break with the Tuskegeean. When Washington, on a trip to Europe in 1910, suggested that American Negroes were better off than many European peasants, Pickens signed a statement, composed by Du Bois, highly critical of the Tuskegeean's remarks. The document, entitled, "An Appeal to England and Europe," attacked Washington for "giving the impression abroad that the Negro problem in America is in the process of satisfactory solution.... It is one thing to be optimistic, self-forgetful and forgiving, but it is quite a different thing, consciously or unconsciously, to misrepresent the truth."[68]

Pickens's increasing identification with the radicals caused the AMA to fear that Washington, in retaliation, would make it difficult for AMA schools to get philanthropic support, and for graduates from AMA schools to find employment. President J. M. P. Metcalf of Talladega also complained to the AMA that Pickens was missing some of his classes to do recruiting and fund-raising for the NAACP. Reprimanded by AMA president A. F. Beard for neglecting his students, Pickens insisted that Metcalf was "hostile" to the work he was doing, and that he had excellent relations with his students.[69]

Despite continued pressure from the AMA and Talladega, Pickens continued his work for the NAACP and was one of its most active southern recruiters. In 1914 he joined with Joel E. Spingarn, the white chairman of the board of the NAACP, in establishing a branch in Louisville in order to test that city's residential segregation ordinance. Their efforts resulted in a milestone decision by the Supreme Court, which unanimously invalidated the restrictive ordinance.[70]

That same year, when the National Conference of Charities and Corrections, meeting in Memphis, deferred to southern prejudice by segregating Negro delegates, Pickens and Spingarn picketed the conference—possibly the first interracial picket line in the South.[71] Du Bois joined Pickens and Spingarn in organizing a public meeting in Memphis's Avery Chapel to denounce the conference for discriminating against blacks and for refusing to include the race problem as one of the discussion topics. All but a few blacks boycotted the sessions, but Washington ignored the NAACP protest and addressed the delegates on the advantages of liquor prohibition.[72]

Pickens's activism was only one reason for the deterioration of relations between himself and the white administrators at Talladega. He seemed to get on well with the students, believing that "Negro students under Negro teachers, especially teachers of the younger generation . . . display an exhilarating freedom of body and soul."[73] He was also on good terms with some of the white teachers, but thought others came to Talladega "principally to spend the winter in a warmer climate. "Some of them," Pickens added, "were at best a hindrance to the advancement of the Negro race."[74]

After several years, however, he began to feel that the northern-based AMA was out of touch with conditions at Talladega. Furthermore, Pickens bridled at what he called "the law," which said that "wherever white people and colored people work together, in such enterprises, even in those that are professedly for the special benefit of the Negro race, the whites must occupy the highest places, regardless of other qualifications."[75] He was convinced that Metcalf and many white teachers disliked him, not only because of his work for the NAACP and his "special" relationship with the students, but because he would not play the deferential toady. "Because of the peculiar genius which has been developed in the white-and-black relationship in America," he wrote, "even the good, conscientious, missionary white people are likely to find a really straight-out, straight-up, manly and self-respecting Negro co-worker inconvenient at times, to say the least."[76]

In the spring of 1914 students at Talladega staged a strike in protest against the paternalism of some of their white teachers and the indifference of others. The strikers demanded more black faculty and a black administration.[77] President Metcalf believed Pickens was partly responsible for the uprising. When white residents of Talladega expressed concern for the safety of the white faculty, especially the women teachers, a local white bank president warned Pickens "as the most distinguished member of your race at Talladega," not to support the students. "I agree with you," he wrote Pickens, "that as soon as practicable the teaching force should be composed of Negroes." But, he added, any untoward action by the students against white teachers would bring "a mob of five thousand or more people from the mountains of Clay, Shelby and Talladega counties . . . shouting for your blood, and men like myself could do next to nothing in such an emergency."[78]

Pickens replied:

> You can be sure that I know no better friends than some of those who have been connected with Talladega College, but our newer teachers are not always so good as some of the older ones, and do not always understand conditions so well. . . . I mean to stand firmly by the right, and if necessary, die for it! But I mean to live and work as long as possible.[79]

Although they won none of their demands, the students returned to their classes; the whites of Clay, Shelby, and Talladega kept to their homes; and Pickens continued to live and work, but not at Talladega College. Washington played a role in hastening Pickens's departure. Shortly after the strike ended, President Metcalf wrote to the Tuskegeean several times requesting financial assistance, but Washington did not reply. In August, Metcalf wrote again, "I do not think I need say that we are more than ever committed at Talladega to making and keeping our education in touch with the real life of the people." "Might I say also," he concluded, "that our Trustees discontinued Mr. Pickens' services at Talladega."[80] Washington then promptly promised to lend assistance. He added:

> Although I dislike to say so, I am heartily glad you have gotten rid of Pickens. As you perhaps know, I have tried again and again to work with Mr. Pickens and to make of him a real force in the state and in the South, but I found that he could not be depended upon. He seemed determined to play the demagogue. I understand that he is going to Texas; perhaps he will learn something there.
> I feel that all of us have done our duty by him. I find that he is fast gaining the reputation among all classes of colored people of being an insincere individual.[81]

The AMA had proposed "promoting" Pickens to the headmastership of their Avery Industrial College in Charleston, South

Carolina, but he declined the offer, considering it a substandard school. The AMA then informed him that it had no further use for his services.

Pickens attributed his dismissal, after ten years at Talladega, to the hostility of President Metcalf, "who never wanted me there."[82] He did not know that Washington had a hand in his removal. Despite their obvious differences, especially from 1910 onward, Pickens had shared a number of public platforms with the Tuskegeean and, as late as 1914, in his capacity as president of the Alabama Colored State Teachers Association, he had "cordially" introduced Washington to southern audiences.[83] Nevertheless, the break was now complete. He had come to Talladega, in 1904, something of a Washingtonian, and was leaving ten years later a full-fledged radical.

In 1934 Pickens summarized his view of Washington's accomplishments and mistakes:

> Booker T. Washington was a pioneer in practical education not only for his own race, but for all races . . . with an influence on the course of education in Latin America, South Africa and China. . . . In spite of the well-known handicaps for a Negro in this country, he succeeded during the last twenty years of his life in attaching to himself a greater number of powerful friends than did any other American, hardly excepting his great contemporary and friend, Theodore Roosevelt.
>
> A public character usually makes his worst mistakes when he yields to the temptation to step aside from the work which he can do so well and to offer his opinions as an expert in problems outside of his special field. Booker Washington, like many other great leaders, made some mistakes in that line.

Pickens, in retrospect, however, recognized the difficulty of Washington's position as the most powerful man of his race.

> It was a dangerous road he had to travel between the white and black races, both of them sensitive and suspicious of any new movement along the color line. The leader of a minority people in such a situation is like a tight-rope walker, with very interested observers and resentful and threatening voices on both sides of him. It is a great tribute to his skill when he does not fall to his destruction on one side or the other.[84]

In his own career as a black activist Pickens learned many times how difficult it was to walk that tightrope.

2
"THE NEW NEGRO," 1914–1919

> Justice cannot be corrupted for black men and remain pure for white men. Government cannot be tyranny to the weak and democracy to the strong. American civilization will be what it is to the Negro.
> —Pickens, *The New Negro: His Political, Civil and Mental Status and Related Essays*

After a brief but perilous stay at Wiley College in eastern Texas, Pickens spent the next five years as dean and, later, as vice president of Morgan College in Baltimore, Maryland. While at Morgan he became increasingly involved in the civil rights movement, and, by the end of World War I, he was a major figure among black leaders and one of the country's most popular black orators. During the period from 1915 to 1920, Pickens reflected in his writing and activities the heightened militancy among a growing number of race leaders, and in his collection of essays, *The New Negro*, he expressed an approach to the race question which, with few exceptions, he would retain for the rest of his life.

When Pickens, after numerous clashes with Talladega's administrators, was dismissed by the parent Congregationalist American Missionary Association (AMA), he joined the Northern Methodist Episcopal Church and accepted a position teaching Greek and sociology at one of its schools, Wiley College in Marshall, Texas.[1] Pickens had misgivings about taking his family to Wiley. In 1905, a year after Pickens had become professor of languages at Talladega, he married Minnie Cooper McAlpine of Meridian, Mississippi, a graduate of Tougaloo College. The following year William Jr. was born, followed by Harriet Ida in 1909, and Ruby Annie in 1911.[2] Wiley College, founded in 1873, had a black president and faculty and was one of the larger and better black colleges west of the Mississippi River. Nevertheless, Marshall was located in the northeast corner of Texas, near the

Arkansas and Louisiana borders and only forty miles from Shreveport. This area was notorious for frequent and particularly barbaric lynchings. Pickens called it "one of the worst sections in all this round world . . . for any Negro to live in."[3]

During the last three months of 1913, at least three Negroes had been publicly murdered near Shreveport. In 1914, the year Pickens moved his family to Marshall, *The New York Times* reported six more lynchings in that area. Pickens personally investigated and reported on several other hangings and shootings which, he claimed, the white press refused to notice.[4]

In one such instance a policeman emptied his revolver into a black youth who had accidentally touched the officer's buggy. Although the killer was convicted, a rarity in that part of the country, he was only lightly fined and set free. Pickens was deeply affected by the fate of a black child who had been seen kissing a little white girl with whom he had been playing. A mob formed, kidnapped the child, and marched with him at midnight through the town. The boy was set on a huge pile of drygood boxes, but, before a fire could be started, he fell asleep. One of the members of the mob, possibly moved by the sight of the sleeping child, persuaded the others to spare the boy's life. "Being persuaded to mercy," Pickens wrote, "the mob simply cut off his ears and mutilated his body in other unmentionable ways and turned him over to his parents."[5]

Twice, during his "eventful year" in Marshall, Pickens narrowly escaped being killed by irate whites. On one such occasion he visited a white resident who owed him six dollars from a minor insurance claim. The man's wife dismissed Pickens, telling him that the debt had been paid. Six months later he confronted the man on the street and asked for his money. The debtor insisted the money had been paid and rebuked Pickens for being insolent. When the black instructor refused to back down, the white man drew a pistol. Possibly because the incident occurred before a number of witnesses, on Marshall's main street, the man hesitated, put away the gun, and finally drove off. Nevertheless, Pickens never collected the six dollars.[6]

He again faced danger when, returning to Marshall from a speaking engagement for the NAACP in New York, he defied "Jim Crow" on a southern train. To save an extra day's travel, he had purchased a Pullman ticket on a night train from Little Rock. Although he was the only black man in the car and the object of menacing looks from the white passengers, he refused to take the black porter's advice to disembark at the next stop. When he retired for the night, Pickens put a revolver, which he always carried with him, under his pillow, and asked the porter to warn him if anyone approached his berth. "I had no expectation of seeing the light of day again," he wrote. "I would not have gone into the car if I knew my life would be endangered. But being in was another thing and being bullied out was impossible." Fortunately none of the whites disturbed the sleeping traveler.[7]

The ever-present danger to Pickens and his family was only one reason why he was anxious to leave Marshall. He got on well with Wiley's president, M. W. Dogan, but he preferred teaching at a school with greater prestige and higher salaries, and that was closer to New York and Washington, D.C., the centers of black activism.[8]

He had an opportunity to become the president of a black college in West Virginia, but lost it when Booker T. Washington interfered. When a member of the West Virginia State Board of Regents wrote to his counterpart in Alabama, asking about Pickens, the letter was passed on to Washington. Because of Washington's unfavorable report, Pickens did not get the position.[9] This time, unlike his dismissal from Talladega, Pickens knew that Washington had worked against him. When a white friend, Andrew B. Humphrey, director of the American Peace and Arbitration League, informed him that "certain educators belonging to your race" were undermining his chances for the West Virginia job, Pickens replied:

> Yours of April 19th came as no surprise. I know these people thoroughly well. They are not so much enemies to me personally as they are hostile to the ideas which I endeavor to support. There is a great effort to throttle independent action and free speech in this country—so far as the American Negro and his interests are concerned. These education monopolists will do all to hurt me that is in their power to do, for I am not a tool, have not been and will not be.[10]

However, despite continued opposition from Washingtonians, he was able to obtain another position. Shortly after his arrival at Wiley, he learned that J. W. E. Bowen, vice president of Gammon Theological Seminary in Atlanta, had suggested him for the deanship of Morgan College, another Methodist Episcopal school, in Baltimore. Pickens exchanged letters with Bowen throughout the academic year 1914–15, and finally on 16 June, Morgan's Board of Trustees offered him the position, which he quickly accepted.[11]

In every respect the new appointment was an improvement

over his position at Wiley. He was promoted to dean—the first black ever to hold that position at Morgan College—and with the new rank went an increase in salary. He was moving to a school with a promising future, one that was about to build on a new campus and was relatively well supported by the Methodist Episcopal Church. He would also have "a safer platform from which to speak," and would no longer have to live in "the most savage and dangerous" part of the country. Pickens looked forward to working with Morgan's white president, John O. Spencer, so that he could "give the lie to the enemy who have tried to make the impression that I cannot work well with white people." He also knew that the Negroes on Morgan's integrated Board of Trustees wanted a black as the school's next president, and he hoped to be Spencer's successor. Furthermore, in Baltimore he could work more closely with other Negro leaders and would not feel cut off from the mainstream of black activism. "You [are] happier there than you could have possibly been this far South," President Dogan wrote. "You feel so keenly when it comes to race matters that you need a better atmosphere than we could give you here in Texas.[12] Still sensitive about his dismissal from Talladega, Pickens wrote about his new position, "It is a promotion, pure and simple, and not a plot, like the AMA's efforts to send me to Avery [Industrial College]."[13]

Pickens went east during a time of great change. By 1915 increasing numbers of Negroes were migrating north in response to worsening social and economic conditions in the South as well as war-induced job opportunities in the North. Blacks were generally divided on how to react to the changing times, and, even after the death of Washington in November 1915, deep antagonism separated his followers from NAACP supporters and other black militants. Most black leaders however, agreed that they had to try to reconcile their differences. When a meeting for this purpose was arranged, in the summer of 1916, Pickens accepted an invitation and temporarily put aside his fund-raising activities for Morgan College.[14]

W. E. B. Du Bois had suggested bringing representatives of the various factions together to "bring about . . . a degree of unity of purpose among Negro leaders.[15] Joel Spingarn took up the idea and offered his summer home in Amenia, New York, for the meeting. The Amenia Conference, which it became known as, began on 24 August and lasted for three days, and brought together more than fifty prominent blacks from all parts of the country. "I doubt if ever before," Du Bois wrote, "so small a conference of American Negroes had so many colored men of distinction who represented at the same time so complete a picture of all phases of Negro thought."[16]

The largest contingent at Amenia came from the Washington-Baltimore area and included, besides Pickens, Dean Kelly Miller of Howard University, the historian Carter G. Woodson, and Municipal Court Judge Robert Terrell and his wife Mary Church Terrell. From the deep South came John Hope, president of Morehouse College; R. R. Wright, Sr., president of the State Colored Industrial College of Georgia; Robert R. Moton, Washington's successor at Tuskegee; and Emmett Scott, Washington's former secretary at Tuskegee. Among those from the Midwest were the noted author Charles W. Chesnutt of Cleveland, and I. Garland Penn of the Freedman's Aid Society of the Methodist Episcopal Church from Cincinnati. New England was represented by Baptist clergyman Garnett R. Waller and William H. Lewis, former assistant U.S. attorney general. Those from New York included James Weldon Johnson (soon to become field secretary of the NAACP); William L. Bulkley, a public school principal; and Fred R. Moore, editor of the New York Age. A number of prominent whites attended sessions of the conference, but only Joel Spingarn, his brother Arthur, Mary W. Ovington, and Roy Nash, all associated with the NAACP, were listed as conferees.[17] Pickens's inclusion among the notables at Amenia constituted recognition as a major figure among American Negro leaders. He was known to many blacks as an educator, a scholar,[18] an author, an activist, and, above all, as one of the most popular black orators in the country.[19]

Despite sincere attempts to set aside personal animosities and ideological differences, the conferees found few points of agreement. "We all believed in thrift," Du Bois wrote nine years later. "We all wanted the Negro to vote, we all wanted the laws enforced, we all wanted the assertion of our essential manhood." Beyond these generalities, however, the participants merely patched over long-standing conflicts by agreeing that all forms of education, academic and vocational, were desirable and that southern blacks had "peculiar difficulties," concerning race relations, which northern blacks did not share. The race leaders also agreed that little could be achieved without greater organization and less factionalism, and that something comparable to the Amenia Conference should become an annual event.[20]

There was not, however, to be another such conference for sixteen years. Du Bois thought that "if the world had not gone crazy" and if America had not been drawn into the world war, the Amenia Conference might have been the beginning of a new era of greater unity among blacks.[21] Most participants shared the view, but the Amenia Conference was, in fact, another futile attempt to find a single banner under which all American Negroes could march. Amenia proved again that Negroes could not agree on the means to achieve the ends they all sought.

Although Pickens's remarks at Amenia, like those of the other conferees, were never recorded, that same year he published *The New Negro*, which dealt with many of the issues raised at the conference. *The New Negro* indicated the mature racial philosophy of the thirty-five-year-old Pickens and placed him in the forefront of the Negro leadership's more militant spokesmen.

In *The New Negro* he rejected the view of many accommodationists who maintained that blacks had to prove themselves ready for equality through self-discipline, hard work, thrift, and impeccable moral conduct. For Pickens the burden was clearly on white America and not on the Negro. America owed the Negro "a large debt" that was "perhaps absolutely unpayable." He stressed the active role played by blacks in building America. Southern slaves had been "the army which attacked the forests, the canebrakes and the swamps."[22] If the black was civilized under slavery, he was also a major force in destroying the institution.

> The runaway slave [he wrote] was the pioneer abolitionist; he was the appointed creator of antislavery sentiment,—an avenger born of the womb of slavery for slavery's own destruction. Wherever he went with the stripes on his back and the eloquence of his tongue he fired the hearts of men. . . . The runaway Negro was the vanguard, the first hero in the struggle to free his race.[23]

Since gaining his freedom the Negro had been "the very best friend which the American white man has in the whole round world." American civilization, therefore, and not the Negro, was on trial. Pickens demanded "a strict application of those principles of morality and justice which the white race has been foremost in formulating and spreading in the human society." "The Negro race," he added, "is God's high challenge and supreme test of American Christian democracy. Will it accept the challenge? Can it stand the test?"[24]

Pickens believed that America had no choice but to meet the challenge, for "God never bound two races more firmly in the same destiny than the white and black people of this country."[25]

Failure to pass the test would result in the ultimate decay of American democracy. "Justice cannot be corrupted for black men," he argued, "and remain pure for white men. Government cannot be tyranny to the weak and democracy to the strong. American civilization will be what it is to the Negro."[25]

For Pickens the race question went beyond America's borders and was the most fundamental problem facing the world. He believed that the European powers were engaged in a bloody and destructive war because they had subjugated colored peoples in Africa and Asia and then, in the same spirit of greed and inhumanity, had turned on each other. America, despite its past failures in dealing with the race problem, still could set an example for the rest of the world. Concerning America's mission he wrote:

> A providence wiser than men has brought the children of Africa and mingled them in goodly proportion in his great melting pot of peoples. After confusion there will be fusion of thought and spirit.... The fight here is decisive. Our success at this point means world-wide victory, our failure world-wide disaster.... No finer ground could have been chosen for freedom's last great battle than this young and virile nation filled with all the elements of the world. The thought should inspire the meanest.[27]

In the half-century since the Civil War, however, America had failed to fulfill its mission, and, as Pickens saw it, the new generation of black leaders did not share the accommodationists' blind faith in the capacity of whites to solve the race problem. This maturing black leadership, to whom Pickens referred as "The New Negro," was the product of a movement, since the turn of the century, of an increasing number of blacks from rural farms to urban centers, from the South to the North, from debt slavery to economic independence, and from ignorance to literacy.[28] The New Negro was no longer the "patient, unquestioning, devoted, semi-slave" of the past, but a "self-conscious, aspiring, proud young man." He was "sober, sensible, ... conscious of his environment, knowing that not all is right." Although still hopeful that "unreasonable opposition to his forward and upward progress will relent," he was "resolved to fight and live and die" for his rights. He was still a loyal American, and, if the United States were to become involved in the world war, he "would stand fast and firm by America against any European state." But, Pickens asked, "how long will his loyalty last?"[29]

Pickens, like most of the Amenia conferees, hoped that white

America would ultimately respond to the just demands of its black citizens and consequently did not develop the theme of possible black retaliatory violence or separatism. Nevertheless, he argued, the Negro must not wait passively for that response. "By no means must [the Negro] stop wanting," he wrote, "for that is the stimulus to his working. He must want life, want civilization, want citizenship, want votes and equal opportunities,—and for all these wants he will work.... The only way to work effectively is through organization." But how would such efforts bring about racial equality? "The white man is human," Pickens concluded, "and if the black man works well he will gain friends and cooperation."[30]

Pickens's concluding sentence seemed to be a retreat from militancy. Moton, Scott, and the other conciliators also argued that the race problem would be solved through favorable white reaction to responsible black organization. Pickens, however, was not slipping back to accommodationism, but was expressing the dilemma all black militants faced when dealing with practical solutions to the race problem. He, like the other leaders at Amenia, generally accepted the existing political and economic system. He did not seriously attack democratic capitalism, but wanted the black to share more of its benefits. He was sympathetic to socialism and believed that exploitative capitalism was a root cause of racial discrimination, but he rejected violent revolution. As an advocate of complete racial integration he also opposed all black separatist schemes, such as a negro state or mass migration to Africa.[31]

What practical solutions to the race problem could a black militant like Pickens offer? He advocated not only black economic cooperation, which the accommodationists favored, but also political activism and nonviolent social protest. Unfortunately, since most blacks had been disfranchised and the federal government had refused to interfere with state-established segregation, black political and social action could not have effected the changes that militants sought. Therefore, by rejecting the use of violence and by demanding integration, Pickens had to accept the fact that blacks had few options available to them, and that meaningful change was essentially in the hands of the dominant whites. What he wanted, in effect, was a radical change in white attitudes and white practices, and the chief weapon blacks had for this purpose was moral suasion. But the use of moral suasion, through propaganda, implied a faith in the capacity of whites to respond to reason and a willingness to break traditional patterns of behavior.

Pickens, it may seem, was forced full circle into accepting a basic tenet of Washingtonian thought—faith in the goodwill of white America. Although this was not quite the case—Pickens's New Negro would not wait passively for the millennium—his program reflected an ambivalence, which resulted from his awareness of the blacks' relative powerlessness. For example, Pickens wholeheartedly supported the black exodus from rural to urban areas. But he also warned that the city was not a black mecca. He wrote:

> If he [the urban Negro] fills the city slums, he also fills the greater proportion of the best homes of the Negro race; if his life is shorter, it is more interesting; if he is weaker, he is wiser. Better twenty years of Atlanta than a century of semi-slavery of the "Mississippi bottoms."[32]

He no longer subscribed to Washington's advice to the Negro "to let down his bucket" in the South. His own migration to the North, during his college years, had been a key to his success and he prescribed it for others. Yet he wrote, "Neither North nor South offer the Negro a fair industrial opportunity, if in the one he can boast and starve, while in the other he may eat but cringe."[33]

He rejected Washington's emphasis on vocational training, advocating instead traditional public school education for blacks. "With brains in his head," he wrote,

> a man cannot ultimately be industrially repressed. . . . But there can be no doubt of the value *right now* of vocational training for a race economically situated as the Negro race is in this country and having the industrial opposition [meaning lily-white labor unions] which it has, and which in many instances must fight first to save its body in order to give its mind a chance.[34]

Pickens's basic theme in *The New Negro* was an "identity of interests,"—the interwoven destiny of the two races—and he appealed to whites to realize that it was in their own and the national interest to fight against racial prejudice and discrimination. For example, writing on the effects of lynching and other forms of racial violence, he reasoned that "if a black man is pressed down to the brute end of society, white men must then be brutal enough to pay his acts with retaliative brutality."[35] Concerning attempts by several northern state legislatures to pass antimiscegenation laws he wrote:

> The primary motive of the black man is not a desire for a mixed family but for the protection of his own colored family. He believes that a law to compel fathers to marry the mothers would break up more miscegenation in a week than a law prohibiting marriage will break up in twenty-five years.[36]

On the question of the relationship between Negroes and organized labor he argued that, by excluding black workers, labor unions were being shortsighted.

> The relation of the Negro to trade unionism shows that he is either a help or a hindrance to industrial freedom in America: he must be in the union in terms of equality, or, if out of the union, he will be a strike-breaker and wage-reducer, a weapon of the employer against the white employee. If the black is pushed down, the least that the white laborer can expect is to be pushed down next to him.[37]

In sum, Pickens articulated an underlying agreement at Amenia among black conciliators and agitators. They could propagandize, lobby, organize, and cooperate; they could exhort, threaten, demand, or explain, but ultimately they had to fall back on the reasonability and goodwill of the dominant whites. Pickens dedicated The New Negro "to the white and black man of tomorrow: a faith in whose essential humanity and justice is the inspiration of these pages." Given the Negro's weak position in 1916, Pickens had little choice but to keep that faith.

Twenty years before The New Negro was published, Du Bois had eloquently expressed the Negro's sense of "two-ness." "One ever feels his two-ness—an American, a Negro—two souls, two thoughts, two unreconciled strivings: two warring ideals in one dark body." Pickens added another dimension to this ambivalent sense of "two-ness"—two races caught in a single national destiny. He reiterated the theme after the United States entered World War I.

> When we put colored men in the front line of trenches, we expected and, for the time being, at least, we ardently wished that they would be the equals of any soldier in the world. We understood in a moment what we had not understood in fifty years: how closely bound up in destiny with all the rest of us is this Negro—that his weakness is our weakness, his strength our strength.[38]

Although many whites saw them as a nonassimilable element, blacks considered themselves Americans as well as Negroes, and, when their country went to war, many volunteered for military service. At first the War Department refused to enlist them, but, when it became clear that massive numbers of troops would be needed to stop the German armies, Congress passed the Selective Service Act in May 1917, which required all adult males between twenty-one and thirty, regardless of race, to register for the draft.[39]

Pickens never doubted that the Negro would support the war effort. "He would fight," Pickens wrote. "There was no debate worth considering on that point."[40] His main concern was that blacks receive equal or, at least, decent treatment in the military service. But it was clear from the outset, that this would not be the case. Blacks were not admitted into the marines, nor accepted as pilots in the air corps. In the navy they served as "messmen, watertenders, gunner's mates, and coal tenders,"[41] none of which required much skill. Although they were eventually admitted into all branches of the army, the majority of black soldiers were assigned to stevedore regiments or other labor units. Furthermore, southern social mores were generally respected in all aspects of military life and, wherever possible, blacks were segregated from white troops, both in training camps and overseas.[42]

They were often harassed and insulted by white soldiers and white officers. On numerous occasions black soldiers clashed with white civilians. The most serious confrontation occurred in Houston, Texas, in late August 1917, when Negro troops from regular army companies of the Twenty-fourth Infantry, stationed at nearby Camp Logan, retaliated against alleged systematic police harassment and killed seventeen whites. Pickens received an eyewitness account of the Houston riot from President Dogan of Wiley College. According to Dogan, the violence was triggered by a white policeman who slapped a black woman and then insulted several black soldiers who had defended her from further attack.

> It is to be regretted [Dogan wrote] that so many innocent people were killed and wounded, but it seems clear that this was not the intention of the soldiers. They went to the sections of the city where the mean police were on duty with the intention of cleaning them out only, but others got in the way, to the regret of all. While the city deserves

credit for holding the rough element of whites in check following the trouble, it is to be regretted that it was found necessary to disarm all Negroes in the Negro sections of the city. This would appear to invite the destruction of the Negroes by the bad whites. . . . Four of the meanest police in Houston are among those killed, including the one who slapped the woman and abused the soldiers the day of the riot.[43]

Dogan commended the War Department for bringing the rioting soldiers before a military court "rather than leaving their fate in the hands of the civil authorities." Nevertheless, after a perfunctory trial, thirteen black soldiers were hanged and forty-one were condemned to life imprisonment. Many black leaders complained that the executions were nothing more than "legal lynchings."[44]

Blacks were also upset at the War Department's unwillingness to increase the number of Negro army officers. Although the prewar regular army included ten thousand black soldiers, very few had achieved the rank of officer. When thousands of blacks were drafted for military service, their leaders demanded that black officers be trained to lead them. The War Department, under pressure from southern officers and civilians, seemed to be moving in the opposite direction. For example, the highest-ranking Negro officer in the regular army, Lieutenant Colonel Charles Young, was found physically unfit for overseas duty and relieved of his command. Furthermore, although Congress had authorized the establishment of fourteen officer training camps, none was designated for the training and commissioning of black officers.[45]

Although Pickens was greatly displeased with the treatment of black soldiers, he was particularly disturbed that qualified Negroes were being denied the opportunity to assume leadership roles in the army and that, as a result, thousands of black soldiers would be under the command of white officers, many of whom were southerners.

Realizing that blacks would not be accepted in white officer training camps, Pickens joined with Joel Spingarn, who was acting privately and not as an NAACP official, in pressuring Secretary of War Newton D. Baker for separate black facilities. To prove that qualified Negroes were seriously interested in becoming army officers, Pickens, Spingarn, and others, recruited black college students for the proposed camp. Secretary Baker, who wished to be fair, tentatively agreed to their demand, but then hesitated when the NAACP and a number of black leaders, including most of the editors of the black press, objected to a "Jim Crow" training camp.[46]

"At the risk ... of the undoubted evil and wrong of segregation," Pickens continued to fight for a black camp. Since Negroes were already segregated in the army, he argued, a separate camp "would provide more opportunities for promotion of Negroes than a predominantly white training camp." Furthermore, since the choice was actually between a segregated facility or none at all, a Jim Crow camp "would not make the world safe for democracy, but it would make the United States Army much less dangerous for the Negro."[47]

In order to maintain pressure on the War Department, Pickens, Spingarn, George W. Cook of Howard University, and others, helped black students organize the Central Committee of Negro College Men, which lobbied in Washington and won the support of over three hundred congressmen. These efforts were successful and, on 12 May 1917, Secretary Baker announced that Fort Des Moines, in Iowa, would be set aside for the training of black officers.[48]

Many black leaders who at first opposed a segregated camp later changed their minds, and Baker's decision was generally hailed as a great victory for the race. Emmett Scott, who was appointed a special assistant to the secretary of war, described the scene at Howard University the day news of Baker's announcement arrived. "The authorization of the camp brought joy unspeakable to the hearts of the committee and students. Smiles and handshakes soon made the campus seem like an old-fashioned Methodist prayer meeting and the news was heralded far and wide."[49]

The War Department announced that Fort Des Moines would begin training black volunteers on 15 June. The Central Committee of Negro College Men sent letters across the nation to black college students and professional men urging them to enroll.

Let us not mince matters [the letter read]; the race is on trial.... It needs every one of its red-blooded, sober-minded men.... If we fail, our enemies will dub us COWARDS for all time; and we can never win our rightful place. But if we succeed—then eternal success; a mighty and far-reaching step forward; 1250 Colored Army officers leading Negro troops. Look to the future, brother, the vision is glorious![50]

Pickens also saw the war as holding great promise for the Negro. On the first day of 1918 he drew up a balance sheet of the Negro's gains and losses during the previous year. "The colored American has every reason to take courage," he concluded. "The past year may have taken something away, but it gave more than it took." If the Houston riot took away "three score of the best soldiers in the world," at Fort Des Moines "we have gained the unprecedented total of 700 colored commissioned officers in the United States army and have an equal status for service in the ranks." The federal government still supported segregation in the nation's Capitol, "but, in substance, we are represented in every department of government service, and have a high civil officer [Emmett Scott, special assistant on Negro Affairs] in the War Department." In the war overseas, Negroes "have earned the hatred of Germany,—but we have deepened the love of France." Although the Negro "stands horrified and aghast at this World War and world murder," he "has gained . . . and will gain proportionately more from this world conflict, perhaps, than any other single element in the world."[51]

Black men in uniform, including officers, continued to suffer under the burden of discrimination, both at home and overseas, but Pickens never lost hope that their loyalty and sacrifice would result in significantly improved race relations. When a young Negro from Mississippi wrote that many of his black friends lacked "patriotic zeal" and spoke of refusing to serve in the army "no matter how beautiful the camouflage," Pickens replied:

> The Negro does not get justice in this country, but he will get more just treatment if he does his duty by the country now. Just as did the Negro soldiers in the Civil War. We are better off today than we would otherwise be, because our brave black people stood by the country then. That is not "camouflage,"—that is fact. My country first now, and my rights first immediately after the war.[52]

Pickens's final theme—"My country first now, and my rights first immediately after the war"—was reiterated four months later by Du Bois in his famous "close ranks" editorial for *The Crisis*. "Let us, while this war lasts," Du Bois wrote, "forget our special grievances and close ranks with our fellow citizens."[53]

In general, Pickens and Du Bois had similar views on the world war and the Negro's response to it. At first both blamed all the European powers for bringing on the war, but, when the United States became involved, they switched to an anti-German position. Although they spoke out against discrimination in the military service, both endorsed acceptance of segregated Fort Des Moines and both insisted that a good showing by blacks would go far toward removing such injustices after the war. Both men also expressed faith in the war as a liberating force among the darker, subjugated peoples of the world.[54]

While Du Bois was supporting the war effort in his *Crisis* editorials, Pickens was making his contribution from the speaker's platform. When he offered his services to Scott, he was appointed to a special "Committee of One Hundred" of the Committee on Public Information.[55]

Scott wanted Pickens to explain the war aims of the United States to Negroes "with a view of stimulating their patriotism where needed, and pointing out to them in a definite and practical way how they may be of greatest service to the nation in the winning of the present struggle for liberty and democracy."[56] Pickens would perform this service again in World War II.

He preached support for the war effort among Negroes, but he also told whites what he believed the Negro was fighting for. On Decoration Day, before a racially mixed audience at Morgan College, he delivered an address entitled, "The Kind of Democracy the Negro Race Expects."

> FIRST. *Democracy in Education.* No other democracy is practicable unless all of the people have equal right and opportunity to develop according to their individual endowments.
> SECOND. *Democracy in Industry.* The Negro asks American labor in the name of democracy to get rid of its color caste and industrial junkerism.
> THIRD. *Democracy in State.* A political democracy is one in which all are equal before the laws; where there is one standard of justice.
> FOURTH. *Democracy without Sex-preferment.* The Negro cannot consistently oppose color discrimination and support sex discrimination.
> FIFTH. *Democracy in the Church.* The preachings and the practices of Jesus of Nazareth are perhaps the greatest influence in the production of modern democratic ideas. The Christian Church is, therefore, no place for the caste spirit.
> *FINALLY.* The great Colored races will in the future not be kinder to a sham democracy than to a "scrap of paper" autocracy. The Negro welcomes the opportunity to lift the "Negro question" out of the narrow confines of the Southern United States and make it a world question. Like many other questions, our domestic race question, instead of being settled by Mississippi and South Carolina will now seek its settlement largely on the battlefields of Europe.[57]

Most black leaders echoed Pickens's demand for greater democracy for American Negroes and for the world's colored peoples. For example, Du Bois wrote:

> This war is an End and also a Beginning. Never again will darker people of the world occupy just the place they had before. Out of this war will rise, soon or late, an independent China, a self-governing India, an Egypt with representative institutions, an Africa for the Africans, and not merely for business exploitation. Out of this war will rise, too, an American Negro, with the right to vote and the right to work and the right to live without insult.[58]

"What the Negro should get out of the war," wrote Scott, "ought to be determined largely by what he put into it."[59] Despite numerous obstacles, Negroes made an important contribution to the war effort. More than 400,000 blacks served in the armed forces. Although most of the 200,000 black men sent to France served in labor units, many fought in the decisive battles of the war's final months. Entire black regiments as well as individual black soldiers won military honors from a grateful French government. On the home front, Negroes supplied needed manpower for the factories producing war matériel, and they also purchased a significant number of liberty bonds and war savings stamps.[60]

"Will the black man," Pickens asked, "who has shown himself so trustworthy in time of war, ever again have doors shut in his face in time of peace and security."[61] The answer came quickly and decisively. With peace restored in Europe the armed forces returned to prewar conditions. Black officers were denied the opportunity to retain their commissions, and black volunteers were no longer recruited. Negro soldiers returning to their homes were thrown off Jim Crow trains and were often harassed and insulted by white civilians. Although, early in 1919, Negro regiments returning from overseas received heroes' welcomes in New York and other cities, by the end of the summer a rash of violent racial confrontations had covered the country. During the "Red Summer" of 1919, more than twenty-five cities, from Washington, D.C., to Longview, Texas, were convulsed by race riots, in which hundreds of blacks and whites were killed or wounded.[62] Among those killed were a number of blacks who had fought in France to "help save the world for democracy."[63]

3
THE FIELD SECRETARY AND "THE EMPEROR OF AFRICA," 1919–1927

> Negroes seem to be held in a state of eternal preparedness for a great number of contradictory opinions—ready to accept one type or another depending on how they are driven by pressures or where they see an opportunity.
> —Gunnar Myrdal, *An American Dilemma: The Negro Problem and Modern Democracy*

During World War I many Negroes expected the millennium, only to find disappointment and disillusionment after the fighting stopped. Black soldiers proved their loyalty on the battlefields of France, but, upon returning to America, they again faced the lynch mob, Jim Crow, the lily-white labor union, and even a resurrected Ku Klux Klan. For such a black militant as William Pickens, the postwar era was a time for reevaluation and decision. He could continue to work for racial justice in nonviolent, nonradical, militant organizations like the NAACP. But in the postwar period there were several new options to consider, among them, Marcus Garvey's back-to-Africa movement and the radical revolutionary Communist party. Pickens also might give up the struggle and join the black ex-patriates who sought asylum in the seemingly nonracist cosmopolitan centers of Europe.

Like other Negro leaders, Pickens was confused and uncertain about which path to follow: whether to remain a race man or seek his own personal destiny; whether to continue fighting for racial equality within the existing political and economic framework; or join the new radicals in trying to overthrow the system; whether to champion the rights of colored men throughout the world or concentrate on the plight of the American Negro.

Like most men, Pickens was something less than a self-sacrificing crusader. Impulsive, ambitious, concerned for his family's economic security, he sometimes acted in ways that might not have been in the best interests of black people. But, for the most part, his desire for self-advancement complemented his commitment to the advancement of his race. This is best illustrated by his brief flirtation with Marcus Garvey.

The year 1919 was a difficult one for Pickens. He felt insecure about his own future as well as that of his race. Although in 1915 he had enthusiastically accepted the deanship at Morgan College, he was never happy there, and from 1916 onward he sought other employment. He worked more harmoniously with Morgan's President Spencer than he had with Talladega's Metcalf, but both administrators complained that Pickens did not devote sufficient time to his official responsibilities. Although Spencer was more sympathetic to Pickens's civil rights work than Metcalf had been, he felt that Pickens's activism interfered with his duties as the dean of Morgan College.

"The time has come," Spencer wrote in 1916, "when I must lean on some strong, brave, unselfish man like yourself. I greatly admire you and trust you. You have qualities that will insure the highest success, but you have forces that need regulation and direction." Spencer reminded Pickens that the school needed financial support for its proposed expansion and that he was expected to participate actively in the fund-raising campaign. Furthermore, as dean, he should "carefully cultivate attention to details in administration."[1]

Pickens, however, lacked the discipline and the disposition to be a good administrator. The qualities that made him a premier public speaker—wit, flamboyance, spontaneity, and individuality—were of little help in running an organization. He was a first-rate fund-raiser, but the NAACP, the National Urban League and, later, the U.S. Treasury Department, benefited more from his talent than did Morgan College. Nevertheless, Pickens brought in sufficient contributions to Morgan so that Spencer wanted to keep him.[2]

The more Pickens became involved in black activism, the less satisfying he found his role as an educator. He preferred the excitement and importance of his work as recruiter and fund-raiser for the NAACP to the more prosaic life of a school administrator. Pickens was an ambitious man and, especially after mingling with the black elite at Amenia, he wanted a place in the black leadership's inner circle. He considered Morgan College primarily as a base of operations, his deanship as a job that provided a small, but steady income and that allowed him time to engage in other race work. When Spencer insisted that he commit himself completely to Morgan's interests, Pickens looked for another job.

In the winter of 1917 he applied for a full-time position with the National Urban League, which, as the name suggests, was primarily concerned with the problems (especially unemployment) of city-dwelling Negroes.[3] The Urban League executives were familiar with his reputation as a public speaker and fundraiser, but they decided against hiring him because, as a friend told him, "some of your close friends stated to the powers that be that your executive ability was below par."[4] Eugene Knickle Jones of the Urban League suggested that Pickens keep his job with Morgan College and work for the league on weekends.[5]

Pickens informed Spencer of the Urban League's offer of part-time work, but intimated that they preferred his services full-time at $2,500 per annum. He insisted that his salary of $1,300 could not cover his family's expenses, but suggested that he would remain at Morgan if promoted to the vice presidency and given a substantial salary increase. In January 1918 Spencer agreed to give him $1,800 per annum and a rent-free house, and to appoint him vice president with "very limited class or administrative work." Under the new arrangement Pickens was to devote all his energies to the school's fund-raising drive.[6] Morgan College's first black vice president, however, did not quite fulfill his part of the bargain, especially after he volunteered to help in the liberty bond drive, and Spencer continued to complain about his lack of commitment to the school. Pickens replied, "It has never occurred to me to assume toward any institution, especially an institution for education like Morgan College, . . . that my services were worth only so much as I might go away and bring back in my pockets."[7]

Early in 1919 Pickens wrote to Mme C. J. Walker, a former Louisiana washerwoman who had become very wealthy by selling her hair-straightener and skin-lightening cream to black women. He offered to escort her on an around-the-world tour and then write a book about her experiences. "The thing can be done," he wrote, "and it would be one of the greatest marks in the history of the American Negro, if managed with honesty and dignity."[8] He also promised to "deliver at least one address in every state of the Union, on our return, on the subject of your tour of foreign countries and its importance to the Negro Race, etc. This would make the book sell like hot pies."

Pickens suggested that idea to Mme Walker because he was unhappy at Morgan and anxious to try something new, especially a project that promised national recognition and substantial economic reward. Nor would he mind returning to Europe, where he and his wife had vacationed in the summer of 1913. Such an explanation provides only half the answer, for Pickens's reference to the projected tour as being "important to the Negro race," was more than an insincere rationalization. He considered Mme Walker a near-heroic figure. She had raised herself from humble origins to become one of the richest women in America and, equally significant, she had made her fortune entirely within the Negro community. Her success symbolized the potential for economic nationalism, or cooperation, among Negroes that had been a prevalent theme among black leaders from the conservative Booker T. Washington to the radical Marcus Garvey.

Pickens never made the grand tour with Mme Walker—she died later that year—but in 1937 he reviewed her significance to the race.

> In Indianapolis she built a great office building and factory, where black people could make not only their own unkinking preparations, but also their own soap, lotions and notions,—all of which things they would otherwise have bought of white manufacturers, without ever having the chance to work at making or marketing them. She built offices for Negro professionals, whom the chauvinist majority excluded from "white" premises; a theatre where blacks would not be segregated; eating places where they would not be thrown out, screened-off or have glass or too much salt sprinkled over their food; and auditoriums in which even the Negro radicals could meet and talk as they pleased. She started in the capitalist world as a black washerwoman and managed to beat some of the white capitalists to some of the "takings" from the black population.[9]

In the winter of 1919 the NAACP asked Pickens to join their organization as an assistant to the field secretary, James Weldon Johnson. The Association's membership and branches had increased enormously since the United States had entered the war, and the NAACP wanted Pickens to help Johnson in recruiting new members, establishing new branches, and maintaining liaison between the branches and the national headquarters in New York.

Pickens was an obvious choice for the job. He had been associated with the NAACP since its founding in 1909 and, while teaching at Talladega, Wiley, and Morgan, was one of its most successful recruiters.[10] He had a particularly close working relationship with Joel E. Spingarn, former chairman of the Board of Directors, having assisted him in establishing the Louisville branch, protesting Jim Crow in Memphis, and advocating the Negro officer's training camp at Fort Des Moines. The NAACP also had asked Pickens to join Spingarn on a potentially perilous tour of Oklahoma in 1915 to gather new evidence of railroad discrimination for a test case against Jim Crow interstate carriers. He was unable to escort Spingarn, but continued his equally hazardous investigations of lynchings in the Southwest and reported his findings to the national office.[11] Pickens also had delivered major addresses at the Association's annual meeting in 1915 and at its National Conference on Lynching in 1919.[12] Pickens could make a valuable addition to the NAACP's staff, because, as the black poet Langston Hughes wrote, "he was one of the most popular platform orators in America." Pickens was popular with both the black masses and more sophisticated audiences. "A man of the people," Hughes wrote, "with a powerful voice, a jolly face, and a smile 'like a lighthouse in the sea,'" Pickens "never lost the common touch." On the other hand, a reporter for Boston's *Congregationalist and Advance* found Pickens most effective before audiences made up of "the intellectuals of his race." The reporter added:

> There is no one comparable with him. For he has a sense of humor and wit that Du Bois lacks; there are more strings to his instrument on which to play the deep chords of racial tragedy; and he has a physical vigor and vehemence of utterance in accurate English phrase, and moral courage . . . that makes him tremendously powerful. He tells a story and adorns a moral with all the humor and wise good sense that Booker T. Washington mastered in his day; but . . . he is educated in the world's best lore as Washington never was, and his irony, while not as cynical and bitter as Du Bois', . . . is all the more effective sometimes, just because the lightning comes out of a sunburst of humor and not from a dark cloud of lamentation.[13]

Finally, Pickens had become, early in 1919, a syndicated columnist and contributing editor of the Associated Negro Press (ANP) and, through his contacts with the Negro press, could publicize and propagandize the Association's work. His columns first appeared in the Philadelphia *Public Journal* and the Boston *Chronicle*, but, by the late 1920s, his byline was appearing periodically in almost every black newspaper in the country.[14] The ANP was founded in 1919 in Chicago by two black journalists, Claude Barnett and Nahum D. Brascher, and rapidly became the largest and most successful black news-gathering service in America. Acting as a clearinghouse for more than one hundred Negro newspapers, the ANP charged a weekly fee for distributing news items and editorials on all subjects that were "of interest to the race."[15] Barnett, the ANP's guiding force, was accused of selling its services to Negro organizations and of operating the ANP more as a paid "publicity agent than as an impartial news services."[16] Nevertheless, during the 1920s and 1930s, at no cost to the NAACP, Pickens used his position as ANP contributing editor "to get over to the public many reams of NAACP material."[17]

The Association had considered Pickens for the field secretaryship before offering the post, in December, 1916, to James Weldon Johnson, a contributing editor on the New York Age. Johnson had less impressive ties with the NAACP—he had become the vice president of the New York branch in 1916—but he was "a good mixer" as well as "a good talker" and, having previously been closely identified with Booker T. Washington, he was still on good terms with many black conservatives. At the time of Johnson's appointment, NAACP Chairman Joel E. Spingarn wrote, "It will seem strange to have us go to [editor of the New York Age] Fred Moore's office for a man, but I rather think that would be a coup."[18]

On 12 January 1920 John R. Shillady, the NAACP executive secretary, officially offered Pickens the position of assistant field secretary. He accepted the post, which brought with it a salary of $3,000, but he did not resign from Morgan College until the end of the academic year.[19]

Pickens joined the NAACP at a time when it had reached administrative maturity. By its tenth year of operation, the Association was the largest, strongest, and most important civil rights organization in the country. It had grown from 10 branches and 3,000 members on the eve of World War I, to 310 branches and over 90,000 members by the end of 1919. The greatest expansion had come between 1917 and 1919, when membership increased tenfold and the number of branches quadrupled. The circulation of the Association's monthly journal, The Crisis, edited by W. E. B. Du Bois, reached a peak of 100,000 in 1919. Although the organization's annual income was still only a modest $61,755, it had more than quadrupled between 1917 and 1919.[20]

The NAACP's impressive growth was due, in part, to a well-organized membership drive, launched in April 1918. Another factor was Booker T. Washington's death, late in 1915, which eliminated the Association's major rival. Furthermore, the world war brought with it the promise of great social change, and many blacks may have looked to the NAACP as the most likely vehicle through which they could achieve postwar racial integration. Finally, when racial violence increased at war's end, blacks may have joined the Association because its legal services and antilynching campaigns seemed to provide their only protection.

By 1919 the NAACP had undergone two important changes—it was no longer a regional organization and it was increasingly coming under black control. In 1914 NAACP membership was heavily concentrated in the East and Midwest; by 1919 approximately 47 percent of the members lived in the South, 42 percent in the North, 7 percent in the West and Far West, while 4 percent were listed as foreign or members-at-large.[21] In 1914 whites predominated on the national board, on the national executive staff in New York, and on branch executive committees. Five years later blacks controlled many of the new branches and were replacing whites in leadership positions throughout the organization. By the end of 1921 all the NAACP national executive officers but two (Board Chairman Mary White Ovington and Treasurer Joel Spingarn) were black. Johnson was executive secretary, assisted by Walter White. Pickens and Addie Hunton shared the field secretaryship. Robert Bagnall was the director of branches and Du Bois was the director of publications and research, as well as editor of *The Crisis*. The shift from white to black control was not yet complete—a majority of the national Board of Directors were white—but the NAACP was no longer a black organization under white direction.[22]

A month after Pickens accepted Shillady's offer, the *Crisis* published an abridged version of the secretary's progress report, entitled, "What Has the Association Done?[23] Shillady tried to present the Association's achievements over a ten-year period in the best possible light, but, in fact, it had made few major advances. The NAACP had won several legal battles, the most significant being the Supreme Court's rejection of Louisville's municipal segregation ordinance and Oklahoma's "grandfather clause," but the South had developed other methods for segregating and disfranchising blacks.

The Association had committed a considerable portion of its meager financial resources to the fight against lynching. It had conducted numerous investigations, held a nationwide conference, lobbied in Washington, and obtained statements from many national figures (even President Wilson) condemning the practice. Yet in 1919 at least seventy-eight blacks were publicly murdered. The NAACP had had little more success in its fight against other forms of racial discrimination.

"The NAACP has organized an effective fighting machine," Shillady concluded, "of nearly 100,000 members in over 300 branches—fighting to make democracy safe for all Americans." Although very significant, this was the secretary's only claim that could not be challenged. During its first years the Association had been attacked by Washingtonians for being too radical and outspoken, yet it survived and eventually supplanted the accommodationists as the leading voice among black activists. By 1919 the NAACP was being attacked again, but this time by Garveyites and black Marxists who considered it too conciliatory.

Not long after Pickens became associate field secretary of the NAACP, he clashed with the Association's board on several issues that also had been sources of irritation between himself and administrators at Talladega and Morgan. Pickens wanted more money, a voice in the organization's operations, and freedom to determine his own work schedule so that he could continue private lecturing, which was an important supplement to his income. The NAACP did not prohibit him from giving private lectures but expected him to do so during his two-month summer vacation, and they objected when it seemed to take priority over his fieldwork.[24] The Association especially wanted Pickens to help establish new branches in the West and Southwest, where membership was relatively sparse, and the board feared that, by designing his itinerary to suit his lecture schedule, he would not give those regions sufficient attention.

Although Pickens's salary as NAACP field secretary was low, averaging over the years approximately $3,300 a year, he had other sources of income, including fees for lecturing, a regular salary as contributing editor for the ANP, royalties from several books,[25] and, in 1925, a $2,000 inheritance from his close friend Mrs. Flora Olmstead Avery.[26] In addition, Mrs. Pickens had money of her own.[27]

This income, plus Pickens's frugal nature,[28] permitted the family to enjoy a comfortable middle-class living standard. Upon arrival in New York in 1920, Pickens purchased a townhouse at 260 West 139th Street, in what was generally considered "the finest group of Negro residences in the country."[29] The two-story house was part of a group of "spacious, luxurious brownstones," built originally for upper-class whites in 1891 by the famous architect, Stanford White. These homes were put on the market in 1919, following the black migration to Harlem, and were all sold to well-to-do Negroes. The homes on this street (139th Street between Lenox and Seventh avenues) became known among blacks as "Striver's Row."[30] Black journalist George S. Schuyler, who often visited the Pickenses, described the street as "one of the most beautiful blocks in New York City."[31]

The Pickenses entertained often and were part of the black social elite during the Harlem "Renaissance" of the 1920s.[32] Mrs. Pickens especially, became involved in the social and cultural life of the community. In later years she was active in the Harlem Adult Education Committee, the Harlem branch of the YWCA, and the Schomburg Branch of the New York Public Library. She was also active in John Haynes Holmes's Community Church and the Metropolitan Museum of Art.[33]

Despite his modest NAACP salary, Pickens and his wife provided well for the education of their three children. They all attended private high schools in New York—William, Jr. at Townsend Harris; Harriet Ida and Ruby Annie at Wadleigh. William, Jr., the eldest, attended City College of New York, but then transferred to Lincoln University in Pennsylvania, from which he was graduated in 1928. His parents also financed his three years at Fordham University Law School, from which he received a law degree in 1931.[34] Harriet Ida received a B.A. from Smith College in 1930. Ruby Annie attended New York University, from which she received a B.S. in 1933 and a M.S. in 1937.[35]

Although the Pickenses lived relatively well, William Pickens unquestionably was underpaid for his work with the NAACP. The Association simply did not have the resources to pay its executive staff more. In fact, during the economic depression of the early 1930s, all staff members took substantial pay cuts.

Another point of contention between Pickens and the NAACP leadership concerned his rank within the organization. In September 1920, while Pickens was away on his first extensive field trip, the board promoted Johnson from field secretary to executive secretary, making him the first black to hold the Association's top administrative position. Pickens expected to be Johnson's replacement as field secretary, but, by December, the board had not filled the vacancy. Pickens wrote to Joel E. Spingarn, the board member whom he most trusted, expressing general dissatisfaction with the way the board had treated him.

> All arrangements for our Field Secretary work during the coming year have been so far kept almost as a profound secret from me. I am not supposed, it seems, to know. That is a bit odd, as I came in as Associate Field Secretary, and the Field Secretary has now been removed. . . . I should never have come into the Association with such a prospect—that arrangements of vital interest to me would be

completed, and that I should be left only the fearful necessity of accepting or rejecting, without any previous chance to influence the character of those arrangements. . . . I should say that I took the Association in good faith last February, gave up my other work, and even bought a home and moved my family to New York. Every impression given me when I came was that as Associate Field Secretary I should be made Field Secretary if that office was vacated while I was associated with Mr. Johnson. Else I should surely not have accepted the position.[36]

Spingarn no doubt carried Pickens's complaint to the board, for three weeks later Pickens and Mrs. Addie W. Hunton were appointed field secretaries of the NAACP. His salary also was raised from $3,000 to $3,500, with the understanding "that he is to give his entire time to the work."[37] The board also ruled that executive officers should clear with it all speaking engagements for organizations other than the NAACP. Pickens accepted the board's offer, but he felt that the executive staff, and not the Board of Directors, should rule on the propriety of officers' appearances before other organizations. "Any rule," he argued, "that even looked like a 'gag' rule is likely to prove embarrassing to the Association at some future time. I think that an understanding among the members of the staff would be the best thing."[38] During the next twenty years Pickens fought with the board many times over this issue.

Pickens proposed that the executive secretary, with a majority vote of the staff, should decide "whether any such engagement is injurious to the policies or interests of the Association." He advocated greater independence for the executive staff for two reasons. First, he believed that the predominantly Negro staff should have greater control over the day-to-day activities of the organization than the racially mixed Board of Directors. Second, he felt that he would have a freer hand in his fieldwork and private lecturing if he dealt with the executive staff, which included his friends Spingarn and Mary Ovington.

The board rejected his proposal and continued to complain that he was not devoting enough time to the organization's work. Even Du Bois criticized his handling of the fieldwork. The *Crisis* editor spelled out his criticism in a long confidential memo. He wrote:

The work which we executives have got to put over for the Negro race is bigger than any personalities. In an organization like ours injustice is bound to be done from time to time by all of us in relation to others. The greater duty calls us to bear it. Believe me, I have had my share.

> Meantime, while you are in the field, will you not let me especially ask you to be tactful and careful. Talk up the general organization in private as well as in public and be loyal to every fellow worker. Do not let anybody get the impression that there are any differences within the organization. Furthermore, will you not try to be especially tactful in the matter of taking sides in local branch difficulties. In some way you "got in wrong" in three different places where I have lectured.[39]

Du Bois went on to admit that he was not sure that Pickens was at fault, but suggested that the field secretary not "talk so much." "Listen, get in the habit of listening to other people." "I know," he concluded, "that all this may seem at first sight like unnecessary interference in your business, but I somehow feel that you will take it in the spirit in which it was intended."

Pickens was annoyed by Du Bois's advice, in part because he never took personal criticism well, and in part because Du Bois himself had had numerous run-ins with other NAACP officers and was not noted for being either "tactful" or "careful" in dealing with people.[40] In replying to Du Bois, Pickens displayed some of his well-known sarcastic wit. Since he had visited "upward of two hundred places" and "got in wrong in only three," he felt he had done quite well. He "got in 'wrongest' in Cincinnati," he wrote, by heeding Du Bois's advice and not taking sides between the membership and the officers, thereby antagonizing both sides.

> As to talking—I may be more talkative than other men I know, . . . but in twenty years of very active work I have never acquired the reputation of meddling or of speaking ill of men or women. But I have some enemies, and you have. . . . I have heard of men without enemies, and have often wondered what they could be doing. I trust I shall not have greater faults than to talk readily the truth."[41]

Pickens came increasingly to believe that he was underpaid, that his efforts were unappreciated, and that his position was being undermined by several national and executive officers. By September 1921 the NAACP field secretary was prepared to reconsider an offer from Marcus Garvey to join the black nationalist leader's Universal Negro Improvement Association (UNIA).

Garvey had established the UNIA in 1914 in his native Jamaica. The organization's motto was One God! One Aim! One Destiny! The UNIA's "Aim" was to unite "all the Negro people of the world into a great body to establish a country and a government absolutely their own"; the "Destiny" of the race was the redemption of Africa from its white colonial rulers. Garvey came to the United States in 1916 and the following year established a branch of the UNIA in New York. By 1919 he claimed thirty branches and over one million followers in the United States and throughout the world. In his weekly newspaper, *Negro World*, and from hundreds of public platforms, he preached black pride, black solidarity, and black separatism. Although the UNIA's long-range goal was a massive back-to-Africa emigration, Garvey also called on his followers, who were predominantly poor, uneducated urban blacks, to pool their resources in great commercial and industrial enterprises such as the Black Star (shipping) Line and the Negro Industrial Corporation, both of which were incorporated in 1919. Thousands of blacks responded to the charismatic leader's call and, in one year, purchased more than $600,000 worth of shares in the Black Star Line. In 1920 the UNIA staged an international convention in New York that attracted delegates from twenty-five countries. Twenty-five thousand people filled Madison Square Garden to hear Garvey say, "The other races have countries of their own and it is time for the four hundred million Negroes to claim Africa for themselves." The convention delegates promulgated a "Declaration of the Rights of the Negro Peoples of the World," which declared "all men, women and children of our blood throughout the world free citizens . . . of Africa, the Motherland of all Negroes."[42]

The NAACP would have been greatly embarrassed if its field secretary were to join the UNIA. Although the Association had refrained from publicly criticizing Garvey, several NAACP executives had privately expressed concern about his program, especially his espousal of racial separatism and his contempt for those who advocated racial integration. Du Bois was the only NAACP officer to break the Association's silence.[43]

In December 1920 Du Bois published in *The Crisis* a comprehensive evaluation of Garvey and the UNIA. Du Bois found Garvey to be "essentially an honest and sincere man with a tremendous vision, great dynamic force, stubborn determination and unselfish desire to serve," but also "dictatorial, domineering, inordinately vain and very suspicious."[44] According to Du Bois, Garvey's greatest shortcoming was that he had "absolutely no business sense, no flair for real organization." Garvey's handling of the Black Star Line's finances was so "essentially unsound" that "the investors will certainly get no dividends and worse may happen."[45] Nevertheless, Du Bois considered Garvey's economic program, if "shorn of its bombast and exaggeration," perfectly feasible. "American Negroes can," Du Bois wrote, "by accumulating and ministering their capital, organize industry, join the black centers of the South Atlantic by commercial enterprise and in this way ultimately redeem Africa as a fit and free home for black men." "But," he warned, "it will take long years of painstaking, self-sacrificing effort." Du Bois pointed out that black economic cooperation had not originated with Garvey, "but he has popularized it, made it a living, vocal idea and swept thousands with him with intense belief in the possible accomplishment of the idea." "Do not let him," he implored, "foolishly overwhelm with bankruptcy one of the most interesting spiritual movements of the modern Negro world."[46]

In his articles on the UNIA Du Bois had expressed an ambivalence toward Garvey that was shared by many black leaders. He feared that the UNIA's continued success would hurt the cause of racial integration, but he also believed that Garvey's failure would be equally calamitous for black people. "Garvey is the beloved leader of tens of thousands of poor and bewildered people," Du Bois wrote, "who have been cheated all their lives. His failure would mean a blow to their faith, and a loss of their little savings [both of], which it would take generations to undo."[47] One reason why the NAACP sought to avoid a direct confrontation with Garvey was its concern that, should the UNIA collapse, the black masses would blame the Association.

Despite the increasing rivalry between the UNIA and the NAACP, on 12 September 1921, Pickens informed Garvey that, under the right conditions, he might join his organization. Pickens wrote:

> You know my position. I am doing well personally,—and the masses with whom I deal like me,—many of them love me. There is no reason why I should seek change, and I do not. There is no personal reason, but the great feeling of the great opportunity to aid the supreme enterprise which you are undertaking, and which you have been urging me for some time to consider. . . . State to me, in so far as you can, the particulars of the work for which you want me. I know you have dealt with many traitors and have still traitors to meet. They infest the world. But trust me. If I never worked in the same organization with you, I should still be your BROTHER. . . . There would be no object in the world in my coming into your work unless it was to help you and to be able to render a greater service than I am at the present rendering. You have many inefficient, and some almost worthless, men about you. It would only handicap me to be put under them. . . . Unless it is in brothership, in full accord, a com-

pleteness of understanding, and a oneness of soul and purpose with YOU, there could be no reason and no good in my coming to your work.[48]

Five days later Pickens submitted his resignation to the NAACP, asking to be relieved of his duties no later than 1 November.[49] In letters to Joel E. Spingarn and Johnson, he hinted at the possibility of working for Garvey. Spingarn asked him to reconsider and, on 10 October, when the board agreed to give him greater freedom in determining his fieldwork schedules, Pickens withdrew his resignation.[50] Pickens had not dealt in a straightforward manner with either Garvey or the NAACP.

By threatening to join Garvey he had pressured the Association into granting him greater independence. If the board had accepted his resignation, he was prepared to work with Garvey, although the latter consistently rejected as "preposterous" the goal of racial integration shared by both the NAACP and Pickens.

In the late summer of 1921, shortly before Pickens submitted his resignation, Johnson had asked him to write a piece on Garvey for the *Nation*. Johnson did not want Garvey's attacks on the NAACP to go unanswered, but thought it best to do so through some medium other than the Association's official organ, *The Crisis*. Unaware at the time that Pickens was considering joining Garvey, Johnson presumably expected that he would be fairly critical of the UNIA and its leader.[51]

Pickens's article, "Africa for the Africans," reflected his desire to ingratiate himself with Garvey without undermining the work of the NAACP or his position in it. Although he was careful to insist that there was "no essential or natural antagonism" between the NAACP and the UNIA, he made a plausible case for Garvey's more controversial activities.[52]

> Many of us [he wrote] have ignored this man from the Indies, his organization, and the masses at his Liberty Hall. . . . There are educated and conscientious colored people in Harlem today who live within five minutes of Liberty Hall but have never been in it, and yet know that the whole movement is disreputable, dishonest, and disgraceful to their group, and that Garvey, whom they have never heard, is a smart thief or a wild fanatic.

Pickens admitted that "honest people have honest doubts" about the UNIA, and he listed and then responded to the most serious questions that Garvey's critics had raised.

THE FIELD SECRETARY AND "THE EMPEROR OF AFRICA" 65

1. "Is a Republic of Africa, controlled by black people, possible?" "Ten years ago," Pickens replied, "it seemed impossible to get the Germans out of Africa," but "something happened, unpredicted and unbelievable. . . . The Irish have struggled for generations for national freedom, but it is not as 'impossible' today as it was when the struggle began. . . . An independent African state of great power may not be realized for hundreds of years; the human equality of Negroes may not be realized for hundreds of years. But neither would be realized the sooner by not preparing, not planning and not striving for it."

2. "Why begin in the United States, and with a West Indian leader?" "A Negro of the British Empire," Pickens reasoned, "citizen of the greatest foreign power in Africa today, is the fittest person, all other things being equal, to lead in such a beginning."

3. "Why emphasize RACE? Is not the trend of social and religious forces toward the ultimate undoing away with racial alignments?" "It is possible," he answered, "that the idea of race may vanish in the future. But how far in the future? Certainly not so near as five thousand years from now. The comfort, convenience and protection of hundreds of millions of Negroes cannot wait on that millennial jubilee."

4. "Why create orders of Knights and Ladies, and have regalia, ceremonies, robes, caps and banners? Is not all that just a silly Negro characteristic?" "This is the outside, the least important side, of an organization," he argued, "and it is primarily human, and not of the Negro. It is of the English rather than the Negro. . . . The difference is that these black people, instead of praying for King George and Queen Mary, pray for Garvey and his officers and organization, as they should."

5. "What of the financial and business management and operations?" Pickens admitted that "sharks and charlatans" had infiltrated the organization and had misappropriated UNIA funds. "It is always one of the risks of such a movement that these self-seeking elements are likely to get hold of it. But the words and actions of Garvey indicate that he is opposed to these elements and grapples with and fights them as readily as he fights for his great idea."

6. "Will not the movement waste for the American Negro strength which he could better employ in relieving his difficult situation in this country?" On the contrary, Pickens argued, "in so far as [their] international racial power grew, it would strengthen the position of Negroes in the United States and

everywhere else. . . . The only hurt would come from fratricidal war between the group that chose to devote its energies to the domestic problem and the group in the international organization. . . . There is no reason why the same individual Negro may not have a membership in the Urban League, the National Association for the Advancement of Colored People, and the Universal Negro Improvement Association."[53]

Pickens's analysis of the UNIA was obviously overly optimistic and generously uncritical. He passed over Garvey's shortcomings, barely mentioned his attacks on other black activist organizations, and ignored the potentially dangerous distinction Garvey drew between dark-skinned Negroes, who were by virtue of their color true brothers of the cause, and light-skinned Negroes, whom Garvey accused of desiring acceptance by the white world and whose reliability was suspect. Nevertheless, in his brief for Garvey, Pickens articulated some of the reasons UNIA supporters were using to justify the movement. In the disruptions and disillusionment of the postwar period, many found those arguments convincing.

Despite Pickens's conflict of interests, his assessment of Garvey and that by Du Bois had some basic similarities: both conceded Garvey's personal honesty and dedication, credited him with having created single-handedly a major black mass movement, and approved of his long-range goals—Negro uplift and African redemption. Pickens and Du Bois also agreed that the UNIA's commercial and industrial enterprises, under proper management, could succeed and would be an important step toward the achievement of black self-respect and independence.

Although rejecting his offer, Pickens remained on good terms with Garvey and on 17 December, his "Africa for the Africans" appeared on the front page of *Negro World*. Garvey praised Pickens for being "honest and fair enough to seek the truth," while at the same time he condemned Du Bois for misrepresenting the UNIA's aims and methods.[54] When the Black Star Line suspended operations, early in 1922, and Garvey was arrested for mail fraud, Pickens did not join the chorus of black leaders who publicly condemned him. "I know Garvey personally," he wrote a friend, "and I do not regard him as a crook. He is somewhat of a visionary; all such men are. . . . Colored Americans will make regretable mistakes, if they help white Americans to fight the 'Garvey idea.' "[55]

Whether or not Garvey's economic program was feasible, the

Black Star Line was a colossal failure. The UNIA had purchased three ships, the *Yarmouth*, the *Shadyside*, and the *Kanawha*, which were to be part of a fleet engaged in a black triangular trade including the United States, the West Indes, and Africa. By January 1922 the *Yarmouth* had been sold at public auction, the *Shadyside* had sprung a leak and sunk in the Hudson River, the *Kanawha* had been abandoned in a Cuban port, and the *Phyllis Wheatley*, for which the UNIA had been accepting deposits for trans-Atlantic sailings, had not even been purchased.[56] Garvey blamed the Black Star Line's demise on dishonest UNIA subordinates and on "certain organizations calling themselves Negro Advancement Associations," which had "paid men to dismantle our machinery and otherwise damage it so as to bring about the downfall of the movement."[57] Garvey's charge against the NAACP was untrue and Johnson demanded a retraction. The NAACP secretary also accused the UNIA of "creating antagonism between black and white people."[58] Garvey refused to retract the statement and branded Johnson's countercharge "a malicious falsehood of the most contemptible sort."[59]

Garvey suffered several damaging reversals in the first seven months of 1922 and his organization was rapidly declining. In February he and three associates were indicted for mail fraud; three months later he was forced to admit in court that the Black Star Line had no assets and had outstanding debts of more than two hundred thousand dollars; in June, Mrs. Garvey publicly accused her husband of infidelity with his private secretary. Most damaging to the movement were newspaper reports that Garvey had established relations with the notorious Ku Klux Klan.[60]

In deep financial and legal trouble, Garvey probably calculated that, by coming to terms with the Klan, which also favored racial separation, he would have easier access to the black masses in the South. As Du Bois pointed out, "the Klan's sympathy would enable him to enter the South, where he had not dared to work, and exploit the ignorant black millions."[61] Garvey did not deny reports that he had gone to Atlanta earlier in the year to confer with Edward Young Clarke, imperial wizard of the Ku Klux Klan. In New York on the night of 9 July, Garvey told four thousand followers: "The Klan is going to make this a white country. They are perfectly honest and frank about it. Fighting them is not going to get you anywhere."[62] "Between the Ku Klux Klan and the National Association for the Advancement of 'Colored' People group," he argued, "give me the Klan for their honesty of purpose towards the Negro. . . . I regard the Klan . . . as better friends to the race than all other groups of hypocritical whites put together."[63]

The next day Garvey invited Pickens to participate in the UNIA's third annual convention, where Pickens would be one of the distinguished Negro guests honored with a knighthood.[64] Pickens by this time was one of the few black militants who had not denounced Garvey, but, after the UNIA leader admitted his alliance with the Klan, Pickens decided to disassociate himself completely from Garvey.

On 24 July Pickens wrote a public reply to Garvey's offer of a knighthood in the UNIA.

> I gather from your recent plain utterances that you are now endorsing the Ku Klux Klan, or at least conceding the justice of its aim to crush and repress colored Americans and incidentally other racial and religious groups in the United States. You compare the aim of the Ku Klux in America with your aims in Africa,—and if that be true, no civilized man can endorse either one of you.
>
> . . . .
>
> If you are trying to fool the Klan, you have employed a losing stratagem. If you are sincere, then you are more unfortunate to the American Negro than the whole Klan. You say in effect to the Ku Klux: All right! Give us Africa and we in turn concede you America as a white man's country. In that you make a poor deal: for twelve million people you give up EVERYTHING, and in exchange you get—NOTHING. For the Klan has nothing to give up in Africa; it does not own or control one square inch of Africa. But the Negro American Citizen has everything to give up in America.
>
> If it is ever to be possible for you to negotiate a worse transaction than the Black Star Line, this must be IT. In the deal for the Line, if at a very great expense, you did actually get some boats that are safe when in a good harbor,—but in this K.K.K. deal, you get absolutely nothing for the group, and for yourself, you only get a little freer hand—perhaps—to exploit the more ignorant parts of the group in the Klux-ridden section of the country.
>
> . . . .
>
> Now, I believe in law and civilized government, and am therefore against the Klan and all of its principles, yesterday, now and tomorrow. I would not therefore accept any special honor from even black people who believe in Klan-principles. Wherein I have thought Marcus Garvey to be right, I have said so, regardless of the opinions of those opposed to him. Now that I *know* him to be wrong, I say so. In this Ku Klux attitude he is just about the wrongest black man that ever tried to lead American Negroes anywhere.
>
> Perhaps, then, you will understand why I have the temerity to turn down my first, and doubtless my last, chance to become a Knight, or Duke, or some other breed of Nobleman.

. . . .
I believe in Africa for the Africans, white and black, and I believe in America for the Americans, native, naturalized and all colors,— and I believe that any of these Americans would be foolish to give up their citizenship for a thousand-year improbability in Africa or anywhere else.[65]

Having openly attacked Garvey, Pickens joined forces with the UNIA president's most outspoken critics. When the UNIA's annual convention convened in August, Pickens, along with A. Philip Randolph and Chandler Owen of the *Messenger*, and Robert Bagnall of the NAACP, staged an anti-Garvey rally several blocks from Liberty Hall. Before beginning his speech, entitled, "What to do when Negro leaders league with Negro lynchers," Pickens notified the audience that he had just received a threatening telephone call from a Garvey supporter. In his address he attacked the idea of a massive immigration to Africa, and charged Garvey with "wasting the money of the ignorant and unsuspecting and with attempting to betray twelve million American citizens into the hands of the Ku Klux Klan. . . . We charge him with tomfoolery, humbuggery, waste and with the great crime of attempting betrayal for the sake of the right of way to a few more dollars." When several West Indian Garveyites began heckling him, Pickens replied, "The best hope of the West Indian in the United States is to ally himself with the better element of Negroes in the United States and forget where he came from."[66]

Garvey responded by warning that "somebody is going to be smashed in New York between the 1st and the 31st of August." He attacked all the UNIA's black critics, but reserved his strongest threats for Pickens and Owen.[67] Pickens, protected by a cordon of policemen, continued to participate, during the rest of the month, in several other "Garvey Must Go" meetings.[68]

Garvey's prediction of violent retaliation was fulfilled by some of his supporters. They disrupted several anti-Garvey meetings, made threatening gestures at Pickens in Toronto and Owen in Pittsburgh, and may have murdered the Reverend J. W. Eason, a former Garvey associate, who was to be an important witness in the mail fraud trial.[69]

Believing that matters were getting out of control, Pickens, Owen, Bagnall, and five other prominent black leaders wrote to Attorney General Harry M. Daugherty. Calling themselves "The Committee of Eight," they urged Daugherty to use his influence "to completely disband and extirpate" the UNIA and "to vigorously and speedily push the government's case against Marcus

Garvey for using the mails to fraud."[70] "Men of brains," Pickens wrote, "are still saying that Garvey ought to be allowed to roam at large. We used to think so too, but we are not still saying so, because we can learn. . . . We gave Garvey the benefit of all doubts," he concluded, "and credit for honest intentions. We were deceived."[71]

Garvey reprinted the Committee of Eight's letter to Daugherty and denied its "vicious lies and misrepresentations."[72] "Like good old darkies," he wrote, "they believe they have some news to tell [the white man] and they are telling it for all it is worth." He tried to discredit his adversaries and to each of the eight he assigned an insulting description. Harry Pace, president of Pace Phonograph Corporation, was "a business exploiter"; Robert Abbott, publisher of the Chicago *Defender*, was "a race defamer"; John E. Nail was "a real estate shark"; Julia P. Coleman, president of Hair-Vim Chemical Company, was "a hair straightener and face bleacher"; George W. Harris, editor of the New York *News*, "maintained a Blue Vein Society Church"; Robert Bagnall, the NAACP's director of branches, was an "unscrupulous politician"; and Chandler Owen was "the grafter Socialist." Garvey reserved his strongest condemnation for Pickens, whom he described as a

> turncoat and lackey who has not enough manhood to stand up and defend his own cause in his relationship to others, but who was so mean and low down as to have approached Marcus Garvey for a job about nine months ago, representing to him that he was unfairly dealt with because of his color, and after he was offered a berth he took that as an opportunity of going back to his old employers to get them to raise his salary, which he never would have gotten raised, but for the fact that he had secured new employment in a rival organization.[73]

Garvey, whose mistrust of light-skinned Negroes originated in color-conscious Jamaica, noted that most of the "Eight" were near-white "octoroons and quadroons." Since Pickens was definitely black, Garvey mentioned that Mrs. Pickens was a light-skinned octoroon. In reply, Pickens called Garvey a "squat, energetic, gorilla-jawed black man."[74]

In May 1923, two months after the Committee of Eight wrote to the attorney general, Garvey's case finally came before the United States District Court (Southern District of New York). Much of the evidence against him was circumstantial, but Garvey may have hurt his chances for acquittal by pleading his own defense. Although his codefendants were acquitted, the jury found Garvey guilty on one count of mail fraud. On 22 June Judge Julian W. Mack, a white NAACP member, fined him one thousand dollars and imposed the maximum sentence for such a crime—five years' imprisonment.[75]

While Garvey appealed his conviction, Pickens and other critics continued their attack. "In a brief six years," Pickens wrote, "[Garvey] has not only made a place, and perhaps laid away a fortune for himself, but he has also wasted at the very lowest figure, one million dollars for Negro washerwomen and workingmen."[76] "We may be sorry that Garvey made it necessary for his career to end in jail," he added, "but we are not sorry to see him go to jail . . . and we fully approve the verdict."[77]

In an article for *Forum* magazine, Pickens tried to explain how "one of the worst enemies of his own race" had managed to retain the loyalty and support of thousands of Negroes. Among Garvey's American Negro followers, Pickens argued, "the dues-paying portion are below the average of intelligence for blacks of the continent." Some of the migrants from the South, he added, "had greatly improved their condition by one move, and as simple minds run, a longer and more daring move to Africa . . . would make their happiness complete."[78] With unintended irony he wrote, "Most of the intelligent Negroes who joined the movement were in it for the sake of salaries, titles and honors."

He also suggested that a disproportionate segment of the movement were Negroes of West Indian origin. Although West Indians had been spared the horrors of lynchings and mob violence, he reasoned, they brought to America a "settled and fixed" sense of color and caste distinctions and a history of "subjection and benevolent paternalism," which made "their future outlook more hopeless than that of the Negro in the Southern United States." Furthermore, they responded to Jamaica-born Garvey's back-to-Africa scheme, because, as colonial British subjects, they were used to being "separated by an ocean from the power which rules over them."[79]

Other black writers also stressed the importance of the West Indian role in the Garvey movement. Du Bois insisted that West Indians made up the bulk of the UNIA and contributed most of its funds. When the Black Star Line failed, "with it," he wrote," went some $800,000 of the savings of West Indians and a few American Negroes."[80] Chandler Owen pointed to the "English character" of the movement, with its royal court and titled gentlemen, its cabinet of officers, its empire-building dream, and its interest in shipping. "The Garvey movement," he added, "is a

British West Indian Association. It does not have a large following even of ignorant American Negroes."[81]

W. A. Domingo, a West Indian and a former Garvey supporter turned critic, denied that his people were the backbone of the Garvey movement. He accused Pickens, Du Bois, and other American blacks of "a belated fight to rid the race of the disgrace of Garveyism" by placing the responsibility for the movement on West Indians. "Who are the bitterest and most persistent opponents of Garvey?" he asked. "Aren't they West Indians like Cyril V. Briggs, Richard B. Moore, Frank R. Crosswaith, Thomas Potter and myself?" He also pointed out that "a majority of those be(k)nighted" by Garvey, such as John E. Bruce, R. L. Poston, and William Ferris, were American-born Negroes. "The naked and bitter realities of race prejudice" in America, and not geographic determinism, explained why blacks responded to Garvey and why many of their leaders had taken so long to see through his schemes.[82]

Domingo reminded Pickens of the *Nation* article in which the NAACP field secretary had described Garvey as being "as brave as a Numidian lion."[83] Nor did he forget that Du Bois had considered Garvey's Black Star Line a "brilliant suggestion." "The idea of establishing a line of steamships," Domingo wrote, "controlled by a politically impotent group, without technicians or a large and experienced commercial class, lacking strong international banking support, is as brilliant as Mr. Garvey's other idea of opposing the armament of the European powers in control of Africa with the wooden guns, high-sounding titles and gaudy uniforms of his Universal Legion."[84]

Domingo's point was well taken. A number of American blacks had fallen back on their anti-West Indian biases in order to avoid facing some difficult questions. Why had the UNIA been so successful in winning support among lower-class American Negroes? Why had many black leaders accepted the feasibility of some of Garvey's schemes? One answer to these interrelated questions is that Garvey struck several responsive cords in all American Negroes—the need for black solidarity, black economic independence, and black pride. The appeal was not new, but Garvey promised the fulfillment of these goals in new, simple, and dramatic forms. Blacks could expect little in a white-dominated society, he argued; therefore they must join together and separate themselves from whites; blacks could not destroy white capitalistic exploitation, but through bold, imaginative, collective enterprise, they could compete with whites on more equitable terms; the shame of enslavement and colonial domination could only be erased by redeeming Africa, thereby restoring racial dignity to all its far-flung sons. In the postwar period of disappointment and disillusionment, the audacity of Garvey's program appealed to the black masses and temporarily silenced some of the black leaders.

One student of the movement has suggested that Garvey failed because his racial chauvinism, his Black Star Line scheme, and his back-to-Africa idea were not "a suitable alternative to the unsatisfactory conditions of American life as they affect the Negro. Escape, either emotional or physical, was neither a realistic nor a lasting answer."[85] Nevertheless, if Garvey had offered "realistic" solutions to Negroes' problems, he might never have won a mass following. The more moderate Negro leaders, who had been unable to gain mass support, knew all too well that such solutions required the enthusiastic support of the dominant white society that most blacks had come to distrust.

Garvey's court appeal was denied in February 1925. With the black leader safely out of the way in federal prison at Atlanta, many of his black critics muted their attacks and began to write of him as a pathetic and somewhat romantic figure. They forgave his vituperative tongue, his attempt to polarize blacks and mulattoes, his finacial blunders, his denial of the possibility of racial integration, his alliance with the Ku Klux Klan, and they joined with the masses in seeing him as a martyr to their cause.[86]

Pickens was one of many who asked that Garvey be pardoned. "He was sent to prison for five years," he wrote, "when perhaps five months would have served the purpose as well. . . . All those who knew Garvey knew that his intention was not fraud. . . . " Garvey, who helped to jail himself by being braver than the others, but less shrewd than the others," Pickens concluded," can now be released."[87]

On 23 November 1927 President Coolidge commuted Garvey's sentence, and ten days later the UNIA leader was deported.[88] He continued to work for his cause, first in the West Indies and, later, in Great Britain, but the UNIA suffered many defections and internal factionalism and never regained the glory days of 1920. Garvey died in London in June 1940, without ever having set foot on African soil.[89]

Pickens found a "moral" in the tale of "The Emperor of Africa's" rapid rise and subsequent fall.

> It must be considered [he wrote] that Garveyism could never happen simply because there was Marcus Garvey. There was an opportunity for him and a response to him. The opportunity consists in the general repression of the Negro and Negroid peoples in parts of North America and parts of Africa. Like all humans the Negro is striving for self-expression and self-realization. And if these normal instincts are abnormally repressed, it will make him a prey to sharks and a menace to society.[90]

According to Pickens, Garvey failed because American Negroes would only consider "plans for progress in America" and not "fantastic schemes for egress from America." "Any movement," he concluded, "pivotal on any outside world is doomed to failure among this people."

In the postwar period of despair, Pickens was sympathetic to new, radical proposals for dealing with the race question, but he never approved of racial separatism or massive emigration to Africa. His brief flirtation with the Garvey movement resulted, in part, from frustration in his work and anxiety about his future, but also from his disappointment in white America. Thousands of blacks had responded to Garvey for similar reasons.

4
THE RELUCTANT REPUBLICAN, 1920–1928

> The party of Lincoln has been fully repaid for its share in slavery and emancipation. When a burglar returns your purse, should he demand a tip?
> —Pickens, 1924

In 1924 Marcus Garvey, who previously had shown little interest in domestic politics, formed the Negro Political Union in order to mobilize black voters toward a position of political independence and away from their traditional allegiance to the Republican party. This was one of the few aspects of Garvey's program with which the NAACP leadership could agree. For example, when, in 1912, Theodore Roosevelt had bolted the Republican party and had run for president as an independent progressive on the "Bull Moose" ticket, the NAACP had considered supporting him. It abandoned the idea, however, when the Bull Moose convention adopted a lily-white policy and ignored the Negro's demands for equal citizenship. A considerable minority of blacks, however, were sufficiently disillusioned with the lily-white policies of the Republican party under William Howard Taft, to break their traditional allegiance to the party of Lincoln and vote for Roosevelt or the victorious Democratic candidate, Woodrow Wilson. In 1924 a similar political phenomenon occurred. Senator Robert La Follette (R-Wisc.) bolted the Republican party and became a presidential candidate under the banner of another progressive movement, this one called the Conference for Progressive Political Action (CPPA). Although the CPPA convention was also racially exclusive and generally ignored the Negro question, a number of black leaders, including William Pickens, W. E. B. Du Bois, and James Weldon Johnson of the NAACP, supported La Follette and some black voters joined them. However, when the Republican, Calvin Coolidge, won handily, the CPPA collapsed. Politically independent black leaders and voters were again faced with the unhappy prospect, in 1928, of returning to the Republican fold, throwing away their votes on weak third parties, or voting for the Democratic party, whose congressional representatives were predominantly southerners. Some blacks voted for the Democrat Al Smith and his southern running mate, but the majority, including Pickens, reluctantly returned to the party of Lincoln.

"There is nothing sacred or inviolate about a political party"; Pickens wrote in 1923, "it is but a machine, a convenience, and [not] deserving of reverence." "It made sense," he continued, "when black leader Frederick Douglass [after the Civil War] spoke of the Republican Party as 'the ship, all else is the sea.' No longer! Today there is very little difference, in fact, for the Negro between these two major parties—and yet the superstition persists, especially in the minds of some of the older colored men."[1]

Like Pickens, many black leaders, during the postwar decade, reexamined their traditional loyalty to the Republican party. They had generally supported Republican candidates, especially in presidential elections, but with resignation rather than enthusiasm. Seeing little difference between the two parties, they voted Republican because a Democrat in the White House meant southern control of the national government. During Woodrow Wilson's tenure in office (1913–21) blacks had been segregated in government offices in Washington, D.C.; they had lost traditional federal appointments; and they had observed the national government cease to be even outwardly sympathetic to their cause.

With increasing numbers of Negroes moving north, however, black leaders realized that, by mobilizing and controlling black votes, they could act as a balance of power in close elections in eastern and midwestern states. With this potential power in mind, they made greater demands on the Republican party and warned that, should the GOP take them for granted, they would no longer accept Frederick Douglass's dictum.

More than Negro allegiance to the party of Lincoln was at stake. Negroes' enthusiastic response to the Garvey movement had shown that, if the dominant political parties remained insensitive to their demands, blacks might lose faith in the existing political system and turn to more radical means to ameliorate their condition. Furthermore, "The American Negro," Pickens wrote in 1924, "has shown little disposition to try to secure his fundamental rights by violence, but he is less patient today than he was ten years ago, and being human, he is ultimately capable of any human expression."[2]

Pickens was one of the NAACP leaders who wanted the organization to become more politically aggressive. Traditionally, the Association, whose membership was predominantly Republican, had maintained a nonpartisan position, preferring to judge candidates by their records on racial matters. In 1920 the NAACP board sent a questionnaire to potential presidential candidates of both parties that reflected the Association's major concerns. Top priority was given to the reenfranchisement of southern Negroes, federal antilynching legislation, and the abolition of segregation in the nation's Capitol. The NAACP also wanted candidates to pledge support for federal aid to the education of children of both races, fair representation of Negro soldiers and officers in the armed forces, and the abolition of Jim Crow on interstate carriers. Indicative of the association's growing interest in international affairs was its request for "a solemn pledge to respect the independence of Haiti."[3] The NAACP had received reports that U.S. marines, who had established a de facto protectorate over the "black" republic in 1915, were killing many Haitian civilians while helping to put down an insurrection against the American-supported government. The Association took a special interest in Haiti because it was the only nation outside Africa with a Negro government.[4]

Acting Secretary James Weldon Johnson and Ohioan Harry E. Davis of the NAACP board visited Republican presidential candidate Warren G. Harding at his home in Marion, Ohio, to ask him to speak out publicly in support of the Negro demands incorporated in the NAACP questionnaire. Harding received Johnson and Davis cordially, agreed with them in principle, but, except for the Haitian question, was unwilling to make campaign issues of any of their demands. When Harding expressed concern that injection of the Negro question into the campaign would lose the Republican party more votes than it would gain, Johnson replied, "The colored people of the United States [are] dissatisfied and have become weary of political generalities." He reminded Harding that, in a close election, Negro votes "might be a decisive factor" in states like Ohio, Indiana, Illinois, New Jersey, Michigan, and New York, and that Harding's endorsement of Negro demands would insure the Negro vote to the Republican party. Harding pointed out that he had condemned lynching in his acceptance speech and that, if elected, he would support legislation to improve conditions for Negroes, but he refused to make any other public statement or to use the pages of the *Crisis* in support of their other demands.⁵

Harding and his running mate, Governor Calvin Coolidge of Massachusetts, generated little enthusiasm among black voters during the campaign, but the Democratic standard-bearers, James M. Cox and Franklin D. Roosevelt, made no appeal at all for their support. As a result, Negroes probably voted overwhelmingly for Harding in his landslide victory over Governor Cox.⁶

As president, Harding gave Negroes little cause to renew their faith in the Republican party. By late spring 1922, Pickens, who had reluctantly supported the Republican nominee, attacked Harding for ignoring the Negro. He accused the president of paying lip service to demands for antilynching legislation and for an end to American involvement in Haiti merely to win Negro votes and, in the case of Haiti, to embarrass the previous Democratic administration.

> Since the [Republicans] have captured the fort they are "back to normalcy," indeed [he wrote] and there is no enthusiasm for these ideas . . . about human liberty and American equality of citizenship. Of course, Mr. Harding is a regular fellow . . . that is a machine fellow. To be sure, such a "regular" has no opinions and principles of his own; he is a great weather-cock. There can be no "ill-wind" for him for whatever wind blows hardest will find him with the wind.⁷

When the president and Senate Republicans did nothing to break a southern Democrat filibuster against Representative L. C. Dyer's (R-Mo.) antilynching bill, Pickens exclaimed: "We must have a Democratic Congress and President in 1925. . . . A frank foe is preferable to a treacherous friend."⁸

"Let us not be so silly," Pickens warned after Harding's sudden death in August 1923, "as to think that Providence has arranged the matter for us by making a Massachusetts man President. Coolidge is from the right section of the world, the right stock, and seems to be the right sort of old-fashioned 'Yankee,' but it is yet to be seen whether he will stand up under the test."⁹ When Coolidge, in one of his first presidential actions, appointed as his personal secretary, C. Bascom Slemp, a Virginia congressman, Pickens wrote: "Well, we didn't have to wait long. . . . Slemp is a wealthy Southern white Republican . . . of the 'lily white' breed."¹⁰ Du Bois, echoing Pickens, considered Slemp's appointment "a blow so serious and fatal that we have not ceased to gasp at it." He further suggested that Coolidge had chosen Slemp in order "to buy up venal Southern votes in the next Republican

Presidential Convention."[11] The Slemp appointment foreshadowed Coolidge's general neglect of the Negro constituency.[12]

Both Pickens and Du Bois called for an end to the Negro's allegiance to the Republican party. "You don't really care a rap who is president," Du Bois wrote to his black readers. "Republican presidents are just about as bad as Democratic and Democratic presidents are little better than nothing."[13] "For my part," Pickens added,

> I feel that it is at present best for the great masses of the Negro vote to join with any party (Republican, Democratic, Socialist, or what not) making the best appeal to their group interests. . . . The minority Negro vote attains its highest potential power in American politics only when it assumes an open-mindedness toward all parties and appeals. Once it is pre-empted and owned, its power disappears.[14]

Pickens, Du Bois, and other black leaders hoped that a viable third party would emerge that would actively seek black support, and they looked with favor on the Conference for Progressive Political Action (CPPA), which, by 1924, seemed to be moving in that direction.

Begun in 1919 as a movement among "die-hard progressives," the CPPA grew in the following years, picking up trade unionists, Socialists, concerned liberals, disenchanted Republicans, old Populists, Non-Partisan Leaguers, and other reformers dissatisfied with the two major parties. The movement's main support came from midwestern farmers, Socialists, and the four Railroad Brotherhood unions.[15]

In the spring of 1924 the CPPA issued a "Call" for nationwide support. Darwin J. Meserole, chairman of the CPPA Finance Committee and a New York resident, wrote to James Weldon Johnson, asking him and other NAACP officers to sign the Call, which read in part:

> A number of men and women . . . have fearlessly and with untiring energy championed the cause of the people against those business and financial interests of whose corrupting power the recent investigations in Washington have given some slight indication. . . . Their labor will have been in vain if now the workers, farmers and forward looking men and women of the great middle class of our nation do not rally to their support.[16]

Meserole invited the NAACP to send delegates to the CPPA's presidential convention on 4 July in Cleveland. The NAACP Board of Directors decided that "in view of the Association's nonpartisan attitude," none of its officers would sign the Call, although it was "in hearty sympathy with the aims of those behind the movement."[17] Two months later, at its annual meeting, in Philadelphia, the NAACP reconsidered its position. The Republicans had nominated Coolidge and General Charles Dawes and had endorsed a campaign platform, which, except for opposing lynching, said nothing on the Negro question. At the Philadelphia meeting John Haynes Holmes, white pastor of the Community Church of New York and an active NAACP member, condemned the Republicans for "straddling" the Ku Klux Klan issue, which, in 1924, was a major political concern. He also called the GOP plank against lynching "a farce." Calling for support of the CPPA, he added, "Negroes in America cannot hope to get anywhere until they rid themselves of the Republican Party superstitition."[18]

Johnson followed Holmes to the speaker's platform and stressed the importance of the Klan question to the Negro. He said:

> The biggest issue before [the Negro] is that of the Ku Klux Klan. Colored America should not be lulled into a sense of security by the fact that the Klan is seemingly no longer anti-Negro. The Klan is as much anti-Negro today as it was the day it was organized. At present it is not spending much time tarring and feathering individual Negroes. It is devoting its energies to the bigger job of gaining political power. If it does this it will again turn its attention to the Negro.

Johnson pointed out that the Klan, which was also anti-Catholic, anti-Semitic, anti-immigrant and anti-radical, had spread its influence beyond the South, having strong organizations from Maine to California. In Indiana, for example, the Republican nominee for governor had recently accepted the Klan's endorsement and Senator James E. Watson "openly confers with Klan leaders." "It is the duty of Negro voters there," Johnson insisted, "to vote against the governor and every Republican candidate who is touched with the tar brush of the Klan."

The NAACP delegates, convinced that both the Republicans and the Democrats were "catering to the Ku Klux Klan," decided that "nothing will more quickly bring the old parties to a clear realization of their obligations to us and the nation than a vigorous third party movement. Such a movement may save us from a choice between half-hearted friends and half-concealed enemies."[19] The NAACP was prepared to endorse the CPPA's presidential candidate, that is, if the CPPA, which was about to convene in Cleveland, chose an acceptable candidate and wrote an acceptable platform.[20]

The NAACP board sent Pickens to Cleveland "to bring such influence as might be brought to have the Convention give favorable consideration to the questions brought to their attention by the Association."[21] This was a difficult and delicate assignment for Pickens. He was to represent the NAACP as an observer rather than a delegate. The Association had made no firm commitment to endorse the Progressive candidate, who in all likelihood would be Senator La Follette, and Pickens's assignment was to get the convention to endorse a platform that the Association could accept. Just before leaving for Cleveland, Pickens and Johnson collaborated on a message that was sent to La Follette.

> Earnestly request that you urge Cleveland Convention to include in platform plank favoring enactment of federal anti-lynching law, plank denouncing Ku Klux Klan specifically and general statement on Negro's civil rights. This much at least the colored voters of the country are looking for from the forces to be led by you.[22]

Although La Follette kept away from Cleveland, he dominated the CPPA convention. There was no serious opposition to his candidacy and the platform reflected his most cherished goals. His son, Robert, Jr., read his prepared statement to the obvious approval of the assembled delegates. "To break the combined power of the private monopoly system over the political and economic life of the American people," the younger La Follette concluded, "is the one paramount issue of the 1924 campaign."[23]

Most of the delegates agreed. As Oswald Garrison Villard observed, "These men and women represented a conscious craving for something else than the self-seeking and hypocrisy and prostitution of the two old parties."[24] William H. Johnston, chairman of the CPPA and president of the International Association of Machinists, reminded the delegates of Republican involvement in the Teapot Dome and other oil scandals, as well as the alleged frauds, during the Wilson administration, related to war contracts and confiscated alien property. "The Democratic and Republican Parties have both forfeited all claims to public confidence," Johnston concluded.[25]

The CPPA platform, which was overwhelmingly approved by the delegates, reflected their desire to break what they believed was big business's stranglehold on the nation. The assembled progressives, Socialists, farmers, trade unionists, and other reformers, agreed that the federal government had to destroy private monopolies, tax the wealthy, place federal controls on credit, assume public ownership of the nation's natural resources and railroads, legislate collective bargaining rights for workers, assist in the marketing of farm products and the establishment of industrial cooperatives, and abolish child labor. In the international field they called for the abolition of war and colonial exploitation. However, except for demanding the withdrawal of American troops from Haiti, the platform was silent on those matters that were particularly important to Negroes—the Klan, lynching, segregation, disenfranchisement, and discrimination.[26]

Pickens was disheartened but not surprised by the convention's refusal to deal with the Negro question. "There was not a single Negro delegate in the affair," he reported to the NAACP board, "and but for the representative of the NAACP, there would not have been a single colored person working, among the delegates or on the main floor, in the interest of colored people."[27] The convention leaders "had evidently decided before they came to Cleveland," Pickens wrote, "not to bring up the Klan issue, because, as they claimed, such a religious and racial issue might becloud the more essential economic issues." "They also had observed," he added, "what a happy time the blessed Democrats were having over the Klan in Madison Square Garden."[28]

Pickens believed that not more than ten percent of the delegates in Cleveland were sympathetic to the Klan and that the Socialists were "actively and decidedly anti-Klan." "Many courageous whites were interested in [condemning] the Klan by name," he wrote, "but were quietly turned down or double-crossed. I have in my bag a copy of a resolution which Norman Thomas tried to get in on the Klan. He failed and gave it to me to use in my work."[29]

He tried to get Chairman Johnston to allow him to present Thomas's motion from the floor of the convention.[30] Johnston, in his keynote address, had criticized the "base expediency and unprincipled compromise" of the other parties in "straddling" the Klan issue, but he was unwilling to support Pickens's proposal. "I saw that there was little hope," Pickens reported. "The masters were disposed to dodge and promise and play politics."[31]

On the second day of the convention Pickens again tried to get permission to offer resolutions on the Klan, lynching, and racial discrimination. The convention leaders refused. "They were diplomatic with us," Pickens wrote, "but I could see beneath their words and faces that there was a great desire both to pacify us and to be rid of our dangerous insistence upon these issues."[32] Johnston did allow Pickens to read to the convention the NAACP's statement favoring a third-party movement. Pickens told the white audience that thousands of Negroes were out of sympathy with both old parties and were ready to support the new party if the CPPA wanted them.[33] One observer praised Pickens's "natural, sincere eloquence," and called him "a gallant and rousing figure."[34] "The delegates cheered him wildly,"[35] but the convention, which had shown compassion for Haitians, Filipinos, and the Irish, adjourned without taking up the Negro question.

The NAACP board, after reading Pickens's report, agreed that the CPPA convention had been "decidedly disappointing." "It seems apparent," wrote James Weldon Johnson, "that Senator La Follette and his advisers are afraid of the Ku Klux Klan question, and as for the Negro, they perhaps felt that they had better not take on any more unpopular causes." Although the CPPA program was "more advanced and more intelligent" than that of the other parties, he added, "it contains nothing that makes any special appeal to colored voters."[36]

The Association had been prepared to take a radical political step in 1924 toward an alliance with white reformers, organized labor, and farmers in the formation of a new political party. The Socialists were willing, but the Progressives and, especially, the four Railroad brotherhoods, which financed the convention, had ignored the NAACP's overture. The brotherhoods, as Pickens pointed out, avoided an alliance with the NAACP because they "specifically exclude the Negro from their union rights."[37] The NAACP decided to retain its nonpartisan position in 1924 and did not endorse La Follette.

Black leaders, in general, were deeply divided on how Negroes should vote in the presidential election. A few joined former assistant attorney General William H. Lewis, in supporting John W. Davis, the Democratic candidate. Borrowing from Frederick Douglass, Lewis wrote: "I am going to step aboard the good ship Democracy. If she brings me safe into the harbor of political rights there will dawn a new day for my race and country. If we do not make the port, we are no worse off."[38] NAACP Board Director Harry E. Davis, who was a Republican member of the Ohio legislature, advised blacks to stay in the Republican fold.[39] Floyd Calvin of the Pittsburgh *Courier* also endorsed Coolidge and considered Negro support of the CPPA "nothing short of foolish." He argued that La Follette represented only "disgruntled western farmers who hate the railroads" and had nothing to offer Negroes.[40] W. T. Francis, a St. Paul attorney, pointed out that "third parties heretofore have met with small success," and he advised blacks to "stick to the Republican Party." The CPPA is not a party, he added, "it is La Follette . . . and its outlook is not bright."[41] Bishop John F. Hurst of the African Methodist Episcopal Church, however, favored La Follette. "Show the Republican Party," he wrote, "that there is a limit to the endurance and the patience of the colored American citizens."[42] "I shall vote for La Follette and [Senator Burton K.] Wheeler," wrote Du Bois. "I do not believe in Coolidge. I despise Dawes and will trust no Wall Street lawyer or any relative of southernized Bryan."[43]

Pickens, despite his disappointment at Cleveland, leaned toward La Follette. The CPPA convention had been "unwilling or afraid to specify the Negro or allow his case to become an issue," he wrote. Nevertheless, "here was a group of people who would be in the main fairer and juster and squarer with the Negro than any other group that had gathered in a political convention since Reconstruction days." However, "La Follette must talk plain and straight to the point," he concluded, "if he expects the unselfish and thoughtful part of the Negro vote to have any feeling of conviction that his leadership and his party are more decently American than the others."[44] When La Follette declared himself "unalterably opposed to the evident purpose of the secret organization of the Ku Klux Klan," Pickens endorsed his candidacy and agreed to serve as a CPPA presidential elector in New York.[45]

Negroes had no choice, Pickens decided, but to support the Progressive candidate. He discounted John W. Davis because of the influence of the South and the Klan in the Democratic party. Coolidge remained silent on the Negro question and his running mate, in Pickens's view, "whitewashed" the Klan by suggesting that, under certain circumstances, extralegal mob action was justified. Pickens called Dawes "a Klansman in spirit—a Ku Kluxer without a pillow-case over his head."[46]

The Negro's "long allegiance and servitude to the Republican Party," Pickens argued, no longer made any sense. The party of Lincoln had been "fully repaid for its share in slavery and emancipation." "When a burglar returns your purse," he asked, "should he demand a tip?" As for La Follette, he was "a real man" who had never committed "an act or word against the Negro race."[47] He could find little else to say in support of the Progressive candidate. Pickens knew that the implementation of La Follette's program against monopoly and corruption would not necessarily affect the Negro portion of the population. Nevertheless, a vote for La Follette was a vote against the political status quo and the "average cog-wheel politicians of the two old parties."[48]

Coolidge easily won the presidency, polling 54 percent of the popular vote and carrying thirty-five states. Davis received close to 30 percent of the vote and, as expected, won the South's electoral votes. Nearly five million voters supported La Follette (17 percent of the total vote), but he only managed to win the electoral votes of his home state of Wisconsin. He won more votes than Davis in eleven western states, but did poorly in the South and New England.[49]

It is not clear how well La Follette did among Negro voters.[50] Du Bois believed that one quarter of the estimated two million Negro voters went for the Progressive candidate.[51] Although La Follette was strongest in states west of the Mississippi, where there were relatively few Negro voters, he also did well in a number of urban industrial counties of Illinois, Michigan, Ohio, Pennsylvania, New York, and New Jersey, where Negroes did reside. If the historian Kenneth Mac Kay is correct in his conclusion that "the Negro vote was not identifiable in the 1924 election," this could be significant.[52] Since black leaders could not agree upon a single candidate, and since the CPPA did not make a concerted effort to win Negro support, the fact that Negroes apparently did not vote as a bloc would indicate that a number of them had broken with their traditional allegiance to the Republican party's presidential nominees.[53] Du Bois probably exaggerated La Follette's black support, but he may have been correct in calling their response "a splendid and far-reaching gesture," and an indication of their growing political independence. However, Du Bois incorrectly predicted that the CPPA "had come to stay" and would develop into a permanent third party. In the aftermath of the 1924 election, the CPPA fell apart, especially after La Follette's death in June 1925, and, by the 1928 election, Negroes had to choose again between the two old parties.

Because Pickens, Du Bois, Johnson, and several board members had endorsed La Follette, a number of the NAACP's regular Republican members criticized the Association for violating its traditional nonpartisanship. These black Republican leaders, a number of whom had benefited personally from party patronage, were willing to criticize the Republicans, but stopped short at endorsing candidates from other parties.

For example, Dr. George E. Cannon, a black Republican national committeeman from New Jersey, in July 1923 had led a group of Negro Republicans from eighteen states in a public attack on President Harding, who, Cannon said, had "given less recognition to the colored race than previous Republican presidents."[54] Cannon, however, remained loyal to the Republican party, and, shortly before the 1924 election, he resigned from the NAACP Executive Board because of "the open hostility of the officials of the Association towards President Coolidge and the Republican Party. In becoming a pro-Democratic and Socialist organization, I fear the Association has reached the parting of the ways."[55]

Cannon was not the first regular Republican to accuse the NAACP, not only of anti-Republicanism, but of leaning toward the radical left. When, in 1922, the Association had opposed the reelection of several Republican congressmen who had opposed Dyer's antilynching bill, Perry Howard, a black Mississippian in the Justice Department, had called Du Bois, Pickens, and Johnson "political bolshevists."[56] But the Association had no direct ties with the Socialist party and certainly none with the newly formed Communist groups. Ever since the Red Scare of 1919, the NAACP had gone to great lengths to insist that it rejected both Communist doctrine and tactics.[57] For example, in May 1920, the NAACP board had resolved to strive for Negro rights "through the press, the platform, the ballot box, legislative bodies and the courts, and by every tried and tested legal and constitutional method . . . *and by no other method*."[58]

Pickens, disillusioned with the Republicans and fearful of southern Democrats, admired the Socialists although he never joined the party. When in 1922 he was accused of being a Socialist by another black Republican officeholder, he called it a "willful and unqualified lie." "If I were a Socialist," he added, "I would not apologize for it."[59] He was sympathetic to the Socialist party program, had a number of Socialist friends, and was a member of the League for Industrial Democracy (LID), originally the Intercollegiate Socialist Society, a group of articulate Socialists and supporters interested in "education for a new social order based on production for use and not profit."[60] In 1923 he was a leading speaker at the LID's Camp Tamiment

Conference in Pennsylvania, where he urged blacks to join with like-minded white workers to fight economic exploitation.[61] In the mid-1920s and 1930s he was a member of the LID's Board of Directors.[62]

Pickens had been impressed with the Socialists' performance at the CPPA convention in 1924. "It was they," he reported to the NAACP, "who . . . declared unequivocally against the Klan and in favor of the impartial recognition of Negroes in all labor unions. . . . The Socialists therefore hold the palm among all party groups."[63] But the Socialists were politically weak, especially after the CPPA's collapse, and they could not mount a serious challenge to the two-party system. Therefore, Pickens, with little enthusiasm, supported the Republican presidential candidate, Herbert Hoover, in 1928 and 1932. His opposition to Al Smith in 1928 was based primarily on southern predominance with the Democratic party.[64] "If today," he argued,

> the Democratic Party were offering the Negro fairer prospects (or, if you prefer, *less gloomy prospects*) than those offered by the Republican Party, then we could say in effect: "To Hell with ancient history!" . . . Well, no honest American in his right mind can say that in 1928 the Negro citizen can look with indifference . . . upon the prospects of Democratic victory.

Both Smith and Hoover were "reputable persons," but, Pickens warned, "if Smith is elected . . . the South is elected to [national] dominance. The South dominates the Democratic Party and will continue to dominate that party for an indefinite future time."[65]

He also pointed out that Smith's election would make Senator Joseph Robinson of Arkansas the vice president, and "there would stand just one little frail human life between the highest office in the nation and a rank representative of the Southern oligarchy." For those reasons "this Democratic ticket is loaded with menace for the Negro." Pickens knew that Smith had considered issuing a statement, drafted for him by Walter White, declaring his intention to be "president of all the people," but Senators Robinson and Pat Harrison (D-Miss.) had convinced the candidate that even the most innocuous statement to that effect would antagonize the South.[66] With this in mind, Pickens said: "If he [Smith] needs the South so badly in the election, he will need their representatives still more in the Congress, if he wishes to be able to achieve anything as President. No Democratic President can ignore the South."[67]

Under existing conditions, Pickens believed, Negroes could

not afford the "luxury" of weighing the parties' positions on such issues as tarriffs, farm relief, or foreign policy. He explained:

> The Negro must properly subordinate all other problems to his citizenship rights: if he is not a citizen, neither tariff nor farm relief nor foreign relations will do him any good. What boots it for him to take the tariff off beans if he cannot get any of the beans in Atlanta? Will bigger profits for the farmer help a Mississippi Negro peon? . . . As to our foreign relations: our dominating attitude toward Hayti and the rest of Latin America got in such a state under Woodrow Wilson, in the last Democratic administration, that the combined liberal and anti-imperialistic sentiment of both parties has not yet been able to recall us to the Constitution and to our pristine favor for freedom and human brotherhood. But who expects Robinson of Arkansas to be more decent toward Negroes in Hayti than he is toward Negroes in Little Rock?

The Democratic party had to be "smashed" at the polls, he concluded, and the only way was for blacks to vote for the Republicans, who were "incidentally" led by Herbert Hoover.[68] Most blacks voted for Hoover (or against the Democratic party) in 1928, but a considerable minority, as in 1924, rejected the party of Lincoln.[69] Hoover, whom Walter White called the "Man in the Lily-White House," did little as president to retain black support, except to initiate the withdrawal of American troops from Haiti that was completed under Roosevelt.[70] By nominating Judge John J. Parker of North Carolina for the Supreme Court,[71] Hoover reflected Republican efforts to dislodge the Democrats from their southern stronghold, and the president refused to undermine this strategy by supporting legislation favorable to Negroes. Pickens, nevertheless, supported him again in 1932 for reasons similar to those he had expressed in 1928.

5
THE NAACP COMES OF AGE, 1920–1931

> Let me hasten to congratulate you on the excellent fight you stirred up against the confirmation of Judge Parker. Whether he is or is not named, I believe the group has won great respect through its stimulated mass protest. The NAACP gets the credit for that and no one can take it away.
> —George S. Schuyler to Walter White, 26 April 1930

The fight, in 1930, to deny the confirmation of Judge John J. Parker to the Supreme Court "was recognized," wrote Walter White, executive secretary of the NAACP, "as the political coming of age of the hitherto-ignored Negro voters."[1] The NAACP, in conducting the Parker campaign, celebrated its twenty-first anniversary by demonstrating how well its leaders could work together in mobilizing black support for a popular cause. This, unfortunately, was not always the case. During the 1920s and 1930s the NAACP suffered from serious tensions and personal rivalries within its hierarchy that threatened to undermine the organization's effectiveness. William Pickens was involved in most of these internal quarrels. The most serious conflict was between Pickens, W. E. B. Du Bois, and the rest of the Association black executives, on one side, and White on the other. When, in 1931, Du Bois led an abortive attempt to purge White, the NAACP board supported White, in part, because the previous year he had personally engineered the campaign against Judge Parker. Except for Roy Wilkins, White's assistant, all of the executive officers who had opposed White, including Pickens, eventually had to leave their posts in the NAACP.

Pickens and Du Bois were outspoken, controversial figures in the NAACP who generated excitement and attracted attention—Pickens with his colorful oratory and Du Bois with his erudition. Although quite different in temperament—Pickens was gregarious, Du Bois aloof—neither fitted comfortably into the NAACP's bureaucracy; neither was a good administrator. On the other hand, White, who joined the NAACP as its assistant executive secretary in 1918, was close to being the quintessential organization man. He was as passionately devoted to the Negro's cause as anyone in the Association, but he had learned early—perhaps in the insurance business in Atlanta—to manipulate and operate within a given organizational structure. White was more skillful at public relations than either Pickens or Du Bois, and he paid more attention to administrative details. Pickens and Du Bois were essentially moral propagandists; White was more a politician, more concerned with the effect of a particular action on the Association's future. While Pickens and Du Bois publicly criticized the Association when they disagreed with a policy decision, White generally worked in closer harmony with the NAACP board and, although he influenced decision-making, rarely challenged a policy once it had been adopted. Furthermore, Pickens and Du Bois were politically more radical than White and sought to broaden the Association's activities to include influence on economic policy, labor relations, and international affairs. It was not surprising, then, that the board in 1930 chose White to be James Weldon Johnson's successor as executive secretary, rather than Pickens or Du Bois. The NAACP needed both propagandists and administrators. The question remained, however, whether the Association could survive the recurrent friction between Pickens and Du Bois with White.[2]

The feud between Pickens and White developed over many years and did not reach a climax until 1942. The two men had little in common. Both were southern-born, but White grew up in relative prosperity in Atlanta, one of the South's more cosmopolitan centers, while Pickens, before he moved to Little Rock, was raised in the rural poverty of South Carolina and Arkansas. Although both went to New York at approximately the same time, White, who was twelve years younger than Pickens, adopted a northern, urbane style more readily than Pickens, who always retained something of the quality of his rural, unsophisticated origins. Pickens, moreover, was very dark-skinned, while White, who had a light complexion, blue eyes, and blond hair, could easily have passed as a Caucasian. In fact, some of Pickens's contemporaries believed that the NAACP board held him back and promoted White because of the differences in their appearances.[3] Although they rarely admitted it to whites, some blacks prejudged members of their own race on the basis of color. For example, J. Max Barber, a Negro dentist and one-time NAACP board director, wrote to Pickens: "I never did trust Walter White. . . . Somehow I never warmed up to—never quite trusted a half-white or near-white Negro. He is under a diversity of complexes which do not help his soul." Mulattoes have "split souls," he added. "Those split loyalties seem to make them shifty, mean, unreliable, treacherous."[4] But although color may have been a factor in the animosity between the two men, Pickens, at least, never referred to it in his correspondence.

Roy Wilkins, who worked closely with both men, believed that they did not get along, in part, because Pickens "could never forget that he was a Phi Beta Kappa from Yale and White only a graduate from Atlanta University."[5] On the other hand, Lemuel Foster, who also knew both men for many years, thought that Pickens "wore his Yale diploma like an old hat" and believed that few men got on well with White, who in Foster's view, was a "one-man show."[6] Whatever the decisive factors—age, background, temperament, color, politics, or occupational rivalry—Pickens and White, both key figures in the NAACP, were antagonists for more than twenty years.

Pickens's personal feud with White was a major, but not the only irritant, in his relationship with the NAACP. For example, throughout his tenure as field secretary he complained that he was underpaid. In February 1921, less than a year after joining the NAACP staff, he had withdrawn a letter of resignation when the board increased his salary. But by 1923 he again was asking for more money. "I could not pay my bills now," he informed the board, "if I did not earn a bit occasionally by work outside the Association." "If comparisons are enlightening," he added," it can be found that other organizations, whose executives do a work much less fraught with peril to their futures and their families, are actually paid more than the NAACP executives."[7]

Pickens's work was indeed "fraught with peril." As NAACP Board Chairman Mary Ovington wrote:

> Few people, at least few white people, realize the danger involved in the field work of the NAACP. Mr. Johnson, Mr. Pickens, Mr. Bagnall, Mrs. Hunton and Mr. White risk their lives again and again. Where there is a lawless element in a Southern community, no educated colored man coming from a distance can be assured of safety.[8]

This was particularly true for Pickens who made more field trips to the South than any other NAACP officer. He found many times that southern branches had canceled meetings at which he was to speak because local whites (often Klansmen) had threatened to harm him or one of the branch leaders. At other times local Negro leaders insisted that he speak without identifying himself as an NAACP representative. Some blacks, he felt, came to his talks out of morbid curiosity or, as Pickens put it, "to see what would happen." In Maysville, Kentucky, for example, a crowd of three hundred blacks attended his talk but none joined the NAACP or made a contribution. "That was not what the crowd came for," he wrote, "but to see the KKK come in with whips and clubs and maybe ropes and tar to drive me out."[9]

In Shreveport, Louisiana, in 1922, the local sheriff and his deputies interrupted a meeting, just after Pickens had left, and demanded to know where "Charley Pickett" was. "The sheriff assured us," one of the participants informed Pickens, "that he would not kill 'Pickett' or hang him, but would start him from town as he had done Mulch, the I.W.W. organizer."[10]

Pickens found similar examples of Negro concern for white reprisals as late as 1930, but "in many places," he wrote, "they stood up bravely." He was sometimes critical of southern Negro cautiousness, but admitted later that "they had to remain and live in that place, while I . . . was going to take the next train out."[11]

The NAACP board recognized the hazardous nature of Pickens's work, but, because of its limited resources, it could never pay what he considered a commensurate salary. More important than salary as a cause of friction between Pickens and the board was his propensity for getting into controversies that were embarrassing to the Association. One such controversy developed out of Pickens's attacks on the major Negro churches. He had been raised as a Baptist, converted to Congregationalism in college, and in 1915 joined the Methodist Episcopal Church. When he moved to New York, in 1920, he also became a member of John Haynes Holmes's nondenominational Community Church, although retaining an affiliation with the Methodists.

Pickens opposed the established Negro churches on several grounds. He rejected their emotionalism and biblical fundamentalism and considered most Negro ministers too conservative, too self-seeking, and too accommodating to whites. After a meeting in Monongahela, Pennsylvania, in 1923, he wrote: "The preachers help here in the usual way—by not hindering much. They do most of the talking, but . . . they do nothing to help. This is not due, I suppose, always to their individual character, as much as to the situation and prejudices of their profession."[12]

In February 1923 Pickens publicly attacked the Negro churches in an article for A. Philip Randolph's Socialist *Messenger*. "No intelligent man will ever believe," he wrote, "most of the superstitious buncombe that is handed out from most of the pulpits today." He challenged a literal interpretation of the Bible, claiming that "nobody believes, though many accept or swallow" the idea "that Adam was made out of nothing, . . . that the whale swallowed Jonah,. . . that there is a materialistic heaven situated anywhere in space,. . . that there is a lake of fire and brimstone,. . . that God would ever consider of the abomination of eternal punishment for . . . human beings," or "that there ever was or ever will be a baby in hell—if there is a hell." "God is not against science;" he added, "He is not on the side of ignorance and bigotry. He has not appointed ultimate and inviolate authorities among men. Every brave and intelligent man is his own mediator."[13]

Since many Negroes were members of fundamentalist churches, Pickens soon learned that he could not advocate a "reasonable religion of humanity" without incurring the wrath of Negro ministers and the enmity of many of their followers. "Were you crazy when you wrote that article for the *Messenger*?" asked Nannie H. Burroughs. Burroughs, president of the National Training School for Women in Washington, D.C., was an active NAACP member and a leading figure in the civil rights movement. She continued:

> I am just as sorry as I can be that you wrote it. I know what you are going to say about your right to think what you think and to believe what you believe, but your article in the *Messenger* is not going to help you nor the NAACP. Your friends are shocked and we are wondering what we can do to save you.
>
> You know as well as I do that Negro ministers are going to shut their doors in the face of a representative of the NAACP who thus expressed himself. . . . You know as well as I do the attitude of the Negro ministers toward the NAACP. Why would you make it any more difficult to get into the churches and to get funds. . . .
>
> You know you have been very popular with the Negro masses and you will lose their respect and support if you write another article like the one in the February *Messenger*.[14]

Relatively few blacks read Pickens's *Messenger* article, but the Baltimore *Afro-American* gave the story front page coverage. The following week twenty-six Negro ministers wrote an open letter to Pickens. "We believe he [Pickens] has been Baptist, Congregationalist, Methodist Episcopalian, and is now an African Methodist Episcopalian. What does the dean believe?"[15] R. R. Wright, Jr., a leading bishop in the African Methodist Episcopal Church, made the same point. "We have seen what Dean Pickens does not believe," he wrote.

> We should like to know what the former dean does believe. . . . Or is the dean one of those so mixed up in his theology that he really has no belief? . . . We have always had a great deal of admiration for the Dean, but if he believes nobody believes in the things which he says, he is very far wrong. . . . The serious side of Dean Pickens' agnosticism is that he represents a growing minority among colored people . . . who could not pass a fair examination on the Bible, but who presume to criticize . . . things they little understand.[16]

The NAACP was annoyed with Pickens for instigating a feud with the Negro churchmen. Mary Ovington told Pickens that several ministers had warned the Association not to expect their support in the future. She asked Pickens to avoid further controversy by not replying to the twenty-six ministers. "Nothing could be more unfair or unchristian," Pickens replied,

> than to attempt to refuse the NAACP anything whatever because some person who is a member of the NAACP, and also a member of one of their churches, has expressed an honest opinion and made a clean and fair statement of a matter which does not in the least concern the NAACP. If you will read my article, you will see that it was not addressed to any particular ministers, and was not done in a vein of malevolence, but of real good will to the church.
>
> It would be queer if I should be misquoted and even abused and slandered and not reply. I would be unworthy of undertaking any work in behalf of the sorely beset American Negro, if I were a coward, or if I were dishonest at heart. I have faced meaner people than these ministers, who make no effort to correct, if they think there is an error, but to destroy, and to do it treacherously. I cannot think that all that opposition to the NAACP is born of anything I have said, but that it seeks its excuse in what I have said.[17]

In a cooler moment Pickens agreed to temper his reply "so as to do the most good under the circumstances."[18] In his second article he insisted that he was not an agnostic and had emphasized a disbelief in a "material," not a spiritual heaven, hell, and resurrection. He added, "The ablest statesmen of the church are warning today that some better motive will have to be advanced for interesting people in the Christian church than the fear of hell."[19] Pickens's reply seems to have been sufficiently conciliatory, for the ministers did not renew the battle. In later years Pickens was on good terms with many Baptist and AME churchmen.

Shortly after the fight with the Negro clergy had been resolved, Pickens was involved in another conflict—with the NAACP's Brooklyn branch, one of the largest in the Association. O. D. Williams, its secretary, also worked in the NAACP's main office and was responsible for sending Pickens his mail when he was on field trips. When Williams misdirected some of Pickens's mail, they had a heated exchange. Pickens complained to Johnson that Williams had been insulting and impertinent. The two clashed again over the collection of funds. Pickens accused Williams of an incorrect reckoning; Williams countercharged Pickens with a "discourteous and overbearing attitude." "We do not propose," Williams wrote to Johnson, "to have our self-respect flouted by the arbitrariness of any representative from the national office."[20] Neither Pickens nor Williams was blameless in what was both a personal disagreement and a jurisdictional dispute between an NAACP official and a branch officer.

The hiring and firing of secretarial help was another cause of conflict between Pickens and the main office. Pickens was frequently on the road and relied heavily on the secretaries for mail, information, and instructions. He repeatedly complained to the board that he had not been consulted when secretaries were either hired or discharged. Over the years Pickens began to believe, with some justification, that Walter White generally fired office help who were not unquestioningly loyal to himself or were too loyal to the field secretary. For example, in April 1923, Augusta Bird, a secretary in the main office, wrote to Pickens: "Did you hear that the Honorable Mr. White was going to fire me when I ran off to Boston a few weeks back, because I didn't notify his majesty (I saw Johnson instead). However, he found that he didn't have as much power as he dreamed he had."[21]

In 1925 Pickens complained to Johnson about the dismissal of another secretary, Winifred L. Webb. Webb had been Pickens' first personal secretary, and he was angered that she had been dismissed while he was in the field. "The whole matter," Johnson replied, "is one that does not merit so much concern."[22] Two years later Richetta Randolph, a mainstay of the NAACP office and White's close friend, informed Pickens, when he was again on the road, that still another of his secretaries, Gladys Flynn, had resigned. Pickens later learned that Flynn had left her post under pressure.[23] Convinced that there was a pattern to these dismissals, Pickens wrote to Du Bois, "A suspicious fellow might think that some one was trying to 'frame' him." He also confided his fears to NAACP board Director Moorfield Storey. "It seems that your position is perfectly sound," Storey replied, "and my sympathy has been with you now for some years. I am sorry that you find your work interfered with as it seems to have been."[24] Pickens felt that Storey was merely trying to mollify him and he continued to press for the right to pick his own secretary.

Tension between Pickens and White heightened when White became acting secretary in 1929. Robert Bagnall, the NAACP director of branches, informed Pickens that White had "started his dirty work" by telling the board that the branches were in "a bad way" and that the board should demand more efficient work from Pickens and the rest of the field staff.[25] The following spring Pickens and White clashed openly for the first time. The office had hired a new secretary for Pickens, a nineteen-year-old boy named Clinton M. Arnold. Pickens reproved Arnold for misdirecting his mail and for being "incompetent, impertinent and impossible to work with."[26] White came to Arnold's defense, accusing Pickens of being discourteous to the young secretary.[27] Richetta Randolph also defended Arnold and wrote to the board chairman: "If ever a mountain was made of a mole-hill, it has been done in the matter of Mr. Pickens' secretaries. I shall feel very much relieved if he is given to understand that he can hire and supervise them himself as he sees fit."[28]

But Pickens also had friends in the main office. Bagnall wrote him, "You are getting rather a raw deal since you are not here to defend yourself." "After all," Bagnall later wrote, "you are the only man around here that [is] man enough to tell the whole outfit to go to Hell. So you are the only one around here I have any respect for."[29] NAACP Director of Publicity Herbert Seligmann informed Pickens that both White and Randolph had been giving Arnold "a hard time" until they found out that he was having trouble with the field secretary. "Then," Seligmann added, "they became conciliatory."[30]

Pickens was not one to suffer silently. He told J. Max Barber of his difficulties with White. "What you write about my 'Friend,'" Barber answered, "does not surprise me. I came to the conclusion that he was not trustworthy. He aspired to the favor of the clique and he will do almost anything to bask in the sunlight of their approval."³¹ Pickens also wrote to Ovington. "Has it any significance," he asked, "or is just a mere coincidence, that for the last half dozen years or so, every time I get far away from the office, on some long tour of work, I am called upon to defend myself against some wrong impression that is given to the Board in my absence?"³²

Ovington denied that White was trying to force him out, but Pickens remained unconvinced and again expressed his fears to Barber. "Hold the fort Old Man," Barber replied. "My feeling is that you are too strong with the rank and file of the Association for them to displace you without seriously crippling themselves. . . . So live that you can tell them to go to hell anytime."³³

By this point White had alienated not only Pickens, but also Bagnall, Du Bois, Seligmann, and most of the office staff. An organizational crisis, however, was temporarily averted, in part, because the board and the executive officers were in high spirits over the role the Association had played, in the spring of 1930, in defeating the confirmation of Judge John J. Parker to the Supreme Court, whom they considered a racist. During the next eighteen months the NAACP was too preoccupied, first, with a campaign to fight the reelection of those senators who had voted for Parker, and later, with the Scottsboro case, to concern itself with the feud between White and the other executive officers. In the winter of 1931, however, when the NAACP was preparing to withdraw from the Scottsboro case, the climax occurred.

White, who in December 1930 had become permanent secretary after Johnson retired, brought the crisis to a head, when he submitted a report to the board that was highly critical of the staff's fund-raising performance. He also recommended that money be saved by dismissing some office help, including Pickens's secretary, and by reducing executive officers' salaries.³⁴ Du Bois, who considered White "absolutely unscrupulous," submitted a letter of protest to the board, signed by the entire executive staff. "It is our solemn and carefully considered opinion," wrote Du Bois,

> that, . . . unless Mr. White is going to be more honest and straightforward with his colleagues, more truthful in his statement of facts, more conscientious in his expenditure of money, . . . the chief question before this organization is how long he can remain in his present position and keep the NAACP from utter disaster. We have never met a man like Walter White, who, under an outward charming manner,

has succeeded within a short time in alienating and antagonizing everyone of the co-workers, including all the clerks in the office.[35]

Du Bois tried to have the letter put in the minutes of the December board meeting, but the motion was defeated.[36] After the board meeting all the executive officers, except Du Bois, withdrew their names from the letter. "I told Walter," Pickens wrote to Du Bois, "that I withdrew my name from any seeming reflection on his moral character, but stand by the facts which I know: the falseness of the presentation of the effectiveness of field work and the wrong of presenting such figures and statements without the knowledge of those concerned."[37]

Early in 1933 Bagnall left the Association. In 1934 Du Bois was forced to resign when he clashed with White and the board over control of the Crisis and his advocacy of voluntary segregation for blacks.[38] Although White "never appeared as the cause," Du Bois wrote many years later, "any employee who opposed him soon lost his job."[39]

White survived the vote of no confidence by his fellow-workers because the board was convinced of his ability as an investigator, propagandist, lobbyist, and administrator. He had demonstrated these talents most conspicuously in 1930 with his skillful handling of the fight against Judge Parker and his congressional supporters.[40] Although Pickens played a minor role in the confirmation struggle, which many blacks considered one of the NAACP's most significant achievements, he worked effectively with White, despite their differences, in the subsequent, and equally important, campaign against Parker's supporters.

Despite some significant court victories, by 1930 the NAACP had not made much progress toward its goal of racial equality. With the economic depression cutting into its membership and resources, the Association needed an issue which, while not overtaxing its limited treasury, would attract national attention, stimulate the branches to renewed activity, and gain support of blacks outside the organization. Parker's nomination to the Supreme Court seemed to be the perfect issue. In the ensuing campaign these goals were realized, but, in helping to defeat Parker, the NAACP also learned some of the limits of its political power.

On 21 March 1930 President Herbert Hoover chose John Johnston Parker to succeed the late Edward T. Sanford as associate justice. Since the Senate had recently concluded a long and bitter fight before approving another Hoover nominee, Charles

Evans Hughes, as chief justice, most observers expected that the nomination of Parker, a life-long Republican from North Carolina and a judge on the Fourth Circuit Court of Appeals, would be quickly confirmed.[41]

The day after the nomination was announced, White sought information about Parker from Dr. A. M. Rivera of the Greensboro, North Carolina, branch. Admitting that he knew nothing about the nominee, White added, "We want to be in a position to work against his confirmation if there is any reason for such action."[42] In reply, Rivera sent White a copy of the Greensboro *Daily News*, dated 19 April 1920, in which Parker, then a candidate for governor of North Carolina, was quoted as saying, "The participation of the negro in politics is a source of evil and danger to both races and is not desired by the wise men of either race or by the Republican Party of North Carolina." Parker went on to say, according to the news report, that the Negro "has not yet reached that stage in his development when he can share the burdens and responsibilities of government." Rivera concluded that "unless he has changed his opinion," Parker should be opposed by the NAACP.[43]

At first, White doubted that Parker's confirmation could be blocked, but he agreed with Rivera that the Association must nevertheless oppose it.[44] "Our protest is, in our opinion," he wrote, "well worth while . . . because it is going to make Parker and other southerners with national ambitions more careful about what they say about the Negro."[45] When the American Federation of Labor also came out against Parker, because he had upheld a "yellow dog" contract,[46] White became more optimistic. "The outlook seems very good," he wrote to Rivera, "that we are going to win out and either force the withdrawal of Parker's name by President Hoover or Parker's defeat on the vote in the Judiciary Committee." "However the matter turns out," he added, "it is going to have the most profound effect of any fight in recent years made by Negroes on so important an issue." White also appreciated the potential for the future growth of the NAACP in waging a major campaign against Parker.

> Let me come back to the matter I have mentioned to you previously,— [he wrote to Rivera] namely, the matter of the distressing condition of the North Carolina branches. This situation ought as nothing else could, convince the Negroes of North Carolina not of the desirability, but of the absolute necessity of having alert, strong and well organized branches to be on guard, ready to handle situations like this.[47]

White sent a similar message to Pickens, who was doing fieldwork on the West Coast. "We are straining every nerve here in the office on the Parker fight," he wrote. "I am asking each one of the field secretaries to concentrate at all meetings upon raising funds and upon getting branches to make remittances as soon as possible of all sums due the National Office." He added:

> Letters of commendation of the Association for its fight against Parker are pouring into the office and indicate a golden opportunity to increase the membership of the Association. We must translate this enthusiasm for the Association into larger memberships and greater financial support. Never has the Association had the widespread approval which it now has and it is up to us to utilize the occasion for increasing financial support of the Association.[48]

Parker's supporters in North Carolina sought to neutralize the NAACP's campaign by finding reputable blacks who would publicly support the nominee. They located three public school administrators, each dependent on state funds, to endorse Parker—Dr. S. G. Atkins, president of Winston-Salem Teachers' College; Dr. James E. Shepard, president of North Carolina College for Negroes at Durham; and C. M. Eppes, principal of the Greenville Industrial High School. Eppes, in a letter to the *Washington Post*, claimed that "thousands of home-owning and thrifty Negroes endorse Judge John J. Parker because they feel that he will reflect that culture and refinement necessary for the court of last resort." He accused the "highbrows of Harlem" of trying to "lynch" Parker and suggested that the Association was being used by unidentified "forces" wishing to destroy the Supreme Court. His deepest concerns were left for the concluding paragraph of his letter. "In this hour of economic depression there are many Negroes who are anxious to see the good work of interracial good go forward without disturbing the turbid waters of prejudice and hatred."[49] H. L. McCrorey, president of Johnson C. Smith University, an Episcopalian college in Charlotte, did not publicly endorse the nominee, but he thought that Parker would "fill the position as well, so far as the Negro is concerned, as any other man who may be appointed from the South."[50]

"Funny world," Pickens wrote to White from Los Angeles. "I see that Sheppard [sic] of North Carolina also apologized for 'Marse' Parker. The treachery and ignorant weakness of some colored people is the chief menace." Pickens informed White that the Parker campaign was going well in California. "The

California branches and other organizations, including the churches, certainly did their duty in worrying the President and the two Senators from this state. Dr. [H. Claude] Hudson [of the Los Angeles branch] and I made form telegrams for many of them."[51]

White found a number of North Carolina blacks willing publicly to oppose Parker's appointment. Among them was another educator, J. H. Johnson, president of Livingston College, an African Methodist Episcopal (AME) Zion institution in Salisbury. Johnson congratulated White on the Parker campaign, adding, "The great bulk of the leading Negroes of North Carolina are with you." R. McCants Andrews, a black attorney from Durham, also spoke out against Parker, as did L. E. Austin, editor of the *Carolina Times*; L. E. Graves, manager of the Eagle Life Insurance Company of Raleigh; and Benjamin Brawley, head of the English department of Shaw University, a Baptist institution.[52]

George Schuyler, a noted Negro journalist, described for White his recent trip to North Carolina.

> Let me tell you, Big Boy, the NAACP is first in the hearts of all articulate and intelligent Negroes I met there, because of the Parker fight. At least one "Big" Negro told me that his banker had called him and asked him to endorse Parker. The Negro refused. I understand that many other "Big" Negroes were called into white offices and asked to praise the Native Son. . . . I think we've gone a long way when "Big" Negroes are scared to be Uncle Toms.[53]

White personally dealt with every facet of the Parker campaign.[54] He repeatedly instructed the branches to flood Washington with telegrams. "Indicate to your senators," he wrote, "that Negroes will watch carefully their vote on Parker's confirmation."[55] He fed a stream of news releases to both Negro and white newspapers, insuring a prominent role for the Association in the daily descriptions of the confirmation fight. This tactic was highly successful. Many newspapers, regardless of their editorial position on the nomination, identified the NAACP as the most effective organization opposing Parker.[56] White wrote to many senators, thanking those who opposed Parker, providing information to the uncommitted, and reminding all who had Negro constituents that their position on confirmation would be remembered on election day. He also wrote to the president, urging him to "strike a blow at . . . race prejudice" by withdrawing Parker's name. As for reports that Parker might issue a denial of the statements attributed to him in the Greensboro *Daily News*,

White wrote, "such a denial by Judge Parker at this late date would be unconvincing and unsatisfactory."[57]

Hoover, however, despite mounting protest within his own party, refused to withdraw Parker's nomination. He had consulted with Chief Justice Hughes and Attorney General William D. Mitchell before selecting the North Carolinian and considered him an ideal choice.[58] Five states of the "Solid South," including North Carolina, had supported Hoover in 1928, and the president knew that many southern Republicans were disappointed that their region had been generally ignored for appointments to the cabinet and major federal offices. With Parker moving up to the high court, Hoover could replace him on the Fourth Circuit Bench, which had not been tapped for a Supreme Court vacancy in over sixty years, with another southerner. Both moves would obviously please the South.

Although, at forty-five, Parker would be one of the youngest justices ever to sit in the Supreme Court, Hoover felt that his nominee had demonstrated sufficient ability as a lawyer and jurist to qualify him for the post.[59] Parker was not considered a liberal, but neither was he identified with large corporations, a major consideration because of the fight over Hughes's nomination. In sum, Hoover chose Parker because the nominee was Republican, southern, and safe.[60]

Parker also saw himself as a noncontroversial figure. When first nominated, he told reporters in Charlotte, "I am not a spectacular person, boys, and make mighty poor copy."[61] But suddenly the unassuming judge found himself under attack by the NAACP and organized labor, and for the next month his name was front page news.

Shortly after the nomination was announced, Senator Arthur Capper (R-Kan.) a member of the NAACP's Board of Directors, in response to a cable from Walter White, indicated that he would "look into the matter carefully before a vote is taken on confirmation." Although he was "a supporter of the Administration" and had "great confidence in the President," he was "surprised at some of the statements credited to him [Parker] in his speech of acceptance of the nomination for Governor."[62] Senators from states with Negro populations larger than Kansas sent White similar replies.[63]

On 11 April Vice President Charles Curtis, in a cabinet meeting, informed the president of the growing concern among Republican senators that Parker's nomination might adversely affect the party in the November elections. Senate Majority Leader

James E. Watson (R-Ind.) urged Hoover to withdraw Parker's name. Yet, even after the Senate Judiciary Committee voted ten to six against recommending confirmation, Hoover would not change his mind.[64]

White was elated by the Judiciary Committee's action but reminded the branches and the Negro press that the fight was not over. "Urge everywhere," he wrote to Pickens, who was still in Los Angeles, "that we must redouble our efforts to insure victory. Success or failure depends largely on the next few days. . . . Urge everybody to send telegrams to [Senators Samuel Shortridge and Hiram Johnson of California] so that we can keep up the pressure. Parker will be defeated or confirmed by a very narrow margin so that every effort counts."[65]

During those last crucial days several disclosures further eroded Parker's chances. First, Senator Thomas Walsh (D-Mont.) revealed that in prosecuting an alleged war fraud case, in 1923, Parker had been reprimanded by the presiding judge for withholding evidence clearly exonerating the defendants of wrongdoing. "I regard this," Walsh concluded, "as a very serious imputation upon either the professional integrity or the professional industry of Judge Parker."[66]

More damaging, perhaps, was the disclosure, on 30 April, of a letter from First Assistant Secretary of the Interior Joseph M. Dixon to Walter H. Newton, one of Hoover's personal secretaries. In the letter, dated 13 March, five days after Justice Sanford's death, Dixon, a native-born North Carolina Republican, suggested that Parker's nomination as Sanford's replacement "would be a major political stroke," which would greatly please the South and "go a long way toward satisfying the unquestioned feeling that the Administration has not yet recognized the political revolution of 1928."[67] Parker supporters were embarrassed by the Dixon letter. Attorney General Mitchell insisted that the president had never seen it. He denied that political considerations had determined Hoover's choice, but added, "While locality is not controlling, it is never ignored, and the Fourth Circuit had not been represented on the Court for sixty years."[68]

The Senate debate on Parker's confirmation was heated and lengthy. Henry J. Allen (R-Kan.) led the administration forces and made the most detailed defense of Parker's record.[69] Robert Wagner (D-N.Y.) was the only senator to attack directly Parker's statement on Negro voting, calling it "an insufferable and unjustified affront to millions of American citizens."[70] With both sides predicting a narrow victory, debate moved toward a final vote. Simeon D. Fess (R-Ohio) accused the anti-Parker forces, especially the NAACP, of "socialistic" sentiments. Fess called Du Bois "a self-confessed Bolshevist," Ovington "a socialist promoting the revolutionary spirit among negroes," John Haynes Holmes "an extreme radical preacher," and Pickens who, Fess pointed out, had visited Russia in 1927, was "a communist, a defender of communism, as well as an ardent advocate of social equality." Fess also accused Parker's opponents of using "bludgeoning" tactics.[71] Henry Ashurst (D-Ariz.) rejoined with a call for an investigation of press reports that the administration was offering ambassadorships and federal judgeships in exchange for votes for Parker. Hiram Johnson (R-Calif.) was the last to speak and he reiterated the points most often made against Parker—that he was unsympathetic to labor, that he lacked sufficient stature for the post, and that, having run for attorney general, congressman, and twice for governor in North Carolina, he was too much "the perennial candidate."[72] When Johnson had concluded his remarks, debate was closed and the calling of the roll began.

At 3:15 P.M. on 7 May, Oscar De Priest (R-Ill.), the only Negro in Congress, called White from a phone in the Senate lobby to inform him that the Senate had just voted 41 to 39 against confirmation of Judge Parker.[73] For the first time since 1894 the Senate had rejected a presidential appointment to the Supreme Court. Congratulatory notes poured into White's office at NAACP headquarters. A. Philip Randolph applauded White's "brilliant and effective fight." Julian Rainey of the NAACP's Boston branch wrote, "In my opinion your work in that case is the most outstanding achievement in behalf of the race . . . by any individual within the last quarter of a century." "I have not seen Negroes so aroused," wrote Elmer Carter of the Urban League, "in the past few years as they were about this case." "In this fight," read a New York *Amsterdam News* editorial, "the Association has been seen at its best." Frank R. Crosswaith, a black Virgin Island-born Socialist, was one of many who called Parker's defeat "epochal." "Future historians," he predicted, "will not overlook this day as they search the record to approximate the period when the Negro first began in an intelligent and vigorous manner seriously to battle in an organized way for his constitutional rights in the United States."[74]

In the euphoria following Parker's defeat, few blacks seriously doubted that the NAACP had played a major role in Parker's defeat. Yet, among the forty-nine senators who voted or were paired against Parker, few would have opposed confirmation solely on the grounds of his lily-white statement. One analyst thought that no more than ten senators opposed Parker from fear of losing black support.[75] This bloc was probably balanced by the votes of eleven southern Democrats, some of whom reportedly switched to Parker because of the race issue.[76] A number of progressive senators, who wanted to move the Supreme Court in a more liberal direction and were frustrated in their attempt to defeat Charles Evans Hughes, found Parker a less formidable target.[77] Several senators probably voted against Parker because of organized labor's opposition to his confirmation. It is impossible to determine how many Republicans opposed Parker to express their disapproval of Hoover's leadership.

Despite all these factors, Parker was defeated by a scant two votes. The NAACP's vigorous campaign may have proved decisive, but only because of the closeness of the vote. Moreover, had the administration succeeded in delaying a final vote until after the November elections, thereby neutralizing the threat of both Negro and labor defections, Parker possibly would have been confirmed.[78]

White, naturally, emphasized the positive aspects of the victory over Parker. "Negroes have delivered an effective blow," he wrote, "against the Republican Party's lily white policy. Negroes know it. So do white politicians. Negroes have had a striking object lesson in the use of organized effort to defend their fundamental rights. They will not forget the lesson."[79]

"This victory is only the beginning," wrote White as he led the NAACP into a new and even more ambitious political campaign, with its goal the defeat of every senator who voted for Parker's confirmation. Some leaders within the Association, including Pickens, feared that the new political militancy of the organization would have some undesirable consequences. In a letter to Pickens, Harry E. Davis, of the Cleveland branch, questioned the wisdom of committing the Association's limited resources and manpower in campaigns against every senator who voted for Parker. Not only was there the danger of getting "someone who is worse," he argued, but the NAACP might soon be recognized as a "mere political organization."[80] Pickens was not opposed to dropping the Association's traditional nonpartisanship, but he believed that "each of these cases ought to be considered separately and on its own merit." For example, in California, Samuel Shortridge had voted for Parker and Hiram Johnson against, but Pickens would "vote for Shortridge against Johnson every time."[81] Shortridge had won the gratitude of Negroes when in 1922 he introduced in the Senate, Congressman L. C. Dyer's antilynching bill and supported it with a "strong and exceedingly skillful speech." In 1926 Shortridge had won reelection with Negro support.[82] Despite Pickens's reservations about the NAACP's all-inclusive campaign against Parker supporters, he agreed to lead the fight against Senator Henry Allen of Kansas, who, in the Senate debate, had been the administration's chief spokesman.

Kansas, with approximately sixty thousand blacks distributed in several urban centers throughout the state, and with a relatively strong network of NAACP branches, was an ideal setting for a test of the Association's newly won political power. White, who wanted to rechannel the enthusiasm over Parker's defeat before it began to dissipate, knew that in three months Allen faced a difficult primary contest. Roy Wilkins, who edited the Kansas City *Call* in neighboring Missouri, and knew Kansas politics well, told White that, although there was little chance that Kansas would elect a Democrat, Allen could be defeated in the Republican primary. Allen, as governor of Kansas, had made several important political enemies, including organized labor, some farmer groups, and former senator Charles Curtis. When Curtis became the vice president, Allen filled his vacated Senate seat. In less than two years on Capitol Hill the junior senator had achieved a reputation as one of Hoover's most loyal supporters, but he had had little time to mend political fences at home.[83]

Before going to the Senate, Allen had been on good terms with Kansas's black leadership. As publisher of the Wichita *Beacon* he had given prominence, in articles and photographs, to successful blacks rather than the criminal element. As governor he had given financial support to Negro schools and had refused the extradition of Robert L. Hill to Arkansas, where the black sharecropper was under indictment for allegedly participating in the Elaine "uprising" of 1919. In fact, Pickens had written an article for the *Crisis*, praising Allen's action in the Hill extradition case.[84]

Despite the opposition of labor and Negro groups to Allen's candidacy, White hesitated to risk the newly won prestige of the Association until he was convinced that there was a good chance of defeating him. Wilkins assured White that Allen was desperate. The candidate, in a bid for Negro votes, had prevailed on President Hoover to appoint David E. Henderson, the Negro assistant county attorney of Kansas City, as the first black assistant

U.S. attorney general since the Taft administration, and the first black Kansan chosen to an assistant cabinet post. The appointment had been announced on 26 June and clearly was timed to win Negro support before the August primary.[85]

Some prominent black Kansans continued to support Allen. W. J. Tompkins of the Kansas City *American* called Allen a "friend of the race" and asked the NAACP not to interfere in the primary. Du Bois, speaking for the Association, replied, "It makes no difference whether Senator Allen . . . sympathizes in general with the aspirations of the Negro race or not; he voted to put on the Supreme Bench a man who was against Negro suffrage, and he did this in defiance of the open protest of American Negroes."[86]

Once the NAACP had decided to enter the fight against Allen, Wilkins recommended that the home office send a spokesman to Kansas to help rally Negro voters. "Is it possible," he asked, "to send William Pickens? With his wit, . . . with his perspective of the Parker fight and its meaning to democratic government, with his knowledge of something of the spirit of Kansas, . . . with all this, Pickens could spike the Allen guns." He would be "good copy" for the Kansas newspapers, Wilkins added, and "would be the catalytic agent in the test tube of Kansas politics, which would prove the undoing of Allen."[87] The NAACP board, at their meeting of 10 July, agreed to send the field secretary to Kansas.

Pickens was, perhaps, the first NAACP executive to campaign actively, in his official capacity, against a candidate for national office. He had little time to prepare for the campaign and relied on W. L. Hutcherson of the Wichita branch for background information on Allen, and on Wilkins for his itinerary, which included stops in Coffeyville, Wichita, Topeka, Leavenworth, Atchison, Lawrence, and Kansas City. With the Senate still in session, it appeared that Allen would not get back to Kansas in time for the primary. Wilkins hoped the senator would return, "for nothing would lend more dramatic effect to the campaign than your speeches against his." "There is nothing," he added, "the colored brethren like better than drama."[88]

Some black Kansans, despite Wilkins's warm endorsement of Pickens, would have preferred to have Robert Bagnall come to Kansas. "The Negroes of Kansas," wrote John H. Grant of the Wichita branch and the Colored Ministerial Alliance, "are not very responsive to the leadership of Mr. Pickens." Grant did not elaborate beyond saying, "There are some personal factors involved." But Bagnall was otherwise engaged, White informed

Grant, and he hoped that Pickens would receive full cooperation when he arrived. Grant need not have been concerned. Pickens's tour of Kansas was a personal triumph.[89]

On 29 July Pickens spoke in Wichita before an overflow crowd of three thousand. Since he found "all of the office-holders and job hunters" among the Negro leaders had joined Allen's "bandwagon," he addressed his remarks "to the man in the crowd with the vote." The following night, in Topeka, he found "Allen money everywhere." The local NAACP branch had neglected to reserve a place for him to speak, so he accepted an invitation from Allen supporters to address their meeting, "where they expected to slaughter me by a whole battery of Allen speeches." Pickens so effectively attacked Allen, according to his own account, that none of the local candidates mentioned the senator. The next night, still in Topeka, Pickens almost managed a direct confrontation with Allen. He hid in the gallery until Allen, who had recently returned from Washington, concluded his remarks. Then, as planned, a call went up from the audience, demanding that Pickens be allowed to answer the senator. When the chairman refused to recognize Pickens, a number of spectators voiced their displeasure, and, in the resulting confusion, Allen left the hall and the meeting was adjourned.[90]

Pickens drew over two thousand to the First AME Church in Kansas City to hear his address entitled, "The Four Horsemen of the Apocalypse—Parker, Hoover, Allen and Henderson." The last mentioned, David Henderson, recently appointed to the Justice Department, had remained in Kansas to campaign for Allen and was in the audience when Pickens accused him of "selling out the rights of his race for a political appointment."[91]

Pickens, preparing for the last speech of his exhausting campaign, received a telegram from White. "Heartiest congratulations on great work against Allen. Negroes of Kansas have golden opportunity to strike blow which will create new respect for the Negro. . . . Success to your efforts."[92]

Pickens's efforts were not wasted despite the fact that Allen, running against three other aspirants, won the Republican primary with a plurality of the votes. Pickens was greatly encouraged that a majority of Negroes, despite an intensive campaign by Allen's black supporters, had voted against the senator. In Kansas City, the city with the largest number of Negro voters, only one fourth voted for Allen. "The Negro mass vote against Allen," Pickens later wrote, "augurs the possibility of Negro political action independent of party control."[93]

Allen had benefited from having three opponents in the primary, but in the November election he was less fortunate. He was defeated in a very close race by Democrat George McGill, the first of his party since 1912 to win a Senate race in Kansas.[94] Enough Negro voters had broken with the Republican party or refrained from voting to help bring about one of the major political upsets of the year.[95] Although McGill himself credited Pickens's campaign with providing his margin of victory,[96] many other factors, as in the Parker fight, contributed to Allen's defeat. The senator had undergone major surgery that summer and was unable to campaign actively. Furthermore, organized labor opposed him for his advocacy, as governor, of a state industrial court, while many farmers voted against him, and other Republican office-seekers, to protest a drastic decline in wheat prices. Although Frank Haucke, the gubernatorial candidate, was the only other major Republican candidate in Kansas to suffer defeat in 1930, in most contests the party lost a considerable part of its traditionally large majority.[97]

The economic depression was primarily responsible for the noteworthy shift in Kansas away from the Republican party in 1930, but without the equally significant switch among Negro voters, Allen would probably have won reelection. During the next two years a number of other senators who had supported Parker were denied reelection, including Felix Grundy (R-Pa.); Roscoe McCullough (R-Ohio); Simeon Fess (R-Ohio); James Watson (R-Ind.); Pickens's favorite, Samuel Shortridge (R-Calif.); while David Baird (R-N.J.) was defeated for governor in 1931. The NAACP home office, because of a shortage of funds, campaigned actively only against Baird and McCullough, leaving the other contests to the local branches.[98]

Baird had defended his vote for Parker as a matter of "conscience," and suggested to Negro voters that, even if he were "lacking in some measure, the record of the Republican Party would be enough to command your loyalty."[99] New Jersey Negroes rejected this appeal to the past and voted overwhelmingly against Baird. Better than eighty percent of their vote was cast against the Republican candidate. Vernon T. Bunche, president of the New Jersey State Conference of the NAACP, called the result "the political emancipation of colored voters in New Jersey."[100]

The Baird campaign indicated, however, that, although blacks were voting against Republican candidates, they were motivated, perhaps, more by dissatisfaction with the Hoover administration and by the economic depression than by the Parker issue. As time passed and economic conditions worsened, the defeat of Judge Parker diminished in importance in the minds of most Negroes. In May 1930, immediately after the confirmation battle, the NAACP enjoyed near-unanimous support among blacks, but, by 1931, the Association was again under attack by black conservatives for being too politically involved, and by black radicals for ignoring economic issues, and by blacks of all stripes for its role in the Scottsboro case.

The Association's slogan in 1930, its twenty-first year, was The NAACP Comes of Age. With maturity came the realization that victories are rarely "epochal." The NAACP was reminded again, in the campaigns against Parker and his supporters, that Negroes were dependent on white support and could not achieve a major political victory entirely through their own efforts.

Two days after Parker's defeat, Hoover named Owen J. Roberts, a noted Philadelphia lawyer, to the High Court. Walter White investigated Roberts's record, found nothing objectionable, and recommended that the Association publicly endorse the appointment. The nominee, best known as a special government counsel on the Teapot Dome and Elk Hill oil lease cases, was unanimously confirmed. However, Roberts, during his years on the bench, proved to be generally unsympathetic to Negro aspirations, while Parker, on the Fourth Circuit Court, displayed a more liberal attitude on racial questions. On the question of Negro voting in the South, a key issue in the NAACP's fight against Parker, Judge Roberts wrote the majority opinion in *Grovey v. Townsend* (1935), upholding a Texas white primary. When the Supreme Court later reversed itself, in *Smith v. Allwright* (1944), Roberts was the sole dissenter. Parker, on the other hand, in 1947, upheld a Federal District Court ruling that set aside a South Carolina white primary.[101] "In Judge Parker's behalf," White wrote that year, "I should like to add this postscript: Since his rejection, his decisions on both Negro and labor cases which have come before him have been above reproach in their strict adherence not only to the law but to the spirit of the Constitution."[102]

White had launched the Parker fight with three major objectives in mind. First, he wanted Negro voters to be more politically aware and more independent. Second, he wanted politicians with national ambitions to be more careful about what they said and what they did on the Negro question. Finally, he wanted to strengthen the internal structure of the NAACP. He made progress toward these goals and, in the process, solidified his position as executive secretary.[103] When Pickens, Du Bois, and the other executive staff members challenged his authority in 1931, he emerged as the dominant force in the NAACP. Pickens made his peace with White in 1931, but they would clash again.

6
PICKENS, THE COMMUNISTS, AND THE SCOTTSBORO BOYS, 1926–1933

> For a Negro protest or betterment organization to adopt a revolutionary program would be suicidal for the organization and damaging to the Negro cause.
> —Gunnar Myrdal, An American Dilemma: The Negro Problem and Modern Democracy

> Communism is not regarded as the enemy. The black folk of America know the enemy, the *real* enemy. They have looked into his hard white face. . . . They have met him face to face in the villages of South Carolina, in the swamps of Florida, on the banks of the Potomac, on the plains of Texas and Kansas, and in the dark ghettos of Detroit, Chicago and New York. After such dread encounters they are not easily aroused by the reputed devilry of Communism.
> —Henry Lee Moon, Balance of Power: The Negro Vote

Some black leaders who applauded the NAACP for its effective work in the Parker campaign turned against it, the following year, when the Association was considerably less effective in competing with the U.S. Communist party for control over the Scottsboro case. The Communists used the Scottsboro case, which involved the trial of nine black boys accused of having raped two white women, as part of its program to discredit the NAACP in the eyes of the Negro community.

In 1920 American Communists were too preoccupied with fighting among themselves and with the Socialists to formulate a coherent policy on the Negro question. In December 1921, however, most Communists united in the Worker's Party of America, under the leadership of William Z. Foster and Charles E. Ruthenberg, and established close ties with the Communist International. The following year the Fourth World Congress of the Communist International instructed American Communists to make a concerted effort to recruit blacks. No specific plans for separate Negro organizations were suggested, however, and, for the most part, the Communists recruited Negroes as they did other workers. When this approach failed, they established, early in 1924, the American Negro Labor Congress (ANLC), which attempted to organize black workers and intellectuals as a separate Negro front under Communist control. When the ANLC also had little success in attracting black recruits, the Communists again switched tactics and attempted to discredit or infiltrate existing black protest groups.[1] The NAACP was a prime target for the Communists' new approach, and two black NAACP executives—W. E. B. Du Bois and William Pickens—seemed to be the most likely prospects for conversion.

Pickens was not unsympathetic to the Communists' program, especially their seeming willingness to accept blacks as equals, but he resisted conversion, in large part, because he could not accept the rigid discipline and unquestioning submission to Russian directives that were required of all party members. Furthermore, he became convinced, during the clash between the Communists and the NAACP over the Scottsboro case, that the Communists, however well-meaning some of their members were, could not help the Negro in his struggle for equality.

Du Bois and Pickens were both outspoken critics of American racism, capitalism, and imperialism. Both were economic determinists and saw the race question, for the most part, in those terms. They were well-known to most politically conscious blacks through their writings and public speaking as well as through their NAACP affiliation. The Communists would have achieved a major coup had they succeeded in persuading either of these men to join the party.

Du Bois was perhaps the more promising of the two for conversion since he had briefly been a Socialist in 1911 and considered himself a disciple of Karl Marx. In 1925 he praised the Russian Revolution as "the outstanding effort which may yet show the world the Upward Path."[2] In 1926, upon his return from a Communist-financed trip to Russia, he declared: "I am in astonishment and wonder at the revelation of Russia that has come to me. I may be partially deceived and half-informed. But if what I have seen with my eyes and heard with my ears in Russia is Bolshevism, I am a Bolshevik."[3] Du Bois, however, was speaking about communism in Russia, and he did not join the party until 1961, when, in his nineties, he repudiated the United States and went into exile in Ghana, West Africa.

The Communists were also impressed with Pickens's militancy and class consciousness. In his writings Pickens often suggested that the root cause of racial prejudice and interracial violence was class conflicts resulting from capitalist exploitation. For example, in a study of lynching, written in 1921 for the American Civil Liberties Union (ACLU), of which he was a charter member, Pickens wrote:

> The race problem in the United States is only an intensification of the wrongs of our economic system. It is fundamentally one with the differences between labor and capital, employee and employer, wages and unearned income. Lynching and mob violence are only methods of economic repression. Lynching is most prevalent where Negro labor is most exploited.[4]

In the same article Pickens gave a class, rather than a racial, interpretation to the "alleged Negro insurrection," which had occurred in 1919 in Elaine, Arkansas. Negro tenant farmers in the area had organized a marketing cooperative in order to sell their cotton at the open market price rather than at the lower price that white landlords offered. When whites fired on one of their meetings, the blacks returned the shots, killing one of the intruders. The governor called on the National Guard and federal troops to crush the "insurrection," and in the ensuing massacre many blacks were killed.[5] The black farmers' "feeble attack upon the debt slave system," wrote Pickens, "made the landlords so nervous that they seized the first opportunity to accuse the Negroes of a general plot of treason and murder, and they shouted for troops, ostensibly to put down rebellion, but in reality to smash the union of Negro farm laborers."[6]

Pickens cited the lynching of Henry Lowry as another case in which economic repression was the underlying cause of racial violence. Lowry, a black farmer, had been lynched in Nodena, Arkansas, in January 1921, after having killed two whites, one a prominent planter, over a wage settlement dispute. Lowry was slowly roasted to death before a large and festive white crowd, in what Pickens described as "perhaps the most barbarous burning of a human being in the history of man." The brutal nature of the public murder suggested to Pickens "some deeper and more primal feeling than mere aversion to color or even anger at homicide in self-defense." "Lowry's act," he concluded, "awakened in the landed class a feeling akin to horror at insurrection. It was like a threat of rebellion on the part of the submerged class to overthrow the system on which the power of the landlords rest."[7]

"Three thousand colored men and women have been burned and otherwise lynched," Pickens argued, "not because Negroes are more criminal than other races, nor because Americans are more criminal than other people, but because black and white in America are victims of a medieval conception of the 'classes' of man."[8]

In 1926 the Communists, who called Pickens "one of the most influential leaders in the Negro liberation movement,"[9] began a campaign to convert him from a Socialist sympathizer to a full-fledged Communist. In July 1926 Pickens received a letter from Lovett Fort-Whiteman of the ANLC, himself a black Communist convert from socialism. "Please write me soon," Fort-Whiteman wrote, "in regard to your sounding sentiment in behalf of a group of three intellectuals, including yourself, making a visit to the Soviet Union. Of course, this [idea], you know is wholly the work of the Worker's Party."[10] "Personally you stand very much in favor in the regard of our Party leaders," Fort-Whiteman subsequently wrote. "This I suppose you know without my telling you."[11]

The possibility of visiting Russia intrigued Pickens, and in replying to Fort-Whiteman he indicated his interest. He also suggested Charles S. Johnson, editor of the Urban League's magazine, *Opportunity*, as a possible companion. "But I am afraid," he added, "that the bourgeois crowd that supports the Urban League would object to one of their servants even SEEING Russia."[12]

Pickens wrote an article for the *Daily Worker* in which he responded to those who feared that Negroes visiting the Soviet Union were being seduced and subverted to communism. "We are not saying or implying that Russian Communists would be doing anything foolish or criminal," he wrote,

> if they were seeking to convert Negroes to Communism by letting them see what it is and how it works. . . . Frankly, it seems to us that Mississippi and New York newspapers are afraid that, if American Negroes see Moscow, they may conclude that it is a darn sight better civilization than what they see in Vicksburg and Yonkers [New York]. . . . Well, what are they afraid of? Draw your own conclusions, Sambo.

Pickens praised Russia's "willingness to be seen, and seen intimately." He was ready to bet his "last dollar" that, "if Mississippi wanted to convert Negroes to a belief in Mississippi methods," they would never do it by inducing them to "come and see how the thing works in Mississippi."[13]

The following month Fort-Whiteman informed Pickens that he and two other blacks—Hubert H. Harrison, a Socialist, and George Weston of the Universal Negro Improvement Association—had been chosen to represent American Negroes at the Brussels International Conference of Oppressed Nations, which had been arranged by the left-wing, but not exclusively Communist, Anti-Imperialism League. The conference was scheduled for November and the Worker's party had arranged for the three black delegates to go on from Brussels to the Soviet Union. The meeting at Brussels was designed as a propaganda vehicle against European and American exploitation of colonial and national minorities, and the Communists were anxious that Pickens "fight hard to go as a delegate of the NAACP."[14] The Communists hoped this tactic would draw the Association closer to the radical camp, or, if the NAACP refused to participate, embarrass them in the eyes of their colored brothers. "If you do not succeed," Fort-Whiteman wrote to Pickens, "you will go as a representative of the Negro people."[15]

Pickens pressed the Association to designate him as their official representative to the Brussels Conference, not because he wanted to embarrass the organization or draw it closer to the Communists, but because, he, like W. E. B. Du Bois, wanted the NAACP to play a greater role in the struggle against worldwide repression and exploitation of dark-skinned peoples. He also had a personal motive—as the NAACP's representative he would not have to sacrifice his salary for the time he was overseas.

By this time, the NAACP Board of Directors were alarmed by Communist attempts to infiltrate or undermine the organization,[16] but they agreed, after considerable debate, to designate Pickens as their official ambassador to the Brussels Conference. Several NAACP leaders, including Moorfield Storey, Joel Spingarn, Bishop John Hurst, and Louis Marshall, gave Pickens both gifts of money and their personal best wishes for the trip.[17] Pickens sailed for Europe on 24 November. "It is fortunate for the NAACP and for the colored people of the United States," Du Bois wrote, "that they are represented at this time by so vigorous a personality and so forceful a speaker and so honest a soul as William Pickens."[18]

Pickens, however, never attended the Anti-Imperialism Conference. After giving a series of lectures for the English Society of Friends, he arrived in Brussels only to find that the meeting had been postponed. He remained in the Belgian capital long enough to confer with several delegates and then made his way across the continent to the Soviet Union.[19]

"Perhaps even hell is not as bad as the opposition reports it to be," Pickens wrote in January 1927, after two weeks in Russia. "I saw the Bolsheviks in their own lair and realized more than ever before how impossible it is to get a fair picture of a people through the eyes of those who are out of sympathy with that people."[20]

The Russians treated Pickens, as they had Du Bois, the poet Claude McKay, and other blacks, as an honored guest.[21] He met Lenin's sister and former president Mikhail Kalinin, and had an audience with Leon Trotsky. The Russian authorities were amazed, Pickens recalled, when he considered passing up meeting Trotsky because the time for the interview conflicted with a showing of Sergei Eisenstein's film, *Potemkin*. The film showing was delayed long enough for Pickens and the Bolshevik leader to exchange some pleasantries.

Pickens's response to Russia was greatly influenced by his experience as a black man in America. The first thing that impressed him about the Soviet Union was the absence of obvious class distinctions. "Deference and servility," he observed, "are resented by those to whom they are offered." He saw no "kowtowing to superiors" either in the Soviet army, the university, the factories, or on the streets of Moscow.

"As to race and color prejudice," he wrote, "there is less of it in New York than in New Orleans; less in London than New York; less in Paris than in London; and absolutely none in Moscow." He found that the four American Negro students were very popular at Eastern University, where more than a thousand students of all races from around the world were enrolled.

"The greatest human gain" resulting from the Revolution, in his view, "was that of the Jews." He contrasted the horrors of the pogroms under the czars, as depicted in Moscow's Museum of the Revolution, with the freedom they seemed to enjoy under the new regime. "At last the Jew is a man in Russia," he exclaimed, "which alone might atone for the horrors of the Revolution."

Pickens was very impressed with the "Workers' Clubs," which were not only recreation centers, "but institutions of liberal culture and of general and special education. Nothing of the sort was ever dreamed of by the toilers under the Czar, and we have not seen such institutions for workers anywhere else in the world."

He was not entirely uncritical of life in the Soviet Union. He found the Leninist cult distasteful. He observed:

> The likeness of Lenin appears in a thousand postures and forms . . . on every wall of every room. Understand me, Russia is not any seventh heaven; it has poverty, inefficiency, demagoguery and some robbery. . . . But, if one has an open heart of goodwill for his fellowman, he feels a thrill when he sees these plain people, who have come up like the bowels of a volcano from the nether regions, now standing there in the sunlight and attempting to achieve their own destiny.

"Although Russians have made, are making, and will make mistakes," he argued, "opposition and unsympathetic treatment from others will cause a people in the present social status of the Russians to make even greater mistakes." "For Britain and the United States to recognize Russia as a free, independent and coordinate state," he suggested, "would draw the teeth and clip the claws of Russian propaganda in those countries." Just like an oppressed group within a nation," he concluded, "so an unrecognized nation among the nations will lose much of its disposition to spread propaganda when once it is recognized as an equal among the others."22

Shortly after Pickens returned from Russia he spoke at the Fourth Pan-African Congress, which met in New York. In his rhetoric, at least, Pickens seemed to have adopted the Communist line.

> The devouring of Africa, the raping of Haiti, and the bullying of Nicaragua will go forward as far as human selfishness will carry them, unless those whose welfare is at stake shall begin to confer and cooperate. The proletariat, the workers, the producers of the goods of the human society are beginning to sense a common interest in a common cause, and a need for mutual support,—in Moscow, in Hankow, in Paris, and in Passaic [New Jersey].
>
> . . . .
>
> Racial organization is simply local fermentation,—a first stage in the evolution of world organization and cooperation along economic lines. Economic lines are societally more fundamental than racial lines. . . . Human science is the miner and sapper which is laying siege to the whole works of nationalism and racialism. In the end human science, rather than religion, will bring to pass, not by persuasion, but through necessity, a condition of universal brotherhood.

> Economic exploitation knows neither race nor color. It will attack that group which is most helpless, most open to exploitation. The Negroes of Africa were not enslaved because they were Negroes, but because they offered the greatest return for the smallest outlay and effort to the slave hunter.... Even an American Negro capitalist, late descendant of raped Africa, is just exactly like other capitalists. He must be like the others. A Negro who owns a thousand acres in Alabama or Texas, pays his tenants and "hands" just as little and charges them just as much as any white farm owner in the neighborhood.[23]

Pickens had come a long way from his student days when, as a disciple of Booker T. Washington, he had advocated American intervention in Haiti and had seen the hand of Providence in the African slave trade. But, to the Communists' dismay, he was still not prepared to join Fort-Whiteman, James W. Ford, William L. Patterson, and the handful of articulate blacks who had become party members.[24] Nevertheless, he maintained cordial relations with several Communists, notably Robert Minor and Earl Browder; wrote for Communist publications such as the *Daily Worker* and *New Masses*; attended several meetings of the International Labor Defense (ILD), the party's legal organ; and worked with them in radical organizations, such as the anti-imperialistic "Hands Off China" Committee.[25]

He was active in the antiwar and anticolonialism movement of the 1920s and, having missed the Brussels Conference, he very much wanted to attend the Second World Congress Against Imperialism, scheduled for the end of July 1929. The Communists, however, were no longer anxious to have Pickens participate. In 1928, on orders from the Soviet Union, they had again shifted their policy on the Negro question. Previously they had considered Negroes as part of the exploited working class and concentrated their efforts on winning over northern urban blacks. Under the new Soviet directive, Negroes were transformed into an exploited nation within a nation, a distinct minority that had to be encouraged to seek self-determination, under Communist guidance, in a separate Negro state, which was to be located somewhere in the southern "black Belt." The Communists also abandoned "boring from within" existing organizations (a technique that had failed) and intensified their efforts to discredit the NAACP and other Negro reformist groups.[26] Pickens, as the NAACP field secretary who had resisted conversion, came under Communist fire, and two black Communist delegates, James W. Ford and William Patterson, secretly planned to denounce him publicly as a bourgeois lackey if he did attend the Second World Congress.[27]

The NAACP board was reluctant to let Pickens attend the anti-imperialism conference or to be the organization's representative, but Roger Baldwin of the ACLU persuaded them that "it would be a serious omission not to have American Negroes represented by their most militant organization." "Otherwise," he argued, "the only Negro representatives there would be Communists, who represent nobody but themselves and the party behind them."[28]

On 10 July 1929 Pickens sailed for Frankfurt am Main, site of the Second World Congress Against Imperialism.

Pickens revealed, in his reports on the Congress's proceedings, some of the reasons why he never seriously considered joining the Communist party. From the outset, he observed, the Communists fought to gain control of the congress and by the official opening "they were evidently, perhaps a bit too evidently, in control of the general machinery and leading policies of the organization."[29] Throughout the week-long conference the Communists, according to Pickens, displayed "an astonishing intolerance and lack of regard for the opinions and rights of those who do not agree with them."[30]

In his report Pickens scoffed at Ford's repeated reference to American Negroes as "a potential revolutionary force." "We always smile at those assurances," Pickens wrote, "These people never will know the Negro and his situation in America. . . . The American Negro is at present such a weak revolutionary possibility."[31] He added:

> When a man adopts a creed, or a party point of view, he is so apt to stop thinking and to run in the party ruts. . . . Many Negroes who get interested in these international movements, while they gain an international ideology . . . they also seem to lose the perspective of the Negro's situation in America. They seem to forget that American Negroes, like all humans, will act first of all with an eye to their own good in America. . . . The Negro of Mississippi will not act against the interests of the Negroes of Mississippi in order to aid white people in Vladivostok, or even to aid black people in Kenya or in Chicago. Only on the common interests can there be cooperation and unity of action. . . . But when the Communists take Negroes into tutelage and tow, they seem not only to put certain things into their heads, but to use a hypodermic needle and put something under their skins which renders them, thenceforward, immune to such everyday thinking.[32]

Shortly before he was to address the congress, Pickens learned that the Communists planned to "muzzle" him. One of the delegates, whom Pickens identified only as "a Boston woman," informed him that Ford and the presiding officer had prearranged to interrupt his speech after he had spoken for ten minutes of a scheduled forty-five-minute address. Ford, seated on the stage behind Pickens, would then humiliate him by ridiculing his partially delivered speech. But Pickens also "resorted to a little strategy." He did not give copies of his address to the translators until just before he was to speak, making it impossible for Ford, who did not know German, to get an English copy. When Pickens addressed the vast audience of fifteen thousand (his estimate), the great majority of whom were Germans, in their native tongue, "they got so enthusiastic," he wrote, "that, when the Russian chairman attempted to stop me after a few minutes, they shouted and threatened a riot, and I had to go to the end of the forty-five minute talk." "The joke was turned"; Pickens added, "the poor critic, seated behind me, had to get up and fill in his time as best he could."[33]

Although angered by the Communists' abortive attempt to humiliate him at the World Congress and critical of their new policy of favoring Negro separatism, Pickens still did not repudiate the entire Communist movement. He praised Ford and Patterson for suggesting a World Congress of Negro Workers and considered passage of their proposal the most significant action taken by the Frankfurt Congress. He supported the idea for a Negro Workers' Congress, whose aim would be the recruitment of black workers into international labor unions, although he knew that the congress would be controlled by the International Trade Union Committee of Negro Workers, a Communist front organization. "If others will not organize the Negro workers of the world," he reasoned, "why should not the Communists do so?"[34]

Just as Pickens had ambivalent feelings toward the Communists—criticizing their intolerance and fanaticism and praising their willingness to organize blacks and treat them as equals—so too did the Communists have mixed feelings about him. They included him in their attack on the NAACP leadership, but they also continued to report his work in anti-imperialist organizations and published his writings in their journals.[35] They probably hoped that, as the Negro's condition worsened, Pickens would lose patience with the NAACP's approach and lose faith in the American system as well. They believed that Pickens was the NAACP leader "who was most receptive to economic radicalism."[36]

Throughout 1930 the Communists kept sniping at the NAACP. The Association, for its part, was preoccupied with two other concerns that year: keeping its organization from collapsing under the pressure of the deepening economic depression; and fighting against Senate confirmation of President Hoover's nomination of Judge John J. Parker to the Supreme Court.[37] In 1931, when, as a result of the famous Scottsboro case, the conflict between the Communists and the Association intensified, Pickens found himself caught in the crossfire.

The Scottsboro case was the most celebrated court battle of the early 1930s. On 25 March 1931 nine young Negores were taken from a freight train at Paint Rock, Alabama, and arrested; they were accused of raping two white women who were found on the same train. The black youths, ranging in age from thirteen to twenty, were taken to Scottsboro, the county seat, to stand trial, and on 9 April were found guilty by all-white juries and sentenced to die in the electric chair. The testimony given at this and subsequent trials clearly indicates that the rape charges were baseless.[38]

Walter White, Johnson's successor as NAACP executive secretary, hesitated to involve the Association fully in the Scottsboro case until he could read the trial transcripts and was reasonably sure that the boys were innocent. The Communists were less cautious. The same night that the Scottsboro boys were sentenced, the party issued a statement condemning the "legal lynching" and calling for worldwide May Day mass protest demonstrations. The International Labor Defense (ILD), the legal arm of the Communist party, dispatched a representative to Scottsboro to start appeal proceedings.[39] By 20 April the Communists persuaded the boys to permit the ILD to handle the appeal. The *Daily Worker* gave the case continuous front-page coverage and also chided the NAACP for not speaking out against the "legal lynching on a mass scale."[40]

Pickens was visiting midwestern NAACP branches at the time of the first Scottsboro trial. He had not communicated with White for some time and was unaware that the NAACP secretary had decided to commit the Association's legal resources to the case. On 19 April, several days before the NAACP made any public statement on the Scottsboro case, Pickens wrote to the *Daily Worker*, congratulating the ILD for its fight "to prevent the judicial massacre of Negro youth in Alabama." Enclosing a small check "for the cause," he unwittingly became the center of attention when he added:

> In the present case the *Daily Worker* and the workers have moved, so far, more speedily and effectively than all other agencies put together.

If you do not prevent Alabama from committing these horrible murders, you will at least educate working people, white and black, to the danger of division and the need for union. In either event it will be a victory for the workers.[41]

In reply to Pickens's letter, Communist leader Robert Minor wrote: "Dear Bill: I have just read your letter sent to the *Daily Worker*. I cannot tell you how much joy it gave me to see you come into this fight. . . . Now I am hoping to hear your thunderous voice raised all over the land."[42]

Several days later Pickens again praised "the white radicals for moving more swiftly . . . than any Negro organizations to the defense of these youngsters," demonstrating, in his view, "the need for cooperation on the part of all the oppressed, white and black." "Wake up, Black Man!" he exclaimed, "If you cannot save yourself, die wide awake anyway."[43]

The Communists made effective use of the NAACP field secretary's public praise of their efforts for the Scottsboro boys. "While Pickens has come out in this letter of defense of the nine Scottsboro victims," wrote the *Daily Worker*, "his organization still maintains an official silence in the face of this murderous frame-up and railroading of Negro boys to the electric chair that amounts to open cooperation with the Southern boss lynchers."[44] "When in the hell," Minor asked the NAACP, "is the proper time to join in defense of boys who are condemned to die on July 10th? Would July 11th be the proper time?" The Association's press releases, he added, have "not one word of call to the masses to defend these boys."[45]

The NAACP leaders, except for Pickens, opposed working with the ILD because they feared united action would result in Communist domination of the case. White insisted that the Scottsboro boys were doomed unless their appeals were handled by an eminent southern attorney. By injecting the specter of class revolution, he believed, the Communists had complicated a case already burdened with the explosive issues of race and sex. While the Communists called for a "united front mass campaign to arouse the whole country," the NAACP worked behind-the-scenes in hope of winning the support of responsible and rational southerners.[46]

Pickens, in his letter to the *Daily Worker*, had inadvertently undermined the Association's plan for action. By praising the ILD, endorsing a united front, and strongly implying that the Association had not been playing an active role in the case, he had given the Communists powerful weapons that they used effectively against the NAACP. When rumors spread that the NAACP was so furious with Pickens that he was going to be discharged, the Communists made capital of these reports.[47] A *Daily Worker* editor wrote, "Such action would be in line with the consistent policy of hamstringing the Scottsboro defense which has marked the attitude of the NAACP leadership towards the fight to save the lives of these boys."[48]

The NAACP had not asked for Pickens's resignation, but it had condemned "the unwisdom and what might be construed as the disloyalty of his action." "This is not a question," board chairman Mary Ovington wrote to Pickens, "of interfering with the political or other opinions of officers of the NAACP as individuals, but it *is* a question of not allowing expression of these opinions to injure the organization to which these officers are responsible."[49] The board, at its monthly meeting in May, accepted Pickens's disclaimer of intentional disloyalty, but voted to "severely" censure him for "a serious indiscretion on his part."[50]

Pickens may have lacked discretion in writing the 19 April letter to the *Worker*. He often became involved in controversy because he acted impulsively. As his good friend, Claude Barnett of the American Negro Press, told him, "Whatever you do, you do impulsively, wholeheartedly and fulsomely."[51] Yet, at the time he wrote to the *Worker*, he had not seen any indication of the NAACP's interest in the Scottsboro case. Furthermore, the Association continued to have difficulty in persuading other black leaders, expecially those of the black press, that it was acting effectively in the case.[52] Barnett suggested to Pickens that the NAACP, as compared with the Communists, was being criticized by the black press because the Communists "have usually been a step ahead of you in the presentation of information; they have been dramatic and graphic in their claims and protests, all of which has the news element which has made editors pick them up." He also felt the Association was becoming "ultraconservative."[53]

In the Scottsboro case, NAACP leaders faced a familiar form of the Negro dilemma. Should they rely on the established legal system and work patiently with the better sort of southern whites, or should they concentrate on agitation and mass protests? Should they plead for justice for the Scottsboro boys or demand it? In a sense, the choices were similar to those Pickens had faced in 1905, during the feud between Washington and his critics, and again in 1920, when Garvey challenged the NAACP. The antagonists were different, the historical parallels were incomplete, but the dilemma remained unchanged and, with it, the feeling that the choice was really not the Negro's to make. Whether it was an Alabama governor, a southern mob, or the United States Supreme Court, ultimately white men would decide the Scottsboro boys' fate.

While the Association probably would have accepted commutation of the Scottsboro boys' sentences to life imprisonment with the hope of an early parole,[54] the ILD insisted on acquittal. "When I say 'saved,'" Minor had written to Pickens, "I do not mean . . . that the prison board or the governor might act so mercifully as to let these innocent children spend their lives in prison instead of being electrocuted. I mean that I believe that the frame-up can be exposed and the boys . . . restored to liberty."[55] Mass protests had failed to save Sacco and Vanzetti, but Minor argued that the anarchists had died because "some soft-minded people were slackening up the public agitation . . . on the ground that the governor or somebody would surely save them, since the case had proven to be a frame-up."[56] "The argument may be advanced," Minor added, "by some mistaken or weak persons that mass agitation and turbulent protests may 'turn people against' the boys. But is it possible for some heartless fool to advance this argument in this case?"[57]

This was exactly the argument that Walter White and the NAACP were advancing, and with some justification. The Communists, White wrote, "had been so abusive in several telegrams to the sheriff and governor [of Alabama] that they had inflamed public opinion against the defendants.[58] "If the Communists want these lads murdered," Du Bois argued, "then their tactics of threatening judges and yelling for mass action on the part of southern workers is calculated to insure this."[59]

Pickens, even after being censured by the NAACP board, still favored a united front. In the long run, he believed, Negroes would benefit from such an alliance. The worsening depression had hit Negroes very hard, and they, by 1931, were concerned primarily with economic, rather than civil, rights. A united front of Negroes, workers, farmers, Socialists, Communists, and liberals, in his view, would make more of an impact on the economic system than the NAACP's emphasis on judicial due process. He hoped that the Scottsboro case would be the means through which such a united front would develop. He tried to bring White around to this point of view, but, in the end, the NAACP secretary persuaded him that an alliance with the Communists was dangerous not only to the functioning of the Association, but also to the Scottsboro boys' chances of escaping the electric chair.[60] The NAACP, White convinced him, had to avoid publicity and seek the cooperation of Southern white leaders. "On the other hand, the Communists," Pickens himself later wrote,

> who clearly saw the sensational possibilities of these cases for political and radical propaganda, could afford to publish everything they were doing . . . and even things they must have known they could only promise but could never do. . . . For a radical party is and will be, and must be, more interested in the success of its party program for achieving power than in the fate of any nine Negroes.[61]

White gave Pickens the difficult assignment of wresting the Scottsboro boys and their parents from the ILD. On 31 May Pickens visited the boys at Kilby Prison, in Montgomery, Alabama, and warned them that they could escape death only if they permitted the NAACP, rather than the ILD, to handle their appeal. "The ILD's chief aim," he told them,

> is to use you as a means for interesting colored people in the Communist Party. . . . They have bewildered and amazed your parents and relatives"; he added, "they have paid their fares to New York and other parts of the country, have put them on platforms and in parades, all for the purposes of their own, and not for the primary purpose of keeping you out of that electric chair."[62]

Pickens left Montgomery thinking that the boys had accepted the NAACP's counsel. The Communists, however, effectively persuaded the boys' relatives to rely on the ILD, and the boys, confused by the jurisdictional dispute between the NAACP and the ILD, generally followed their relatives' advice.[63]

On 7 June, at a fund-raising meeting for the Scottsboro boys in Chattanooga, Pickens turned the full force of his oratory against the Communists. In a fashion reminiscent of his about-face on Marcus Garvey, he called the ILD's activities in the case detrimental to the boys and to the cause of all black Americans. Admitting that he had been originally misled, he added, "It has since developed that their chief aim is communistic propaganda." He predicted that their threats against public officials would create "a new and more serious race problem in the South." The NAACP had been unable to get the cooperation of the boys' relatives, he explained, because the Communists had "corralled, abducted, fenced in and hidden" them from "agents of law-abiding organizations." "Whatever . . . efforts are put forth by the NAACP to defend these cases," he concluded, "must first wipe out the mischief-breeding impression already made by the Communists."⁶⁴

When Pickens finished, two young black Communists rose from the audience and demanded time to reply. Joe Burton, identified by the *Daily Worker* as a "militant young Negro worker," criticized the NAACP's interference in the Scottsboro case, despite the parents' request that the organization keep out. He also claimed that the NAACP's collection of funds was "unauthorized" and was being used for other purposes. Gene Braxton, a party "organizer," spoke directly to Pickens. "My [Negro] blood," he charged, "will never let me get down on my knees to beg the white rulers of Alabama for mercy for these nine innocent boys. These boys cannot be saved by such slave tactics as yours. . . . To refuse to fight is to condemn these boys to death."⁶⁵

The *Daily Worker* called Pickens's "somersault" a surrender to "the reactionary wealthy white people who now control the NAACP," and who "pushed him in line with threats to discharge him from his position." The Communists, like Garvey a decade before, called Pickens's reversal of position a "contemptible and cowardly betrayal . . . of the Negro people." The *Daily Worker* concluded:

> Pickens advances the theory of "be good," be white man's Negroes and get favors from the slave owners. We have heard that before from Booker T. Washington. We have heard it again and in still coarser and more depraved form from Marcus Garvey, when he made overtures to the Ku Klux Klan. And now from William Pickens. The class to which Mr. Pickens belongs—the petty bourgeois, hangers on and worshippers of the capitalist system, even if sometimes wavering and discontented with the masters—cannot be trusted of the masses against blood-sacrifices to their oppressors.⁶⁶

Pickens must have appreciated the irony of being linked with Washington and Garvey, two black leaders he had first praised and later attacked. He had switched sides or contradicted himself on a number of occasions and would continue to do so. His critics accused him of insincerity and self-serving; his friends attributed his changes of position to an intense desire to do what was best, in a given situation, for the Negro people. There was some truth in both explanations. Nevertheless, many other Negro leaders, such as Frederick Douglass and Du Bois, during long and active lives reversed themselves on numerous occasions. As Gunnar Myrdal said, "Negroes seem to be held in a state of eternal preparedness for a great number of contradictory opinions—ready to accept one type or another depending on how they are driven by pressures or where they see an opportunity."[67]

Having accepted Walter White's view on the Scottsboro case, Pickens found it difficult to understand why the black press continued to support the ILD. "It is easy to understand that the first approach of the Communists to the Negro Question might deceive even a veteran newspaperman," he wrote, "but how any sensible Negro leader can stay fooled by them, in the light of their later procedure, is a great mystery to us."[68] In referring to the Communists' "later procedure," Pickens had in mind the Camp Hill, Alabama, race riot of 1931. Several Communists had moved into a predominantly Negro section of the area to organize a sharecroppers union and to rally lower-class Negro support for the Scottsboro boys. On 16 July, when the local sheriff interrupted one of their meetings, some shots were fired and for the next few days whites, in hunting for the organizers, killed at least one black and arrested sixty more.[69] The NAACP sent Pickens to investigate the riot and, if possible, to help prevent further violence. Afterward he wrote:

> Whenever they [the Communists] enrage the minds of the abused Negro and stir him to action and into trouble, it is the Negro that remains to do the dying and languishing in jail, while his white Communist leaders escape from the scene. This is what happened at Camp Hill, Alabama. . . . When the police began to shoot, only the Negro was there to get hit.[70]

While the Camp Hill Riot and other interracial disturbances were "good copy for the Communists," Pickens later wrote, "they are very bad for the Negroes involved. Verily will it be better for the Negroes to manage their own affairs a few more generations, than turn [to] wild propagandists who know nothing of the psychology of the South."[71]

Despite similar incidents, including Communist disruption of NAACP fund-raising meetings, Pickens, White, and Du Bois could not win over the black press to the NAACP's point of view on the Scottsboro case.[72] Since the ILD had procured written retainers from the boys or their nearest relatives, the Association announced, on 4 January 1932, that "much against its wishes, it was prevented from further participation in the defense."[73]

Withdrawal from the Scottsboro case was a severe blow for the NAACP. Not only the Communists, but many black moderates also criticized the Association for abandoning the boys. In March, for example, the Denver branch of the NAACP threatened to boycott an address by Pickens because, according to the branch president, "the National Association withdrew from the Scottsboro Case or was forced out by the Communist Party."[74] Pickens heard similar complaints during his circuits of the branches. "I wonder if the people in the office realize," he wrote, "how wide-spread and deep-seated an impression had been made that the NAACP had fallen down on the Scottsboro cases." "Many honest and intelligent people," he went on, "white and colored, have been in error, due to the persistent lying of the Communists and the Negro papers who supported them. The *Amsterdam News* and the [Baltimore] *Afro-American* both did great harm in that way."[75] He repeatedly found a "general lack of information among some of our faithful branch workers respecting the NAACP role in the Scottsboro Case."[76]

The Association defended its actions in the case and insisted, after the boys were found guilty in a retrial, that "had the defense ... been entrusted to it a different verdict would have been obtained."[77] "Perhaps the most decisive factor in determination of a verdict which is contrary to all the evidence," they argued, "was that Communism was on trial as well." Nevertheless, many blacks felt that the Association, by failing to operate decisively in the Scottsboro case, had relinquished to the ILD its most important role—that of defender of the Negro in the courts—and was in danger of becoming an organization without a function. As the Denver branch president put it, "If the National Association is to survive you must institute and maintain an ... aggressive campaign, locally and nationally, for the rights of our group.[78]

The Communists, without acquiring many of the NAACP's members, had used the Scottsboro case to expose the Association's weaknesses. The NAACP had never had a mass following, had never been directly concerned with economic matters, had little interest in an interracial labor movement, and had just begun to establish ties with Negro youths. The NAACP leaders, under pressure inside and outside the organization, decided that the time had come for a reevaluation of its approach to the race problem, and Joel Spingarn offered his country estate for a second Amenia Conference. Roy Wilkins, of the Kansas City, Mo. *Call,* who had recently been appointed NAACP assistant secretary, sent invitations to approximately fifty black leaders.

> The world is in a crisis [Wilkins wrote]. Great changes are occurring almost overnight. The problem of racial adjustment in America and the world is a constantly shifting one.

> How adequate is the present program of the NAACP in this changing state? In 1910 the Association's program was regarded as radical, as being a generation ahead of its time. How is the program regarded today? How should the program be changed or enlarged or shifted or concentrated toward certain ends? The Association wishes these questions to be on the theme of a second Amenia Conference.[79]

The conference, as Joel Spingarn pointed out to Pickens, was intended

> to ascertain what the young members of the colored race are thinking and aspiring toward. . . . You and I, [he added] and all the others who have already served in the good fight of the last two decades should, in any case, merely act as auditors and leave the youngsters to express themselves as they (and not we) see fit.[80]

Only Pickens and Du Bois, among the black leaders present, had attended the first Amenia Conference. In 1916 they were among the "radicals," but in 1933 they, along with White, were accused by the younger blacks of being too conservative and out of touch with Negro aspirations and needs.[81] The "Young Turks," such as Wilkins, E. Franklin Frazier of Fisk University, and Ralph Bunche, Charles Houston, and Abram Harris of Howard University, none of whom were Communists, claimed that they did not intend "to disparage the older types of leadership." "We appreciate their importance and contributions," they wrote,

> but we feel that in a period in which economic, political and social values are shifting rapidly, and the very structure of organized society is being revamped, the leadership which is necessary is that which will integrate the special problems of the Negro within the larger issues facing the nation.[82]

The young blacks felt that the NAACP had failed to realize, especially since the impact of the current depression, that the Negro's primary problem was economic. "In the past there has been a greater exploitation of Negro labor than any other section of the working class," they pointed out, and "there has been slight recognition by . . . Negro leaders of the significance of this exploitation." They advocated "an entirely new labor movement, with Negroes taking the initiative." They also strongly urged that Negroes, "regardless of seeming class differences within the race, . . . unite more closely in the interests of the group's economic welfare." The new labor movement they envisioned would be a political as well as an economic force, which would press for "such social legislation as old age pensions, unemployment insurance, [protection of] child and female labor, etc. These social reforms may go to the extent of change in the form of Government itself."

Neither Pickens nor Du Bois, both of whom were singled out for criticism at Amenia, disagreed with the young blacks' emphasis on economic concerns. There was nothing new in the "Young Turks'" contention that it was impossible to improve the "status and security of white labor without making an identical improvement in the status and security of Negro labor." Pickens had been making that point since 1916. He strongly supported their charge that "the interests of the Negro cannot be adequately safeguarded by white paternalism." He advocated, as they did, "reformed democracy," rather than fascism or communism as the best form of government. He had long supported the idea of a politically active interracial labor movement.[83] Pickens, however, would not abandon or de-emphasize the importance of securing the Negro's civil rights in the courts. The Young Turks were silent on this matter.

Despite general agreement on long-range goals, there was an undercurrent of antagonism at Amenia between young blacks and the established black leadership. Du Bois saw the conflict between Pickens, White, and himself on one side, and the young blacks, such as Ralph Bunche, E. Franklin Frazier, and Abram Harris, on the other, as "the difficulty with age and youth . . . to find a common language, an attitude in which they can approach each other." The young blacks' "difficulty," in his view, was the "difficulty of all youth. Inspired and swept on by its vision, it does not know or rightly interpret the past and is apt to be too hurried carefully to study the present." He added:

> It is hard for age to admit or understand that it has not thought of everything, or attempted everything, or done what it has done as efficiently as it might have done. It is equally difficult for youth to know that age has thought of some of the various problems which bother youth; has tried and failed and succeeded and for reasons not explained altogether by either stupidity or cowardice.[84]

In a postscript Du Bois complained of the "lack of self-discipline" and "ruthlessness" of some of the young people at Amenia. Some did as they pleased, he wrote, "with regard to noise, sleep and enjoyment, with utter disregard of the perfectly evident desires of the rest, and to cap the climax, the rest uttered no protest." "I have seen evidence of this sort of thing among young colored people elsewhere," he concluded. "It is for us and the race a new and pressing problem."

Youth and age were separated at Amenia by more than style, attitude, and historical perspective, or, in Du Bois's view, the young blacks' lack of historical perspective. Pickens and Du Bois supported the idea of a black mass movement, but also believed that the NAACP had a unique and vital role to play in that struggle. They resented the young blacks' cavalier dismissal of the Association's accomplishments as legal defenders, propagandists, and political lobbyists. They feared that the NAACP would be consumed by a mass movement which, past experience had taught them, would accomplish little if it alienated white support. This, for Pickens, was the lesson to be learned from the Scottsboro case. He became convinced that the boys' lives were in jeopardy because they had become "mere pawns" in a fight between the Communists and the ruling powers of the South."[85] "From its experience in many cases in the South," he wrote, "the Association knew it would be necessary to get Southern lawyers and Southern people to be prominent and active in the cause of the defense." Such action may have been, "conservative," he argued, but it would have been the boys' best chance for freedom. "As it was," he added, when the Communists took over the defense, "all Alabama and the entire white South abandoned active participation in the cases." "Three years ago," he concluded, "the cases could have been won by a non-political, non-partisan group. Today it is a question as to whether any group can achieve more than a modification of the threatening horror,— perhaps a prison sentence as a substitute for death."

The Young Turks at Amenia saw the NAACP's response to the Scottsboro case as indicative of the organization's failure to change with changing conditions. As one of the younger conferees put it: "The older policies for Negro advancement had failed and were inappropriate to the changed order impending. There should be a resolute decision to junk these policies, followed by a clear-cut outlining of basically new . . . policies." He also suggested that some of the older leaders "were much more interested in protecting their personal security as individuals in the existing order."[86] Ironically, in view of this criticism, both Du Bois, in 1934, and Pickens, eight years later, had to leave their posts because they publicly disagreed with the policies of the NAACP.[87]

Although the Scottsboro case was not a major topic of discussion at Amenia, it exerted considerable influence on the deliberations. The young blacks may have had reservations about some of the ILD's tactics in the case, but they appreciated the Communists' aggressiveness. They did not fear communism, as did a number of the older NAACP members, and were unwilling to repudiate a group that professed and, to an extent, demonstrated a belief in complete racial equality. Few, if any, of them every joined the party, however, in part because they believed that communism could not work in America "without a fundamental transformation in the psychology and attitude of white workers on the race question and a change in the Negro's conception of himself as a worker."[88]

Pickens, despite being repeatedly attacked in the Communist press, did not completely repudiate the Communists either. As late as 1934 he admitted to "agreement with many of the professed objectives of the Communist Party."[89] But he felt that the Negro had little to gain from the Communist movement. In 1931 he made a statement on that theme that closely paralleled the one made by the young blacks at Amenia. "Even if Communism were established here," he wrote, "the Negro would need to take care of himself against prejudice—race and color prejudice—just as he has to do now. Communism could not immediately change the history and psychology of the American white people."[90]

Pickens also indicated some other reasons why he had never joined the Communist party. "By training and by temperament I am a democrat," he wrote, "believing in the compromise of the ballot after agitation and discussion, and having no favor for class warfare. Narrow discipline never suited me. Therefore, although I could work . . . side by side with any humans, I could never become a member of minority political parties, with the limitations implied."[91] He cautioned Negroes not to be misled "by false prophets and false promises of a future." He wrote:

> Just as [the Negro] once thought that the only way to improve his miserable life, as experienced in this world, was to die and go to heaven, so now is there the danger that he will be persuaded that the only escape from the nightmares of the past and the tortures of the present leads through an uncritical and undiscriminating acceptance of the Utopias of radicalism.

Pickens admitted that the Communists "had some very excellent plans in their blue prints" for the future, but any dictatorship, "whether that dictatorship rests in an individual, in an oligarchy or in the proletariat, is bad for a segregated minority like the American Negro, hemmed in by the traditions, attitudes and prejudices of three hundred years." The only hope for such a minority, he reasoned, "is some form of democratic (non-dictatorial) control, wherein the minority may become at any moment the balance of power between rival factions of the majority. Any dictatorship deprives the minority of this occasionally realized and always immanent power and influence."[92]

The Communists promised the Negro equality, Pickens argued,

> but it is sure bunk for them to pretend to be about to invest Negroes in America with equality. . . . The Communists do not have equality themselves. . . . The Negro will get only what he *takes*, ... and when he takes it, he must take it from the dominant society. That dominant society may or may not in the future be Communist; at present it is *not* Communist.[93]

Pickens was not sure how blacks would "take" their rights, but he knew that the Communists, with their weak political base, inflammatory tactics, subjugation to a foreign power, and unwillingness to work with existing Negro groups, did not have the answer.

In 1935, with the rise of Hitler, the Communists made another policy switch and sought a united front with the NAACP and other nonradical groups. The Association rejected an alliance but cooperated, to a limited extent, with the ILD and other groups in the Scottsboro Defense Committee, which, in July 1937, obtained the acquittal of four of the Socttsboro defendants (they were no longer boys). The other alleged rapists were given long prison sentences, but in 1950, nineteen years after the incident at Paint Rock, the last of the Scottsboro "boys" was freed.[94]

During the 1930s, especially the years of the liberal-radical united front against fascism from 1935 to 1939, Pickens, like many other liberals and non-Communist radicals, was affiliated with a number of anti-imperialist and antifascist organizations which, subsequently, proved to be fronts for Communist activity. Although his main function for these organizations, such as the American League Against War and Fascism, the Medical Bureau and North American Committee to Aid Spanish Democracy, and the Council for Pan American Democracy, was as a speaker advocating civil and human rights for all oppressed minorities, the House Committee on Un-American Activities, in 1943, would use his ties with these front organizations to brand him a subversive.[95]

7
NEW DEAL OR "OLD" DEAL?
1933–1940

> Roosevelt is no god and no superman. An overwhelming number of little men like Smith of South Carolina and big bags of wind like Robinson of Arkansas will override any good intentions of Roosevelt in the future, as they have overridden them in the past, in all matters affecting the equal citizenship of colored people.
> —Pickens, 1936

William Pickens was a consistent, vocal critic of President Franklin D. Roosevelt and the New Deal. Although most blacks by 1936 had come to see Roosevelt as a second Abraham Lincoln, Pickens, as late as 1940, when he briefly led a citizens' committee for Wendell Willkie, the Republican presidential candidate, considered Roosevelt as just another Democratic president, dependent on southern support and unwilling or unable to take decisive action in support of Negro rights. He also believed that Negroes were paying too high a price for the relief, employment, and low-cost housing they were getting under the New Deal. He feared that Roosevelt, by expanding the powers of the executive branch, by running for a third term, and by challenging the Supreme Court, was leading the nation toward dictatorship. Only when the nation entered the Second World War did Pickens join the tide of Negro support for Roosevelt. But by then some black leaders were moving in the other direction.

Pickens, on 3 August 1934, delivered an address entitled, "A Century of Negro Progress," at the Chicago World's Fair.[1] Chicago was celebrating its hundredth anniversary and Pickens's subject was derived from the fair's theme, "A Century of Progress." Several exhibits depicting Negro life were displayed at the fair, including a proported model of the log cabin built in 1779 by a French-speaking Negro, Jean Baptiste Point du Sable, regarded as the first settler in the wilderness of "Eschicagou." Negroes who came to the fair also could see a Department of Interior film on Howard University, a photographic display of manual training classes at Bethune-Cookman and Florida A & M colleges, and a National Urban League exhibit about black migration from the South to the North.

But the fair also displayed, in a more subtle manner, another facet of Negro life—racial discrimination and segregation. Although one Negro was given the washroom concessions and blacks "had a monopoly on all porter jobs in toilets," the fair's managers systematically discriminated against black workers, hiring them only as entertainers and menials. In general, despite the high level of Negro unemployment in Chicago, blacks were bypassed for skilled and semiskilled jobs. Furthermore, black visitors to the fair, who otherwise were free to see the exhibits and spend their money, were denied service in the fair's restaurants. In April 1934, after strong protest by Chicago's black leaders, segregation in public accommodations was lifted, but nothing was done to achieve more equitable employment for Negroes.[2]

Pickens nevertheless found some evidence of Negro "progress," despite the impact of the economic depression on blacks and the extent of racial discrimination, even at a "world's fair" in a northern, cosmopolitan city. "Speaking in dollars and cents," he began, "a language which Americans understand, it is a marvel in economic history how an ex-slave group, proscribed, segregated and almost outlawed, starting empty-handed and almost one hundred per cent illiterate, in a competitive, unsentimental and selfish civilization, could get title to two billion of dollars in two generations." Two billion dollars represented only a tiny fraction of America's wealth, which Pickens estimated at 440 billion dollars, and was only 5 percent of what it would be if Negroes shared the nation's wealth in proportion to their numbers. But it was, Pickens explained,

> a symbol of the progress of the race to which Du Sable belonged, and which [has] moved forward from chattels to men; from slave labor to a position of power in so-called free labor; from universal poverty to the ownership of wealth, which is astonishing when measured against the difficulties in the way of acquiring it; from legally enforced illiteracy to a condition wherein between 80 and 90 per cent can read and write, from an inculcated inferiority complex to self-respect; from drudgery to art.

He also referred to a "slight upturn" in the past decade in the Negro's share in self-government. For example, since 1925 "many

Negroes have been elected to state legislatures and other posts in local government." He attributed this "chiefly to the migration of Negroes from the South and the consolidation of their communities in regions of less prejudice." He reminded his audience that Oscar De Priest (R-Ill.), a Negro, represented a Chicago district in Congress. "That is another landmark in the progress of the colored people of this magic city,—from Du Sable to De Priest."

No discussion of Negro progress would be complete without reference to the New Deal of President Franklin D. Roosevelt, who had been in office for more than a year. Pickens spoke candidly and critically of the New Deal, expressing a view that he maintained long after most black voters had shifted dramatically to the Democratic party. "Strange as it may sound," he told his audience, "the first effect of the New Deal halted and set back the economic progress of the Negro race,—and economic progress is very intimately related to all other forms of progress, artistic, civil, political." He was most concerned that the New Deal involved "certain elements of dictatorship," which was dangerous for any minority, but

> especially for a minority which popular prejudice places somewhat outside the pale. . . . When the federal government took over the supervision of work and wages in America, every classification and every rule of procedure became far more important and consequential for the Negro minority than it could ever have become under private and separate competitive control.

Pickens did not object to greater governmental control over the economy, but the New Deal, "while recognizing the existence of an economic problem, scorned or failed to recognize the existence of a race problem." Therefore, the Roosevelt administration

> while blithely issuing orders about wages, refused flatly to issue orders against the violation of the letter and spirit of the 14th and 15th amendments to the Constitution. . . . By red tape and rigidity of system, the government's procedure . . . naturally resulted in pushing the weakest element, the Negro, out of many of the places to which he had advanced by long and painful struggles in the competitive order.

The New Deal, in his view, "seemed somewhat worse than the 'old deal!' "[3]

Pickens was not surprised by the deterioration of the Negro's position under a Democratic regime. Six months after Roosevelt was installed, Pickens was convinced that his fears concerning a

Democratic administration were fully justified. "I Told You So!" he reminded his readers.

> We said plainly that we would prefer any of the other groups, even the Communists, to the Democrats, from the black-American standpoint.... This Administration, with its extraordinary peace-time powers, is even more disdainful of the claims of the Negro race than was the administration of Woodrow Wilson.

He was particularly critical of Harold Ickes, the secretary of the interior, for doing nothing to "help Negroes to get their just share of work on public projects," and for "giving a free hand" to contractors engaged in Mississippi flood control construction, who were working Negroes from twelve to eighteen hours a day for less than a dollar a day. Pickens was particularly upset that Ickes had appointed Clark Foreman, an "obscure Southern white" to advise the government on Negro affairs.[4] Pickens was amiss in considering Ickes "the most brazen one of the lot" of New Dealers. He later realized that Ickes, a former president of the NAACP's Chicago branch, was, along with Eleanor Roosevelt, among the Negro's best friends in the national government.[5]

Pickens concluded that most of the New Deal's legislative innovations for relief and recovery, including the National Industrial Recovery Act (NIRA), the National Recovery Act (NRA), the Agricultural Adjustment Act (AAA), the Civilian Conservation Corps (CCC), the Tennessee Valley Authority (TVA), and the Public Works Administration (PWA), either provided little or no assistance for Negroes or worked to their disadvantage. For example, he branded the NRA as the "Negro Removal Act."[6] "Consistent with this idea of not advancing the Negro's status," he wrote, "One of the first effects of the NRA programs to raise wages is to oust many Negroes from employment altogether." Minimum wage rates imposed by the NRA were generally higher than Negro workers were receiving and employers preferred replacing previously cheap black labor with whites. In some cases, the NRA codes froze wages at a pitiably low level. "This tangled wilderness of verbiage," Pickens wrote of the codes,

> means simply that . . . the low wages which black field hands up and down the Mississippi Valley accepted in lieu of starvation, are now to be preserved for the benefit of the contractors with the sacredness of law and upheld by the strong arm of the State. . . . That Alabama official was not much in error who banked on non-interference by the national government in behalf of local justice, even where money from the Federal treasury is being expended.

He predicted, however, that the NRA would not function well as a Negro Removal Act. Reiterating one of his basic theses, he wrote, "Prosperity will have to be shared with the Negro or it will be innocently undermined by him."[7]

One of Pickens's fundamental objections to the New Deal was that it had not dealt, in his view, with the underlying cause of the economic depression—laissez-faire capitalism. The NRA codes for industry-wide wage and hours standards, he thought, were not only discriminatory against Negroes, but represented a false, or "bastard," form of governmental economic planning. The "Blue Eagle" insignia symbolized compliance with NRA wage and hours codes, and NRA Administrator Hugh Johnson organized Blue Eagle marches in many cities to bring pressure on industries such as steel, automobiles, oil, coal, and lumber, which had not submitted to industry-wide agreements.[8] Pickens called the Blue Eagle marches a reversion to primitive "rites" and "incantations," and he depicted Johnson as a "medicine man."

> We civilized people [he wrote] when we cannot understand the relationship of cause and effect in the evils that beset us and know not what to do,—we resort to incantations, signs, symbols, "Blue Eagles," and big talk. By marching up Fifth Avenue a quarter of a million strong, with banners and slogans and insignia we expect to change the laws of economics. We might as well expect to change the law of gravity in the same way.

He feared that, in the aftermath of such "performances," people would grow frustrated and desperate when they realized that "the Blue Eagle sorcerers had not been able to drive away an economic depression in a few weeks." They had been promised millions of new jobs, but "they are still on breadlines." "It would be better for them," he added, "if they had been skeptics and had never trusted to sorcery. Some are really getting angry. . . . Pretty soon they may threaten to hang the medicine men."[9]

"We have descended into this depression," he wrote,

> by generations of error. By at least some years of patience and hard work we must clamber out again, unless we can start another fool war and get out in a few days,—to get in deeper after the war is over. . . . We need not trust the medicine men. We must alter the methods of distributing income and must share the ownership of the mighty "machines" of civilization. The Blue Eagle might be any other bird. He has no real power. Economic law must be respected and observed. It cannot be altered.[10]

Pickens supported automobile manufacturer Henry Ford in his fight against compliance with an NRA code. He pointed out that Ford paid higher wages and provided better working conditions than would be guaranteed under the code. "Why should he join the Blue Eagle crowd," Pickens asked, "and help the Administration to further fool the people?" He added:

> If the government wanted to socialize out and out, the great industry of Henry Ford and of the others, we would be with the government. But when the government seeks only a pretense of socialization, so as to keep the people unaware of the true nature of the arrangement, we are with Henry Ford and his lawful resistance to this sort of bastard socialization. . . . If Henry Ford can be bullied and coerced, so can labor unions, strikers, and all others. We hope he will sit tight and give the Supreme Court and the people a chance to set this NRA dictatorship in its proper place.[11]

In his oft-repeated concern about the New Deal as a proto-dictatorship, Pickens echoed the view of white New Deal critics, many of whom were of the political left, but a number of whom, such as Newton D. Baker, Al Smith, John W. Davis, and John J. Raskob, were conservative Democrats and members of the anti-Roosevelt American Liberty League.[12] "Perhaps Newton D. Baker, ex-Secretary of War, and the other so-called reactionaries and anti-New Dealers," Pickens wrote,

> have some sense on their side when they say that pay without work is working havoc in the American character. . . . That at least a large part of us will be expecting to live on the rest of us. . . . The radicals say we already have a parasitic class in the interest-drawing, bond-clipping rich. But, my brother, those parasites are a picnic compared with the consuming power of twenty or thirty million jobless poor. . . . Such a vast army, unfriendly to the idea of working for a living, would be ready-made Myrmidons . . . for some fascist dictatorship.[13]

Pickens, however, parted with the Liberty Leaguers in his prescription for economic reform. While they longed for a return to the halcyon days of private enterprise, Pickens wanted a planned economy as part of a socialist democracy. "The only hope against this insidious change [to fascism] is to reconstruct our economic society," he argued,

> so that, with the assistance of our machines, every able-bodied person can have a job . . . even if the working hours must be shortened to two or three hours a day. And then every person able to work, and old

enough to work, should be required to do his share of the work or allowed to starve. . . . At present, with no opportunities for work for the great masses, men cannot be allowed to starve. And workless income [relief] will transform the characters of these men. We have either to change our system or change our characters.[14]

In 1934 Pickens, because of his interest in providing work for the idle masses, supported Upton Sinclair's bid for the governorship of California. Sinclair, author of *The Jungle* and one of the best-known muckrakers of the progressive era, was a Socialist of the romantic, utopian school. His EPIC plan (End Poverty in California) aimed at establishing a "Cooperative Commonwealth" in which the state would acquire land and abandoned factories and turn them over to unemployed workers who would grow their own food and make their own shoes, clothes, and other material needs. Although regarded by many observers as merely one of California's ubiquitous social and economic cranks, Sinclair surprisingly won the Democratic primary.[15]

"We hope he [Sinclair] will win the governorship," Pickens wrote. "Of course he will not be able to make California into a 'Utopia.' But, . . . by his trying, he can expose the sham of both the Old Deal and the New." Pickens suggested that Roosevelt and "his crowd" would look upon Sinclair as a "Jonah." "The New Deal," he added, "pretends to be liberal or even socialistic in its tendencies and aims. . . . Can the New Dealers follow Sinclair? He has real socialistic and communistic ideas about property and goods and wages and work, and about the rights of the masses of men. We will see how much support he can get from them." Sinclair's "Cooperative Commonwealth" intrigued Pickens, but he was also interested in seeing how the New Dealers dealt with "this unwelcome stepchild to the family circle." "It is a pretty mess for them," he wrote, "and we like it. . . . We just love to see fakes and pretenders brought to light and called up for a showdown."[16]

Although most analysts agreed with Socialist leader Norman Thomas, who called the EPIC plan "economically and politically absurd," President Roosevelt thought that the experiment might have some merit if applied at a local, rather than a state-wide level. Roosevelt, however, had refrained from involving himself in state elections, and his advisers cautioned him to "say nothing and do nothing" in behalf of the controversial Sinclair. When California Republicans, aided by some Democrats, launched a massive smear campaign against Sinclair, in what Schlesinger has called "the first all-out public relations *Blitzkrieg* in American politics," his early lead vanished and Roosevelt dropped any thought of endorsing him. Sinclair lost the election to Frank Merriam, a conservative Republican, by two hundred and fifty thousand votes.[17]

Roosevelt's timidity in the Sinclair campaign was, in Pickens' view, indicative of the New Deal's response to politically explosive issues, especially those that were of vital importance to Negroes. Pickens learned firsthand on his circuits of the NAACP branches that, although many of the New Deal relief and recovery measures included antidiscrimination safeguards, local administrators often ignored the safeguards or, under pressure from whites, consciously violated them. He discovered, for example, that Louisiana Negro home-owners were being systematically denied assistance to which they were entitled under the Home Owners Loan Act. "The extent of the robbery," he reported to the home office, "committed against colored people by mortgage holders under the New Deal is appalling." "Too bad," he added, "that they [Negroes] had no home-buying organization of their own to save them from the sharks."[18]

He learned from the NAACP's Buffalo branch that white residents of Lackawanna, a suburb, had blocked the Federal Subsistence Homestead Corporation's attempt to establish homes for fifty Negro families.[19] Lackawanna was to be one of the New Deal's pilot projects for moving urban and rural slumdwellers into new, government-built, suburban communities. Of the original seventeen projects planned by the Federal Homestead Corporation, only Lackawanna and another in Tuskegee, Alabama, had been designated for blacks. But, as the corporation's general manager explained to the NAACP, local residents "were best situated to determine the type of project with respect to racial make-up which should be established in any community."[20]

New Deal administrators applied the same criterion to the CCC, whose purpose was to provide unemployed young men with work in the nation's neglected forests, parks, and other recreation areas. The CCC camps were, with few exceptions, racially segregated and, wherever local white residents complained, Negro camps were either canceled or removed to army reservations. The CCC director, Robert Fechner, "a Southerner by birth and raising," ignored demands from the NAACP that he should enroll more black corpsmen. President Roosevelt, who by 1935, according to the historian John Salmond, considered the situation "political dynamite," refused to alter Fechner's discriminatory policy. Two hundred thousand blacks ultimately benefitted from employment and training in CCC camps, but about one third were enrolled in the last years of the New Deal, when white youths, attracted by war-related industrial jobs, were no longer interested in the CCC. Salmond has written of the CCC, "The Negro never gained the measure of relief from the agency's activity to which his economic privation entitled him."[21]

The NAACP had hoped that the president, prodded by his wife and Harold Ickes, would support passage of a federal antilynching bill, but here too Roosevelt disappointed the Negro. On 20 February 1934 Walter White testified before a Senate Judiciary subcommittee in support of the Wagner-Costigan antilynching bill, which the NAACP had drafted and that these Democratic senators from New York and Colorado had introduced the previous winter. As part of his detailed statement, White told the subcommittee that, since 1922 when the Dyer antilynching bill had been filibustered to death by southern Democrats, 277 lynchings had occurred.[22]

Pickens congratulated White on his performance in Washington. "God, I hope they will pass the bill this time," he wrote. Pickens predicted that, despite the New Deal's obvious shortcomings, the Democrats would win overwhelming support among black voters in 1936 "if they have sense enough to correct this, . . . by passing it while they have a majority in Congress. We shall see."[23]

White soon learned from Eleanor Roosevelt that the NAACP could not expect much assistance from the president on the Wagner-Costigan bill. On 2 May she wrote: "The President talked to me rather at length today about the lynching bill. As I do not think you will either like or agree with everything that he thinks, I would like an opportunity of telling you about it." In November, however, Mrs. Roosevelt was somewhat more optimistic and informed White that the president "hoped very much to get the Costigan-Wagner Bill passed in the coming session," despite the Justice Department's doubts concerning its constitutionality. In closing she wrote, "The Marianna lynching was a horrible thing."[24]

The Marianna lynching had occurred on 19 October. Claude Neal, a young Negro under arrest for allegedly murdering a white man, had been taken from a Brewton, Alabama, jail and then brutally and publicly murdered in Marianna, Florida. Neal's death was particularly significant because he had been carried across a state line before being murdered, an apparent violation of the federal antikidnapping Lindbergh Law. Furthermore, the local press had publicized days in advance that Neal would be lynched in Marianna, without law enforcement agencies doing anything to stop the crime. Finally, Neal's murder underscored White's testimony before the Senate subcommittee that, after a period of decline from 1922, lynchings were occurring again with increasing frequency.[25]

Shortly after the Marianna incident Pickens wrote to President Roosevelt. "The law-abiding citizens of America," he stated, "have been supporting and applauding your relentless pursuit of the criminals, whom the recent acts of Congress gave you the authority, the power and the duty to pursue and prosecute (i.e. [John] Dillinger ['Pretty Boy'] Floyd). Are you going to chagrin [sic] that applause and discourage that support by lying down under a test like this Florida case?"[26]

Roosevelt's response to the antilynching bill was still in doubt when the NAACP asked Pickens, who was already in the vicinity, to investigate the Neal lynching. Despite warnings by the Jacksonville branch that his life would be endangered, Pickens took on the assignment. "So this is Brewton, Alabama," he wrote to the home office, "the measly little town from which the Florida mob took Claude Neal. Seems I'm tracing Claude Neal all around; Marianna where he was finally hung up; Pensacola where he was in jail; Brewton where the mob got him. I wonder how much further I'm to go on his trail."[27] In Pensacola Pickens had learned that Neal's mother and aunt were being held in jail for "safekeeping, or safely keeping them from talking, I suppose." He started a movement among local blacks to get them released. In the lynching's aftermath, the mob had destroyed the Neal's home and all their possessions. "It's a wonder," Pickens wrote, "they were not burned."[28]

Pickens had "quite a long stop" in Marianna. "Got out and talked to colored people around the station," he reported. "All seems quiet, as if no madness had ever been—until you attempt to elicit any *real* information. Then you are answered by a nonsensical grunt and a vacant stare. They are afraid to talk about it. Even 'big Negroes,' some professional people, are afraid to talk out in Florida."[29]

President Roosevelt, like the blacks Pickens interviewed, remained silent for fear of southern reprisals. In an interview with Walter White arranged by Mrs. Roosevelt, he explained his reasons for not actively supporting the Wagner-Costigan bill. Southern congressmen controlled key committees, he told White, and he was unwilling to antagonize them. "If I come out for the antilynching bill now," Roosevelt admitted, "they will block every bill I ask Congress to pass to keep America from collapsing. I just can't take that risk."[30]

After the Wagner-Costigan bill was tabled, Mrs. Roosevelt wrote to White: "I am so sorry about the bill. Of course, all of us are going on fighting and the only thing we can do is hope that we will have better luck next time."[31] When a similar bill was introduced in 1938, however, the result was the same—a filibuster in the Senate and silence in the White House.

Although the president and his advisers would not jeopardize their legislative program or the Democratic electoral monopoly in the South by championing Negro civil rights, New Dealers did act when they could do so without political risk. For example, Pickens and some friends were arrested in the spring of 1936 at Boulder Dam for refusing to leave an elevator when a party of whites entered it. The whites did not protest, but the elevator operator insisted that Pickens and his group wait for the next vacant car. Pickens would not move and the operator called a policeman who took the Negroes to a Las Vegas jail for "questioning." When Pickens identified himself at the jail, he and his party were released, given an apology, and one of the supervisors gave them a guided tour of the dam.[32] Pickens reported the incident to Secretary of the Interior Ickes. "In view of the facts disclosed," Ickes replied, "I wish to express my regret over the incident at Boulder Dam. I have accepted the resignation of Inspector Edgar E. Long, and Ranger W. E. Lukens is being instructed to avoid any partiality or discourtesy toward visitors in the future." Pickens answered, "The steps which you have taken insures treatment of blacks as human beings at Boulder Dam, or at least extends toward that result, and I am sure that the American Negro citizens will be glad to know it."[33]

Ickes's personal courtesy and Mrs. Roosevelt's interest in the Negro were not enough, however, to persuade Pickens to have faith in the New Deal. Neither the president nor the Democratic Congress, he believed, had done enough to warrant the Negro's trust. He viewed the Supreme Court, "whatever defects it may have," as the "only barrier standing between the Negro's citizenship rights and those who would at any time destroy those rights for political expediency." When the Court came under attack, in 1935, after finding the National Industrial Recovery Act unconstitutional, Pickens warned Negroes against "joining the pack seeking to destroy, to weaken or to discredit the Supreme Court." Should that happen, the Negro minority "would be at the sole mercy of Congress and the President—both of whom are political weathervanes subject to the winds that blow."[34]

He was not, however, entirely uncritical of the Court. On 1 April 1935 the Court had handed down two significant decisions, only one of which was favorable to Negroes. In *Grovey* v. *Townshend*, the Court upheld a Texas white primary. Yet, in *Norris* v. *Alabama*, it called for a new trial for Clarence Norris, one of the Scottsboro boys, because Morgan County, Alabama, had systematically excluded all Negroes from jury service, thus depriving Norris of the equal protection of the law guaranteed by the Fourteenth Amendment. Pickens, convinced that these decisions were contradictory, wrote, "If one were suspicious of the Court's motives, it would look as if they made a trade."[35]

Pickens, nevertheless, was adamant in his support of the Court's independence. "The members of the Supreme Court hold office for life," he argued, "and do not need to seek votes or to appease that many-headed beast which dominates republics and is known as 'the majority.'" No American governmental institution could be "absolutely fair and impartial to the Negro race, but, in his view, the Supreme Court was "the agency of our government best constituted and situated to approach nearest to that fairness, as its history and decisions would show."[36] Pickens was referring, no doubt, to recent history, and to several cases that the NAACP had successfully argued before the Supreme Court. As a New Deal critic, Pickens was little concerned that the Court, after putting down the NRA and the AAA, might proceed to throw out the rest of the New Deal's legislative program.[37] When Roosevelt criticized the Court, after it had invalidated the NRA, for its conservative or, as he put it, "horse and buggy," interpretation of the Constitution's commerce clause, Pickens was one of many who feared that the president planned some kind of assault on the Court's independence.[38] Anticipating Roosevelt's abortive "court-packing" maneuver by one year, Pickens warned, "But for the supremacy of this court, all the constitutional guarantees to the Negro would have been discarded long ago—by hungry politicians seeking re-election to Congress."[39]

His concern for the Supreme Court's independence was only one reason for Pickens's opposition to Roosevelt's re-election in 1936. He had seen how New Deal agencies had ignored Negroes or, through callousness or cautiousness, had exploited them or denied them their rightful share of assistance. His firsthand observations were corroborated by John P. Davis, whom the NAACP sent to investigate the Tennessee Valley Authority's (TVA) treatment of Negroes. Davis, executive secretary of the Joint Committee on National Recovery (an independent Negro group acting as a New Deal watchdog), made two trips to the South, in 1934 and 1935, and discovered systematic discrimination against Negro workers in their wages, hours, and job opportunities. He also reported that blacks were denied housing in the TVA model villages. The best that Davis could say for the TVA, as far as Negroes were concerned, was that "for a year or so it has furnished bread for a few thousand workers."[40]

Most blacks agreed that bread and jobs were the main benefits Negroes had realized from the New Deal. For some this was enough to justify voting for Roosevelt; for others, like Pickens, the economic relief Negroes had received was insufficient and too unevenly distributed to warrant support for the New Deal. The black leadership, as reflected in the black press, was deeply divided in the 1936 presidential campaign. Of the leading black newspapers, five supported Roosevelt and three opposed him.[41]

The black NAACP leadership offered conflicting counsel, with Walter White and the assistant secretary, Roy Wilkins, endorsing Roosevelt, and Pickens opposing him. White was highly critical of the New Deal, but he had come to know Roosevelt personally and was impressed with the president's vitality, candor, and, most importantly, the enormity of the political and economic problems he faced. White admitted that Roosevelt's administration had shown "great deference to the second and third-rate politicians who in most instances represented the South." But he supported Roosevelt, in part, because of "the failure of the Republicans to offer any sound and appealing programs or candidates as an alternative to the present administration."[42]

Pickens preferred the Socialist candidate, Norman Thomas, whose "moral and intellectual superiority" as compared with Roosevelt and Alfred E. Landon, the Republican candidate, "was obvious." "Any critical mind has seen all along," he wrote, "that the set of principles advocated by Norman Thomas and the political group which he heads, are principles which are far in advance of those which either Roosevelt or Landon and their associates even dare to be suspected of."[43] He wanted Americans to have the "healthy experience" of a Socialist government, but, he added, "since that is at present impossible, my second choice . . . would be the Republican Party, and the last choice of all is still . . . the crowd that dominates the Democratic Party."[44]

Robert Vann, editor of the Pittsburgh *Courier*, and one of most influential black leaders in the country, was incensed by Pickens's repeated attacks on the Democratic party. "I am enclosing some of the 'stuff' Dean Pickens is scattering around the Country," he wrote to Walter White. "Ask him, in my name, how in hell he expects Negroes who are Democrats to contribute anything, through his efforts, to the NAACP."[45] After being a staunch Republican for many years, Vann had switched to Roosevelt in 1932, and was rewarded with appointments, first, as special assistant to the attorney general in the New Deal's "Black Cabinet," and, in 1936, as head of the Negro Division of the Pennsylvania State Democratic Committee.[46]

Pickens and Vann had clashed before. In 1924, when the black NAACP leaders had supported Senator La Follette for president, Vann, then active in the Republican party, had criticized James W. Johnson, Pickens, and Du Bois for abandoning the GOP. He also suggested, in a *Courier* editorial, that the NAACP and other Negro activist groups soften their protest for "a season of rest and quiet," in order to ease racial tension and give Negroes "a chance to labor and play." Pickens had attacked Vann's "soothing syrup," and called him a "political job-hunter" and an "Uncle Tom."[47] In January 1936, with the old feud apparently forgotten, Vann had asked Pickens to participate in a new feature he was adding to the *Courier*. Vann wanted black leaders of differing views to write articles for a weekly forum. He was seeking "some common denominator of thought for the great group of ours," and wanted Pickens's opinion of the new feature. Pickens called it a "great idea" and agreed with Vann that W. E. B. Du Bois would be the "best man" to initiate the series. He added one suggestion. "Allow no blue-penciling editor to suppress the thinking, to modify the expression or to determine the objectives and the course of this forum column."[48] Six months later Vann was asking White to silence Pickens.

"I am a Democrat," Vann wrote, "and if the Dean is going to cuss out all Democrats, then I am one Democrat who is going to take him to the public and pull his pants off just like I know I can do it." "Get in politics or get out," he warned, "but don't ride the Donkey with the Dean and the Elephant with somebody else. The truth of the matter is, Walter, the NAACP has no business in politics at all."[49]

White defended Pickens, pointing out that the articles of the director of branches (Pickens's title since 1935)[50] did not express the NAACP's position, which was still nonpartisan, "any more than some statements I have made favorable to the President." The Association "should not have the right to tell its officers,"

White argued, "that no one of them can express an opinion on any subject." He did not "personally agree with some of the statements made by Mr. Pickens," but he would not "deny him the right to say them."[51]

Although he had supported Pickens, White nevertheless did have misgivings about NAACP officers expressing their political preferences, especially when they were hostile to the New Deal. A year after his exchange with Vann he persuaded the NAACP board to pass a resolution forbidding such activity.[52] For the moment, however, he only cautioned Pickens not to reply to Vann and suggested that some of his statements had been "a little too sweeping, or, at least, sweeping enough to give some people the notion that you are engaging in partisan political activities."[53]

"I suppose," Pickens replied, "that a citizen could only properly be accused of being 'partisan' in politics, when he is getting something out of it,—like Robert L. Vann, for a fine example." "Vann may continue to do his own thinking," he added. "I will certainly continue to do mine." Pickens concluded by reaffirming his belief that "the Democratic Party is to date about the worst bet,—the worst of a row of evils, with the Republican Party ranking as evil number two."[54]

Several days later, in defiance of Vann, Pickens wrote:

> Roosevelt is no god and no superman. An overwhelming number of little men like [Senator Ellison "Cotton Ed"] Smith of South Carolina and big bags of wind like [Senator Joseph T.] Robinson of Arkansas will override any good intentions of Roosevelt in the future, as they have overridden them in the past, in all matters affecting the equal citizenship of colored people. We might as well face the truth: in national politics the Negro has a choice only among evils, and the most evil of these evils is the National Democratic Party.[55]

The dispute between Pickens and Vann reflected the division among Negro leaders in the 1936 presidential campaign.[56] The black mass of voters, however, were united in support of the New Deal agencies that provided jobs, housing, and sustenance, and a substantial majority voted for Roosevelt, who easily defeated Alf Landon. In 1932 they had resisted the current that carried Roosevelt into the White House, but by 1936, as one observer wrote, "Colored voters in the urban centers of the North and East had caught up with the procession.[57] "The great tide of votes," wrote a *Crisis* editor, "can be explained only by a deep feeling on the part of most [voters] that Mr. Roosevelt offers an avenue to better things for the vast majority of Americans." The editor did not believe the black vote was for the Democratic Party. "They voted for Roosevelt, *in spite of* the Democratic Party."[58]

Pickens, who did not share this trust in the president, covered his disappointment by making light of the election's outcome. He pointed out that Landon had been as silent on civil rights as Roosevelt, and that the Republican convention had seated lily-white southern delegations and ignored the Negro question in its campaign platform, "So far as the American Negro is concerned," he wrote,

> it would not have made enough difference to worry about, as to which candidate should become President. The Negro will have to fight for everything he gets under anybody's administration. . . . Whatever their party affiliations, the black people of the United States must stand as one for all things affecting their collective welfare and their rights as a group.[59]

Shortly after the election, Pickens himself became an employee, in a minor way, of the New Deal. Dr. John W. Studebaker, U.S. commissioner of education, asked him to become a part-time lecturer in the Federal Forum Project pilot program. The Federal forums were a New Deal innovation, a kind of government-sponsored Chautauqua, designed to establish a network of adult education centers throughout the nation. The project was federally funded but directed by local sponsoring boards, generally boards of education. The project was envisioned, according to one local director, as a means of "making democracy work by developing an open-minded, civic-minded electorate."[60] The forum leaders were free to choose from a wide range of topics, and, according to Pickens, "No subjects seemed to be taboo." Pickens was expected to concentrate on Negro history, culture, problems, and contributions, but other lecturers discussed communism, fascism, the World Court, the Spanish Civil War, consumer cooperatives, and other timely subjects.[61]

As an outspoken critic of the Roosevelt administration, Pickens wondered "why the devil the national authorities ever wanted me for this work. There must have been some mistake or accident somewhere."[62] Whatever the reason for Studebaker's offer, Pickens accepted it because it would give him an opportunity to "get our message over to people whom we couldn't reach except under such auspices as the U.S. Government." Since the government would pay his salary and expenses, Pickens could do NAACP fieldwork on weekends at no expense to the Association.⁶³

Pickens's first assignment was a three-week lectureship in Morgantown, West Virginia, home of the University of West Virginia. He found the experience, "in some respects, the most extraordinary three weeks we have ever had with southern white people." One hundred "leading" white and black residents came to his first lecture, which was followed by a "real inter-racial banquet— in West Virginia!" On his first Sunday in Morgantown, all the white churches suspended evening services and met at the First Methodist Church to hear him speak and to collect money for the NAACP. His white hosts told him that he was the first Negro to dine in the university's faculty club.⁶⁴

In May 1937 Pickens made a similar trip to Seattle, Washington, where he spoke on "Abraham Lincoln, Man and Statesman," "American Race Problems and the Future of Democracy," "Mysterious Africa in Today's World," and "An Evening with Negro Humor." Speaking generally before white audiences, he used the forum to explain the importance of the NAACP in the fight for Negro equality and to dispel white misconceptions about the nature and capacities of black men. In "Contributions of the Negro to American Civilization," the lecture he most often delivered, Pickens recapitulated his basic theme—the interdependence of the races. "It is the mission of the Negro in America," he would assert, "to prove that we cannot have Jim Crowism, segregation, disfranchisement, inequalities of citizenship, and at the same time have justice, civilization and peace." The speech was written in 1926, but Pickens had to make few revisions to bring it up-to-date.⁶⁵

During his stay in Seattle, Pickens visited the site where Grand Coulee Dam, the New Deal's most ambitious construction project and the world's largest man-made structure, was being built. He was awed by "the greatest engineering achievement of the human race." He was also dismayed to find that the New Deal had failed to cope with the human problem of racial discrimination. Negro workers made up less than one percent of the six thousand workers at the dam site; those who were employed held unskilled or semiskilled jobs; they were paid discriminatorily low wages; and were forced to live in Grand Coulee, several miles away, rather than at Mason City, the construction town adjacent to the dam.

Pickens informed the NAACP home office of the conditions at

Coulee Dam and reminded Walter White that the situation was identical with that at Boulder Dam, during the Hoover administration, which the Association had strongly criticized.[66] "It seems," he wrote, "that the Roosevelt Administration, which had less excuses for its policy than Hoover had, because they had before them the record and the history of the Boulder Dam situation, had nevertheless registered the same failure to look out for colored workers in this new and greater project." He suggested that something be done by the NAACP, even if it was only "to expose the situation to the embarrassment of the administration." "It would be very simple," he reasoned, "for the Government to write in the contract that there should be no discrimination against workers on account of race, color or creed, by the contracting companies on the Government project."[67] The NAACP took up the matter with Secretary Ickes, but, as late as 1940, nothing had been done.[68]

Pickens was at his best on the public platform, away from administrative cares and daily routines, and Studebaker was sufficiently impressed with his work to ask him to continue as a forum leader for another six months. He was one of only twelve leaders retained from the original hundred, and the only Negro.[69] The NAACP also thought he was doing an effective job for the race and granted him six months additional leave, covering the first half of 1938. During that period he made more than one hundred speeches in Washington and in South Carolina, his birthplace. Among several letters praising his lectures was the following from the chairman of the Seattle Chamber of Commerce: "Dr. Pickens is one of the cleverest and most effective speakers we have had the pleasure of presenting in some months. His use of humorous illustrations of serious points was remarkably effective."[70] Seattle's Forum project director wrote:

> Dr. Pickens is a dynamic speaker with such sincerity of purpose and with such understanding of human nature that he establishes a perfect rapport with his audience. . . . In districts where there was some prejudice he took the audience by storm, and after the first week the entire city and many of the neighboring communities were doing everything in their power to get him to talk in their districts.[71]

Pickens continued to criticize the Roosevelt administration. His speech in April 1938, before the Seattle Chamber of Commerce, included an attack on the president's dependence on the southern wing of his party. When White criticized Roosevelt for having allowed the Senate to filibuster to death an antilynching bill, Pickens wrote:

> Say, that's a peach of a telegram to Roosevelt connecting America's attitude toward European persecution of Jews . . . with the lack of enthusiasm to smash lynching, our own domestic sin. Keep that up Boy, and they'll all be in love with you down there in Washington. But they will respect you and the rest of us.⁷²

When Roosevelt decided to seek an unprecedented third term in 1940, black leaders were as divided as ever in their advice to Negro voters.⁷³ Editorials in the *Crisis* clearly reflected the ambivalence many blacks felt toward the New Deal. Roosevelt's record on the Negro was described as "spotty," but, "hobbled as he has been by the Dixie die-hards," he managed to include Negro citizens "in practically every phase of the Administration's program." Failure of the antilynching bill was "a black mark against him," yet "for the first time in their lives, government has taken on meaning and substance for the Negro masses." The New Deal's program for low-cost housing was "no more than a beginning," nevertheless, "Negroes had shared in it in a most equitable manner." Although Negroes had been discriminated against by the Federal Housing Administration, the CCC, and other agencies, the New Deal merited "high marks" in federal relief measures, public works employment, and the National Youth Administration. Roosevelt's acceptance of the War Department's "notorious" Jim Crow policy for the armed services "was heavily on the debit side," but his appointment of a "Black Cabinet" and of the first Negro to a federal judgeship (William H. Hastie) were major achievements for the race.⁷⁴

By 1940 the New Deal, in economic terms, had been a boon for the Negro without precedent in American history.⁷⁵ But little had been done for his civil and political rights, especially in the South, where most blacks still lived. Nor had Roosevelt been willing to risk using his potential power of moral suasion to effect a social revolution in the minds of whites toward their black countrymen. By the end of his second term whites were no more willing to accept blacks as equals than they had been at the New Deal's inception. For example, the New York World's Fair of 1939, as far as Negroes were concerned, was similar to the Chicago "Century of Progress" Fair of 1933–34 at which Pickens spoke. When the New York fair managers discriminated against Negro workers, the NAACP sent the following letter to Grover Whalen, President of the fair:

The National Association for the Advancement of Colored People, which for thirty years has sought opportunities for American Negro citizens without discrimination on account of color and has worked for their integration into all phases of American life, is alarmed at the rigid exclusion of Negroes from employment with the New York World's Fair, 1939, except in the capacities of maids and porters. In an exposition which purports to indicate the trend toward the world of tomorrow, this Association believes that among the first considerations should have been a recognition of the unfairness of discrimination between peoples and the justice of opportunity for all on the basis of merit. This Association believes that New York particularly, being in the forefront of cosmopolitan and liberal thought in America, should set a pattern for the rest of the country. We, therefore, condemn the restrictions on employment at the New York World's Fair, 1939.[76]

On the eve of the 1940 presidential election, the *Crisis* editors posed the following question for Negroes: "Do they believe that, in spite of admitted mistakes and failures, the Roosevelt Administration is tending toward the kind of government that is best for the majority of all the people; or, has the Roosevelt record on the Negro specifically . . . been such that a new administration should be voted into power?"[77] White and Roy Wilkins of the NAACP, stressing the gains made by blacks during the previous eight years, supported Roosevelt. Pickens, back with the Association on a full-time basis, was concerned more with the opportunities for advancement of the race that had not been realized, and he worked for the Republican candidate, Wendell Willkie.[78]

Except for 1924 and 1936, Pickens had supported Republicans in presidential elections. But Wendell Willkie was the first GOP candidate since Theodore Roosevelt for whom Pickens had any enthusiasm. Originally a supporter of New York District Attorney Thomas E. Dewey, Pickens was won over when he met Willkie at his home in Rushville, Indiana, at a meeting arranged by John Martin of *Time* magazine.[79] He was impressed by Willkie's charm, candor, and informal manner. Furthermore, Pickens considered the main issues of the campaign to be the record of the New Deal, the European war, and the race problem, and he was satisfied with Willkie's views on all three. Willkie was highly critical of the New Deal, opposed American isolation, and favored greater governmental action to secure Negroes' civil rights. Pickens could not have known then that, as the campaign progressed, Willkie would embrace much of the New Deal and temporarily retreat from his internationalist views on foreign policy.[80] At the end of their interview, Pickens agreed to head a nonpartisan Colored Citizens Committee for Willkie. The Republican leadership, anticipating a close election, planned to make a strong bid for Negro votes and was pleased to have Pickens's assistance in the campaign. Pickens, a consistent critic of President Roosevelt, was happy to cooperate. He knew that the NAACP frowned on partisan political activity by its salaried officers, but he believed that they would not oppose his leadership of a nonpartisan citizens' committee.[81]

A number of prominent Negroes joined Pickens's group, including Frederick Patterson, president of Tuskegee; Charles Wesley, the noted Howard University historian; Claude Barnett of the ANP; and C. A. Franklin of the Kansas City *Call*.[82] Pickens, as head of the Citizens Committee, reminded blacks of Roosevelt's failure to support the antilynching bill and other legislation demanded by the race. He also published several statements by Willkie in support of such legislation. Willkie had called lynching "a hideous crime," promised to end discrimination in the armed services and Jim Crowism in the nation's Capitol, and told Negroes "to expect every consideration" from him, whether they supported his candidacy or not. Pickens also stressed the "third term" issue. "A change in our national administration is most desirable," he wrote, because it would "save the sensible . . . tradition of limiting the executive to eight years in office and would lessen the threat of dictatorship."[83]

White quickly disassociated the NAACP from Pickens's political activities, but did nothing, at first, to prevent him from leadership in the Willkie campaign.[84] However, when a number of black leaders inside and outside the Association complained that Pickens was compromising the NAACP's nonpartisan policy, White insisted that he resign from the Willkie committee. Even a staunch black Republican, Roy Garvin, an advertising man from Washington, D.C., thought that Pickens was "cheapening the organization and dissipating its influence."[85]

NAACP Board Director William H. Hastie, who would shortly become civilian aide to the secretary of war, also questioned Pickens's leadership of the Willkie committee. He considered political activity by NAACP directors and nonsalaried workers "wholly proper," but drew the line against such activity by salaried employees because

> our membership will properly inquire whether the money of the Association is paying for time used for political activity. . . . I think the situation is particularly embarrassing in the case of a Director of

Branches who will be doing field work for the Association at the same time that he is serving as leader of a group organized to support a presidential candidate.... Is there not some legislation of the Board covering such a situation?[86]

The NAACP had come under fire several times before in regard to paid employees engaging in political activities, notably in 1924, in the aftermath of the Parker fight in 1930–31, and in the presidential elections of 1932 and 1936. Generally, the Association's policy was to support or oppose individual candidates rather than political parties. However, as late as December 1936, when one board member had moved that "no paid employee of the NAACP be allowed or permitted to become actively engaged in any political campaign," the board had rejected the motion. It felt that it should not "lay down hard and fast rules," but rather "trust to the tact and good judgment of the individuals concerned."[87] The following year, however, the board reversed itself and prohibited paid executive officers from any partisan political activity. The resolution read: "They may not sign or issue statements in support of party candidates or party policies and programs. They may not speak at meetings called by partisan political groups."[88] Nothing in the resolution prohibited nonpartisan political activity.

Pickens was absent when the resolution was passed, but, in a letter to the board, he strongly opposed its action. "I can see no reason why a paid worker of an organization like the NAACP should have less of political and citizenship rights and privileges than any unpaid worker." Since the Association sought "enfranchisement, citizenation [sic] and political freedom of colored people," he believed that "honest, open and above-board political life and activity should be encouraged rather than forbidden." He thought that such a resolution would "do all harm and no good; that its evil precedent is far greater than any possible good that it can do; and that it is unnecessary."[89]

In 1940 several other NAACP employees besides Pickens had interpreted the prohibition to include only partisan activity. Director of Publicity George B. Murphy, Jr., and Acting Youth Director James H. Robinson had joined a nonpartisan committee supporting the American Labor party candidate, Alfred K. Stern, for Harlem's congressional seat. However, when Hastie raised the question of the NAACP's position on such activity, the Committee of Administration interpreted the 1937 prohibition to cover nonpartisan activity.[90] Pickens felt that White had pushed through an "ex post facto" reading of the resolution in order to muzzle those NAACP officers who opposed the Roosevelt administration.[91] But, when given an ultimatum by White to resign from the Willkie committee or the NAACP, he, like Murphy and Robinson, gave up his committee post.[92] Informing John Martin of his decision, Pickens wrote, "I will go on working, personally, to do the good thing which I was aiming to do through this Committee."[93]

NAACP members were divided, generally along political lines, on the Committee of Administration's interpretation of the 1937 resolution. For example, in the Cleveland branch, two Democrats, Grant Reynolds and L. Pearl Mitchell, favored the directive, while two Republicans, Harry E. Davis and W. O. Walker, accused the national office of restricting Pickens "just because he was out for Wendell Willkie."[94] Reynolds, president of the Cleveland branch, was particularly critical of Pickens's leadership of the Willkie Committee. "In lieu of your unwise commitments in this campaign," he wrote to Pickens, "your value to us in the near future is of no consequence."[95] Pickens informed Reynolds that he had resigned from the Willkie committee, but defended his political activity as "open, honest, unafraid and without guilt—and without selfish aim." Without mentioning names, but clearly referring to White and Wilkins, who were supporting Roosevelt, he pointed out that, while he had "worked in the open, some others work under cover."[96]

Pearl Mitchell, an NAACP board director, agreed with Reynolds that salaried officers should not engage in political activity, but she felt that there was some justification to Pickens's charge that White and Wilkins had identified themselves with the Democratic party. She suggested that the *Crisis* editors (which included White and Wilkins) were using the journal to push Roosevelt's candidacy and that Wilkins was clearly partisan in allowing the Democratic National Committee to reprint and distribute his letter urging Negroes to vote for Roosevelt. Mitchell was also for Roosevelt, but she warned White and Wilkins that many blacks were angered by the inconsistency of the national office's policy. "I still feel that you, my two friends," she wrote, "must watch and be careful if we are to be considered fair and consistent."[97]

White had refused to work for a nonpartisan committee favoring Roosevelt, which had been organized by Fiorello La Guardia, mayor of New York, and he tried to make a distinction between endorsing a candidate and working for him. But many black leaders, especially Willkie supporters, felt that he and Wilkins had used the prestige of positions in the Association in a partisan manner. The New York *News*, a black Republican paper, accused Wilkins of being Roosevelt's chief Negro booster and called for his resignation from the NAACP.[98]

The debate on the role of NAACP executives in political campaigns had little effect on Negro voters, who again supported Roosevelt in his successful bid for a third term. But it did cause renewed tension between Pickens and White. By 1941, with the United States being drawn into the war in Europe, another source of friction developed between Pickens and White. Throughout the New Deal years Pickens had been a consistent critic of the president, while White, although at times disappointed by Roosevelt's cautiousness, generally supported him. After the United States entered the war they switched roles. White became more critical and Pickens more supportive of Roosevelt as commander in chief of the armed forces.

8
A WAR ON TWO FRONTS, 1934–1942

> The United States is our ship on which we have been fighting for generations, on which we will fight with conservatism during this war, and on which we will go on fighting for more generations. But if any outsider, of any kind or color, proposes to sink this ship, all except the idiots among us realize that it is an equal threat to the lives of all of us, whether we have been riding in the cabin of this ship or in its steerage.
> —Pickens, 1942

Both major presidential candidates in the 1940 election promised to keep America out of the Second World War. President Roosevelt and his Republican opponent, Wendell Willkie, privately favored some form of intervention, but they realized that most Americans, despite abhorrence of Hitler and shock at the ease with which Germany had overrun Western Europe, were against American belligerency. William Pickens, however, was one of the few Americans, and possibly the only black leader, who openly advocated intervention. As early as 1934, when he became convinced that Hitler posed an immediate threat to world peace, democratic institutions, and the freedom of nonwhite peoples throughout the world, he called for international collective action against Germany. By 1938 he was vigorously advocating an end to American isolationism. When America finally entered the war in 1941, Pickens was willing to place a partial moratorium on Negro protest against racial injustice at home in order to face the enemy with a united front. Because he consistently maintained this view throughout the war, some blacks called him an "Uncle Tom" and others suggested that he had forfeited his place in the vanguard of the Negro protest movement. His position also conflicted with that of the NAACP, which continued to protest all forms of racial discrimination in the armed forces and on the home front. As a culmination to years of intermittent feuding with Walter White and the NAACP board, Pickens's refusal to abide by the Association's policy resulted in his dismissal from his position as director of branches.

Pickens was one of the first black leaders to point out the potential danger of German fascism. While vacationing in Germany in 1932 he had become close friends with a Jewish couple, Arnold and Erna Kalisch. The Kalisches kept him informed of Germany's political deterioration and its persecution of its Jewish minority. When, in April 1933, shortly after Hitler's rise to power, the Kalisches fled to Denmark, Pickens became convinced that Germany posed a threat not only to all minority groups, but to world peace.[1]

In a radio address in September 1934, Pickens warned Americans that "the racial bigotry of the Hitler party in Germany was dangerous not only for German Jews or Jews anywhere else in the world, and not only for the German nation," but for "the entire world." "We may say that the Versailles Treaty and the blind bigotry of the victorious nations [of World War I] brought Germany under the mad leadership of Hitler. Quite true: but to explain the origin of madness does not secure us against it." He also feared that, although "Hitlerism had infected but a small element in America, . . . those who still believe in the way of human brotherhood have not been so active and vocal as have the imitators of the dictators." Pickens concluded with a moving defense of democratic government.

> When Americans grow impatient with their ignorant, log-rolling House of Representatives and their stubborn and talkative Senate, a good cure for them all is to go and live a while under Hitler or Mussolini. They may soon conclude that the way of liberty, equality and human brotherhood is slow and cumbersome, but it is also the surest way, and that it is better to fight forward through shortcomings of democratic methods, even if it takes thousands of generations, rather than to reduce mankind to a beehive or an anthill. For America, better a thousand government grafters and a million gangsters than one Hitler![2]

Hitler's violations of the Versailles Treaty, Italy's invasion of the African kingdom of Ethiopia, the establishment of the Berlin-Rome Axis, and its support of the fascist forces in the Spanish Civil War, alarmed many black leaders, who saw the analogy between German persecution of Jews and southern treatment of Negroes, but Pickens, almost alone, was advocating American intervention.[3] In the summer of 1938 he visited Barcelona, one of the last strongholds of the Spanish Loyalists against Franco's army. Three thousand Americans, members of the Lincoln and Washington "Battalions" of the International Brigade, fought for the Loyalist cause. Some fifty of them were Negroes[4] and Pickens met a few of them while visiting a military hospital. "All honor to those boys!" he wrote. While they were defending freedom, "the democracies had run out on all the democracy that is left in Spain," and, in effect, were aiding "what they ought to hate: Fascism in Spain." He scored England, France, and the United States for their neutrality, a word, he wrote, "that I shall not respect so much in the future as I have respected it in the past. Where there is a human fight going on, other humans cannot be neutral." He understood the democracies' fear of a greater war. "What sane government heads are not afraid of war?" "But is war being avoided," he asked, "or its ultimate horrors . . . increased by yielding to the bullying" of Hitler, Mussolini and Franco? "Today these Spanish people are fighting in the front," he concluded, "for popular government, for self-government. It is our fight.[5]

In 1939, despite their attempts to appease Hitler, war came to England and France. After France fell, in the summer of 1940, leaving England to fight the Germans alone, Pickens wrote: "What a fight those British are putting up! And I am always conscious of the fact that they fight for me, and for you and for all of us who believe in international decency and human freedom. . . . We scorn neutrality!"[6]

However, many Negro leaders were not debating intervention or isolation, but rather whether blacks should fight even a defensive war or withhold their support until their citizenship rights were guaranteed or, at least, until they won equal treatment in the armed services.[7] George Schuyler and Frank Crosswaith, writing in the Pittsburgh *Courier*, presented the opposing arguments. Crosswaith, a Virgin Island-born radical Socialist and chairman of the New York Labor Committee, thought that the Negro risked what freedoms he already had by taking a "disinterested" attitude toward the war's outcome. He confessed little sympathy for "Perfidious Albion," a common attitude among blacks, but he was convinced "that the fate of the Negro . . . will be far more cruel and inhuman under Hitler and his totalitarian partners." "This is a white man's war," Schuyler rejoined. "Negroes have nothing to do with it." He saw no "basic difference" between the Axis powers and the British "as regards their attitudes toward the darker races." Crosswaith's prediction of the dire consequences to Negroes under fascist rule was, in Schuyler's view, "an exact description of the sort of existence so-called democracy had brought to colored people everywhere." "It is difficult to recall," he added, "what rights now possessed by the ten million Southern Negroes would be jeopardized by Nazi rule here." Since the federal government, "regardless of its political complexion," pursued an anti-Negro policy, "let us first prove its loyalty to us before we rush to its aid."[7]

The American Negro, according to black journalist Metz Lochard of the Chicago *Defender*, realized that the fall of England "cannot but foreshadow a total eclipse of democracy and representative government," but, because of his exclusion from full citizenship in his own country, "the strident cry for national preparedness leaves him unresponsive." Lochard found the Negro's "habitual emotionalism," in the midst of a contagious war hysteria, "conspicuously restrained." He thought that blacks supported aid to Britain, such as the destroyers-for-bases and lend-lease agreements, but only "as an inescapable alternative to actual engagement."[9] Even James Peck, a twenty-eight-year-old black aviator who had fought for the Loyalists in Spain and was eager "to get at Adolf," expressed the belief, in December 1940, that the "battle on the home front [was] of more immediate import."[10]

As German expansionism and racism became more apparent, the NAACP became more alarmed. But at no time, prior to the attack on Pearl Harbor, did the Association advocate American intervention. "It might as well be set down now," read a *Crisis* editorial of May 1938, "before any hostilities come to the front, that Negro Americans are not very enthusiastic about going to war for the Stars and Stripes. If war should come, "why should the Negro fight?"[11] Just before the German invasion of Poland, however, the *Crisis* asserted, "We want to fight for our country, [but] we want no bars in any branch of the army, navy or air corps."[12] By July 1940 the *Crisis* was "sorry for brutality, blood and death among the peoples of Europe, just as we are sorry for China and Ethiopia. [But] the hysterical cries of the preachers of democracy . . . leave us cold. We want democracy in Alabama and Arkansas, in Mississippi and Michigan, in the District of Columbia—in *the Senate of the United States*."[13]

In the summer of 1940 the question of Negro support for American intervention in World War II added to the already tense relationship between Pickens and the NAACP leadership, especially Walter White. Their sharp differences on the war and the Negro's response to it, coupled with White's dissatisfaction with Pickens's performance as director of branches, led to a permanent break between Pickens and the NAACP secretary. Although

Pickens and White had achieved a truce in 1931, after the attempt to oust White had failed, in 1935 their feuding had resumed when White again expressed dissatisfaction with Pickens's field work, in particular his inability to bring in to the home office as much money as Daisy Lampkin, the field secretary. Reminding Pickens of the economic depression, White wrote: "In times like these good will alone cannot pay salaries. Everybody would be more receptive to your request for an increase, . . . if more concrete returns from your work were visible."[14] He accused Pickens of doing too much private lecturing and of taking time at branch meetings to sell his book, *Bursting Bonds*. White told Pickens that several branches had complained that his speeches were too long and that, while "they are interested in your philosophy of race prejudice, they want definite information regarding what the Association is doing. Daisy's forte is raising money; . . . yours is perhaps inspiration." In "normal times" such a division of labor would be acceptable, he argued, but the Association was hard pressed to meet its expenses and White insisted that Pickens alter his methods in order to bring in more money.[15]

Pickens had heard this kind of criticism before and, confessing that he had never learned brevity, he denied the other charges. He pointed out correctly that Lampkin concentrated on a few, large, financially stable branches, while he visited over two hundred branches a year, not specifically to raise funds, but to keep them alive and in touch with the home office.[16] To Mary Ovington he wrote, "It has never seemed to me in these sixteen years that my best service to the cause of the Association could be in directly raising money." He thought that he was most successful as an organizer, trouble-shooter, publicist, and inspirational leader.[17]

Lampkin, whom White had helped up for admiration as a model fund-raiser, seemed to support Pickens's position. "As to the work you have been doing all these years," she wrote, "I think your service has been invaluable. There must be someone whose full time is given to the type of work you are doing if we hope to contact four hundred branches with only two persons in the field to do it."[18] Bishop J. A. Gregg of the Kansas City branch concurred. "These regular visits of Dr. Pickens," he wrote, "go far toward stirring up enthusiasm for the Association, centering the minds of his hearers upon the great work accomplished and the possibilities for the future." "Keeping the Association and its accomplishments before the people," he added, "by sending Dr. Pickens throughout the country, will be more than justified in the good will that he inspires."[19] Ovington felt that the Association was not making the best use of Pickens's talents. "You are a brilliant lecturer"; she told Pickens, "a man especially able to meet an opponent and get the better of him. If we possibly can, we should have you as a lecturer, an interpreter in the white world and one who arouses enthusiasm and courage in the colored."[20] But White was more concerned with fund-raising and administrative functions and, in his view, Pickens was not indispensable.

Pickens and White did not clash openly again until 1940. In the interim, however, Pickens received several letters from friends warning him that White was looking for some excuse to force him out of the organization.[21] Pickens had a number of friends within the NAACP hierarchy, including Archie Weaver, founder and former president of the Chicago branch; Thomas J. Griffith, Jr., president of the Los Angeles branch; Isadore Martin of Philadelphia; Harry Davis of Cleveland; Carl Murphy of Baltimore; John Haynes Holmes of New York; and Sidney Redmond of St. Louis. Martin, Davis, Murphy, Holmes, and Redmond were all NAACP board directors. When White and Wilkins insisted in 1939 that Pickens "subordinate all other activities" to an intensive campaign in a few large branches "that would yield the greatest amount of money," he refused, contending that "it would be dishonest for me to even pretend to be an intensive campaigner."[22] Board Director Redmond came to Pickens's defense. "Many of us feel that this would be an unwise move," he informed the board. "Dean Pickens draws the largest crowd of any speaker in St. Louis and we consider his appearance here somewhat of an institution. Strong supporters are won at these meetings and I trust that you will continue his present practice of speaking as well as working on memberships."[23]

Although some NAACP leaders thought that Pickens was being victimized by a domineering, manipulative secretary, others felt that White had some justification for considering him more of a liability than an asset to the organization. For example, Pickens lost a number of friends by his behavior in Philadelphia at the 1940 NAACP annual conference. When delegates from Los Angeles and Houston contested for the honor of hosting the annual meeting for the following year, Pickens actively and openly lobbied for his friends from Los Angeles. Many delegates thought that this was unseemly conduct by one of the national officers.[24]

Much more damaging for Pickens at the Philadelphia conference was his handling of the NAACP's Youth Council, which was made up of members between the ages of eighteen and twenty-five. He clashed with members of the council on the question of Negro support for American intervention in World War II. At issue was a resolution that the council planned to send to President Roosevelt. The resolution called on the president to support one piece of legislation before Congress—the antilynching bill—and to oppose another—the selective service bill. Compulsory conscription, according to the Youth Council's statement, "was contrary to the democratic principles of a free people"; a peacetime draft was a curtailment of constitutional rights "under a guise of national defense." The council was "wholly in accord with the defense of Democracy at home," but was "equally as strongly opposed to the sending of American soldiers abroad."[25]

Pickens, while chairing what was ostensibly a business meeting on branch problems, infuriated young delegates by calling their message to the president "the biggest fool thing" that he had ever read. The resolution, in his view, was Communist inspired and he argued that young blacks could not demand government protection of their rights and at the same time refuse, if necessary, to fight the Axis powers that posed the greatest threat to their freedom. Communists had infiltrated the Youth Council to some extent and, until 1941 when Hitler violated the nonaggression pact and attacked Russia, had advocated strict American neutrality.[26] Nevertheless, Pickens's reference to Communist influence was unfortunate and inflammatory, since most blacks, both young and mature, did not need prompting from subversive infiltrators to oppose American involvement in the European war. Pickens's hard and insensitive line in the ensuing confrontation with the younger delegates stemmed in large part from his desire for American intervention. However, the other NAACP officers attending the meeting, including White, Wilkins, and, especially, Youth Director Robinson, supported the spirit of the resolution and they tried, unsuccessfully, to resolve the tension that developed between Pickens and the young delegates. Pickens's performance in Philadelphia foreshadowed the extent to which the war had become his overriding concern.

After he had thrown down the gauntlet, a young woman from Philadelphia responded, "I don't think that we have been misguided and foolish in expressing our feeling to the President about lynching and about conscription." "We may make mistakes," she added, "but the youth delegates decided on those resolutions of their own free will, and I think we deserve credit for thinking out these things for ourselves and not to be called stupid and foolish for doing so." Pickens replied:

> There is a post card downstairs and there is a resolution on it which states to the President of the United States that the youth do not want to support the United States if it gets in the European war. Nobody wants to get in that war. I think our statesmen have done more than they ought to stay out. . . . This statement that you are not going to support your country if it gets in the war implies you are not going to help it. . . . Your country can be attacked and torn to pieces without a shot being fired on its shores. . . . If anybody starts that, Mr. Roosevelt can depend on me. And if anybody wants to join the fifth column, you can depend on me to be an enemy. . . . I know that anybody who would persuade the colored youth to act against the interests of this country in this emergency is a very foolish friend.[27]

"If . . . the senior branch vetoes everything we try to do," another young woman argued, "it is going to kill the interest of the youth. What will we do in that case to interest the young people?" "We have already said, and say again," Pickens answered, "that when the youth council is right, they should try to convince the seniors they are right. But if they fail . . . then the senior branch has the right of way." Several other young delegates criticized Pickens for denying youth a voice in the Association, but to each he replied, "Somebody has got to be the head in every house and as I understand it the senior branch is the head in the house when the row is over."

At this point James Robinson intervened.

> There has been [he said] a great deal of discussion and dissension here about the resolution on that post card. . . . Now it seems to me that when young people take a stand on any subject, you have to say "that is your right," and then we have to sit down and think our problem through correctly. The young people have got to respect the older people and the older people owe a certain amount of respect to the younger people. . . . I am certain the majority of the national officers believe in the youth movement. . . . As a national officer and as one who has worked with young people, I endorse the attitude of the young people at this conference.

Put on the defensive by Robinson, Pickens responded: "I don't care much about Franklin D. Roosevelt, but I don't think he used 'guise' in his fight for national defense and I don't think it wise to tell him he is using a trick and then tell him to defend your antilynching bill. If they re-write [the resolution], I think it will be sensible."

Walter White joined Robinson in endorsing the Youth Council's resolution and, in terminating the two-and-one-half-hour debate, he stated what was to become the Association's position on the Negro's proper role with regard to the world war. White said:

> For thirty-one years the NAACP has stuck in the face of opposition, of attack, of criticism, to one single principle. That we are fighting for the same privileges, for the same rights, and full integration of the Negro into every phrase of American life, without segregation, discrimination or exclusion from any phase of it. *There is no compromise. There will be no acceptance of any temporary phase or temporary cure.* We are fighting for complete integration of the Negro in American life. We are interested in America; we are interested in seeing Democracy preserved.[28]

The Philadelphia meeting was a low point in the relationship between Pickens and some of the other national officers. When some of his friends suggested an NAACP fund-raising drive for 1941 in honor of his sixtieth birthday, the Committee on Finance rejected the proposal "in light of the unfortunate controversy which had arisen during the 1940 annual conference."[29] Several board members also nominated him for the Spingarn medal, awarded annually to Negroes who made major contributions in various fields. John Haynes Holmes, a member of the award committee, received many letters supporting Pickens's candidacy. "I want to congratulate you," he wrote to Pickens, "upon the ardent and devoted friends that you seem to have here and there and everywhere." But, according to Archie Weaver, Pickens had made enough enemies in high places at Philadelphia to deny him the prize.[30]

Pickens, in his reply to Weaver, defended his action at the annual meeting. "I had no more confidence in Roosevelt than they had," he wrote, "but he is a human being, and besides all that, he is President of the United States. Besides, I opposed having our Youth Council led always by radicals and the radical elements." He informed Weaver that, following the debate, many adults who were "afraid to express themselves" had congratulated him on the position he had taken. He admitted that he was not popular with the Youth Council or the NAACP home office. But, he added, "the people have always been with me,—the great majority of them." "Some of those with whom I have worked for a quarter-century," he concluded, "have been trying to kill me for a quarter-century. Perhaps they will succeed at last, if I do not die naturally first."³¹

If White was looking for a safe way to remove Pickens from the executive staff, the means was provided when, in April 1941, James Houghteling of the Treasury Department asked White to recommend someone to head its Savings Bonds Division's Negro section. War with the Axis powers was a distinct possibility and the Treasury Department wanted a popular and articulate black spokesman to sell bonds and patriotism to Negro business, religious, fraternal, and civil rights groups. White and Judge Hastie, both critical of Pickens's work as director of branches, nevertheless recommended him for the Treasury position. On 30 April Houghteling, a fellow Yale graduate, broached the subject to Pickens. When Pickens expressed considerable interest, Houghteling asked the NAACP board to grant Pickens a year's leave. The board agreed and on 15 May 1941 Pickens took on his new duties.

When asked by journalist Helen Boardman why Pickens had been chosen, Harold Graves, head of the Treasury Department's Defense Savings Division replied, "We needed a man who knew and understood the Negro people; but, far more, we needed a man whom the Negroes knew—knew and trusted." Boardman believed that Pickens also was chosen because he recognized "the life and death importance of the present emergency." She added, "Those who take the position of the President—and in this he has no more ardent advocate than William Pickens—feel that more than the life of a nation is at stake."³²

In granting Pickens's leave, the NAACP took the opportunity to criticize "the discriminatory treatment of Negro Americans in all phases of the national program." They cited, in particular, restrictions on Negro enlistment in the Navy, "except as mess attendants," and the failure of industrial plants holding defense contracts to hire Negro workers. "Nevertheless," the board announced, "this Association is willing to grant Dean Pickens a leave of absence for one year with an option for renewal, since the government believes he can be of assistance in its program."³³

The black press had differing views on White's role in Pickens's shift to the Treasury Department. The Washington *Afro-American* traced the appointment to "the slick hand of Walter White," who used the influence of the Spingarns and other white backers "to win the ear of Treasury Secretary [Henry] Morgenthau."³⁴ William O. Walker, editor of the Cleveland *Call and Post* and an NAACP board director, thought that Pickens was being "bought off or shoved off," and considered the appointment "a polite way of firing him from his position" with the Association. Walker, a critic of both the Roosevelt administration and White, was "frankly surprised" that Pickens, the Association's "ace speaker" and "as much a national institution as anything we have," had accepted the job. He added:

> It has been evident during the past few years that Pickens' Republicanism was not sitting well with the New Deal Democrats who were in the majority at NAACP headquarters. . . . How much pressure was used at NAACP headquarters to convince him to make the move, we don't know. We know this—the NAACP is the loser in the deal. The government doesn't need Pickens. We as a race are so poor that he never will sell enough bonds to pay his own salary. But his fiery logic and platform eloquence have more than kept alive the NAACP, and have been a constant source of encouragement to the growing militancy among Negroes. In shelving William Pickens the NAACP has hurt its own program that, in these hours of national defense scare, needs every experienced fighter it can command.³⁵

Pickens, deeply distrustful of White's actions, was convinced that he had tried to block the appointment and had recommended Judge Hastie in his place. White denied this and told Pickens that both he and Hastie had recommended him "because we believed that you could do the job and . . . because we wanted to give you a chance to accept or refuse the $5600 salary the Treasury Department was offering."³⁶ The truth lay somewhere between White's version and that of the Cleveland *Call and Post* editor. White was instrumental in getting the Treasury job for Pickens, but his motives were not entirely altruistic. Once Pickens was out of the national office, it might be possible to keep him out.

Pickens accepted the Treasury post for several reasons. First, he was relieved to get away from his critics on the NAACP staff. He had enjoyed his work for the Federal Forum Project, and anticipated a similarly rewarding experience with the Treasury Department. Nor could he ignore the salary, almost twice as much as he was receiving from the NAACP, or the prestige that went with the new position. Perhaps most important, Pickens, a champion of national defense and American involvement in the world war, could use his role as chief bonds salesman to persuade blacks of the importance of uniting behind the national government. He felt that the Treasury Department had chosen him because he "did not have to be converted to the belief that the security of the United States involves the security of all of us." That belief was "one of the threads in the web of all the speaking and writing I have ever done,—especially in the old World War, and more especially, since World War II broke out."[37]

By the winter of 1940 White, like Pickens, thought that the overwhelming majority of blacks "regard the United States as a country they helped to build, and which, rebuffed or not, they are prepared to help defend." However, like Lochard, Crosswaith, and other black leaders who supported national defense, White did not share Pickens's desire for American intervention in the war unless the enemy attacked first.[38] However, two events significantly affected the debate on the Negro's role in the war. The passage of the Selective Service Act in September 1940 subjected all adult males, regardless of color, to a military draft. And on 7 December 1941 when Japan attacked Pearl Harbor, all Americans were at war. Once the question of intervention had been settled, the *Crisis*, echoing a theme that Pickens had been stating for years, called on Negroes to support the war effort. "If Hitler wins," the *Crisis* wrote, "every right we now possess . . . will be wiped out. If the Allies win we shall at least have the right to continue to fight for a share of democracy for ourselves."[39]

The day following the Pearl Harbor attack the NAACP announced its "two front" policy, which it steadfastly maintained throughout the war.

> Though thirteen million American Negroes have more often than not been denied democracy, they are American citizens and will, as in every war, give unqualified support to the protection of their country. At the same time we shall not abate one iota our struggle for full citizenship rights here in the United States. We will fight but we demand the right to fight as equals in every branch of the military, naval and aviation services.[40]

Consistent with this uncompromising position, the Association went on record in opposition to segregated training camps for black soldiers and aviators. The War Department and military leaders, with Roosevelt's concurrence, refused to desegregate the camps and were reluctant to enlist blacks, even on a segregated basis, in the air corps.[41] The Association had faced the same Hobson's choice during World War I. Only after Pickens, Joel Spingarn, and Du Bois had worked for the establishment of segregated Fort Des Moines so that black officers could be trained at all, had the rest of the NAACP leadership reluctantly accepted the compromise.⁴² White, Wilkins, and a majority of the NAACP board were determined not to make that compromise again. They had been disappointed by the absence of racial progress in the military after the First World War; they had not seen any improvement in the Negro's status in the armed services between the wars, and they refused now to follow Du Bois's World War I dictum that they should close ranks and defer social change until after victory. The NAACP could not prevent blacks from being trained in segregated camps and aviators' schools, but they would not give such segregation their moral sanction.

Pickens, however, consistent with his position in World War I, was willing to accept segregated training facilities. Furthermore, as head of the Negro section of the War Bond Division of the Treasury Department, he wanted to instill enthusiasm among blacks for the war effort, rather than criticize it. This was a war, in his view, that warranted the undivided support of all Negroes. If they could not train in integrated camps and fight in integrated regiments, he argued, they still could prove themselves equal to white soldiers, officers, and pilots. Blacks could demand their full citizenship rights after Hitler and the Axis powers had been defeated. "Everything must be sacrificed, if need be," he wrote, "to the winning of this war. Such sacrifices are not really sacrifices at all."⁴³ After twenty years of intermittent conflict with the NAACP hierarchy, it was this issue—segregated training camps—that brought about a permanent break between Pickens and the Association.

In January 1942 Pickens visitd Fort Huachuca, Arizona, where thousands of Negro soldiers and officers were training. He had been at Fort Huachuca in 1930 and was so appalled by its inferior equipment and facilities and by the way white officers humiliated and exploited Negro soldiers, that he had written a long, critical letter to President Hoover, describing the conditions at the camp.⁴⁴ But in 1942 Pickens found the camp's facilities and the black soldiers' morale much improved. He also visited Tuskegee, Alabama, where Negro pilots of the Ninety-ninth Pursuit Squadron were being trained. He had heard reports that the camp was a sham perpetrated by the War Department to halt Negro demands for Negro aviators, but he was impressed with the camp's modern structures, air fields, living quarters, and recreational facilities.⁴⁵

Incorporating his observations at Huachuca and Tuskegee into an article for the New York *Amsterdam News*, Pickens took the opportunity to take a slap at the NAACP's uncompromising position on segregated camps. "The Negro in the Army and in the air"; he wrote, "so much is said about it nowadays and so much on mere imagination and theory. Some people's passion against 'racial segregation,' for example, blinds them to any excellence in the Negro's military record and to his starting [sic] participation in the air force." He predicted that segregation, "the old American mischiefmaker," would be part of the military life "for some generations to come." "But, by heaven," he added, "this 99th Pursuit Squadron [does] nothing to increase or promote segregation, but will make a dent in it. Those boys are going into the air and prove their equality." Segregation based on skin color was "damned nonsense," but the army, he reasoned, was not interested in making a social revolution. "It is planning to win a war, in spite of segregation or of those who oppose segregation."[46]

The NAACP board took great exception to Pickens's article, especially the last sentence. Ten days later they voted not to reappoint him to the executive staff at the end of his year's leave, because "his stand on the matter of segregation in the United States is contrary to the repeated stand taken by the NAACP."[47] The board informed Pickens that he could appeal their decision at the next meeting. Ovington, who had attended the meeting, described for Pickens what had happened. She was "entirely at sympathy" with him on the segregated camp issue, but Judge Hastie and NAACP President Arthur Spingarn had been "especially excited" about the last sentence in the article, which, to them, implied that the Association was against the war effort. The other board members agreed, she added, that "you had criticized the NAACP and that in an employee was unforgivable." "I hope you won't try to stay on with us," she concluded, "because this war work will give you more prestige than ever and when it is over you should get something better than being ignored by your senior officer."[48]

Blacks' responses to Pickens' discharge depended as much on their attitude toward White and the NAACP as on the segregation issue. William E. Taylor, dean of Negro Lincoln University Law School, wrote to Pickens: "I do not know what the facts are in the matter, but whatever they are as between you and Walter White, I am with you." "My opinion is," he added, "that this is the finest thing that has ever happened for you. I was never able to see how a man of your ability and outstanding accomplishments could afford to work under a narrow official like Walter White."[49] "The charge seems to me," wrote Tuskegee's President Frederick Patterson, "to be a trumped up one, for you rightfully said that you did not endorse segregation. The position which you took was in my opinion both reasonable and sound and has merely been used as an excuse to do probably what it was planned to do at the first opportunity anyway."[50] Patterson publicly blamed the affair on White's "ego," which he said was "undermining the effectiveness of the NAACP."[51] The Pittsburgh *Courier's* Percival Prattis, for many years Pickens's colleague in the ANP, thought that the segregated aviator's camp at Tuskegee was "a marvellous victory" for the race, one that meant "as much or more" than the establishment of Fort Des Moines for Negro officers' training in World War I. He believed that the NAACP rank and file was proud of the Ninety-ninth Pursuit Squadron, and he criticized White for "sneering" at the project and for dismissing Pickens for "trying to make the most of it." The NAACP should fire White, Prattis argued, instead of Pickens.[52]

On the other hand, C. F. Richardson, Jr., of the Houston *Defender* agreed with the NAACP's "uncompromising attitude." "It is impossible for a man to serve two masters," he wrote, "and men like Pickens . . . are able to secure governmental jobs in order that the government can capitalize on their good will and contacts. 'Ere long they are forced to choose between their loyalty to their principles or the lure of federal lucre. In far too many cases they have been more practical than idealistic."[53] "Our pal, William Pickens," wrote "Charlie Cherokee" of the Chicago *Defender*, "is fit to be tied. The NAACP has promised him an early hearing but everyone within half a mile has already heard him. Boy, is he boiling, but from here it looks like he's more loud than right."[54]

The reports of Pickens's dismissal proved to be somewhat premature. Having worked for the NAACP for thirty-three years, twenty as a salaried officer, he was not inclined to accept the board's action without protest. At a meeting with the board on 13 April he denied having advocated segregation or any other wrongdoing. "I have been fighting for my race," he read from a prepared statement,

> never hostile to my country, for nearly half a hundred years. For forty years I have repeatedly risked my life in the fight against undemocratic and unnecessary public discrimination based on race. . . . Therefore, it was . . . astonishing to me . . . that some of the Board members . . . were of the opinion that one article of mine, after

forty years of article writing, had one phrase in it which "advocated segregation."

Pickens was referring to the sentence, "The army is planning to win the war, in spite of segregation, or those who oppose segregation." What he meant, Pickens explained, was that

> it is the business of the army, especially in time of war, to win that war; that it is neither the duty nor the capacity of the army to settle our peace-time societal problems; . . . that regardless of who favors segregation or who opposes it, all of us together must support the army in doing its job; and that this war, the greatest of all our wars, enhances the logic and sense of that position.

In the article he had indicated "incidentally" that he was "with the antisegregationists, for it did not seem necessary, after forty years, to say so at all." "Our domestic struggles," he concluded, "should not be abandoned, but should be tempered and directed in such wise as to give no aid or comfort or hope to the enemy."[55]

On the motion of Carl Murphy, which was seconded by Isadore Martin, both friends of Pickens and critics of White, the board voted to rescind that part of the resolution passed at the February meeting, which had terminated Pickens's positions as an executive officer. John Haynes Holmes and Mary Ovington, preferring that the whole resolution be withdrawn and expunged, did not support the motion. The new motion read, "That Mr. Pickens be notified that his article on the matter of segregation in the United States Army is contrary to the repeated stands taken by the NAACP and officially taken by the Association's Board of Directors."[56]

President Spingarn, reminding the board that the press already had discussed the matter and, wishing to avoid further publicity, suggested that the new motion be the only information made public. Pickens informed Spingarn that, although he had maintained silence on his dismissal for two months, he had given copies of his statement to Treasury Department officials and to Claude Barnett of the ANP. But he agreed to ask Barnett not to publish the statement. The next day he changed his mind. He had promised the press some kind of statement after the issue was resolved, he informed Spingarn, and, if he failed to say anything, "it will seem like a violation of that implied pledge." "And worst of all," he added, "it would be a great injustice to myself. I have been publicly criticized by NAACP executives, and I ought to make a public statement about it." Spingarn was "surprised and shocked" by Pickens's decision.[57]

When the board met on 11 May, they had before them a request from the Treasury Department to extend for one year Pickens's leave of absence. Pickens's friends favored granting the request, but a motion to this effect was defeated. His critics, especially White and Robinson of the Youth Council, argued that the Association could not function indefinitely without a branch director. White had taken over Pickens's duties during his absence, but had found the additional work too burdensome. Both White and Robinson suggested that there had been some improvement in the branch work since Pickens's departure, but that a full-time director was needed. It was clear, after another motion further to extend Pickens leave was defeated, that a majority wanted him to decide between the Treasury Department and the Association. The unexpressed hope of many was that he would resign from the NAACP. The board finally voted to grant Pickens a leave of one month, at which time the matter would be reconsidered.[58]

When the board granted him only a limited extension on his leave, Pickens suggested that a director of branches be chosen in his place and that he be granted indefinite leave, "with the understanding that, if and when I return to work in the NAACP, the character of my work will be determined by the Board."[59] He may have been hinting that he intended to leave the NAACP permanently, or that he wished to return in some nonadministrative capacity, such as a touring spokesman. More likely, in the event he could not reach some mutually acceptable arrangement with the board, he was protecting himself against the possibility of again being dismissed. However, he had written a letter to Virginius Dabney, white editor of the Richmond (Va.) *Times-Dispatch*, which antagonized the majority of the board and made rapprochement impossible.

Dabney, a southern liberal, had written two editorials in which he had sharply criticized the black press for, in his view, exaggerating reports of whites harassing black soldiers. Fearing that heightened racial tension would develop into armed violence, he cautioned blacks that they should temper their protests until the war's end. He predicted not only that racial violence would hamper the war effort, but also that "the Negroes will be the worst sufferers. They always are."[60] Although many blacks took exception to Dabney's editorials, Pickens, in an open letter to the editor, found them "full of good will for the Negro race." He was astonished that anyone could "interpret them otherwise." "Of course," he added, "I know the Negro masses better than you . . . and I know that they are loyal as a group, *but with some few traitors and some very foolish persons in their midst.*"[61]

Pickens did not identify the "traitors" or "foolish persons" or make clear whether they were disloyal to the race or the nation. Possibly he was referring to small, pro-Axis, anti-Semitic Negro cults, such as the Ethiopian Pacific Movement, the World Wide Friends of Africa, or the Brotherhood of Liberty for the Black People of America, which were active during the war.[62] He may have had in mind some black newspapers that published, without verification, every report of white hostility against Negroes in uniform. Or, he may have carelessly and impulsively used the term to include NAACP leaders and others who refused to tolerate, for the duration of the war, any discrimination against the race.

Some blacks interpreted Pickens's remark literally. "Mr. William Pickens," wrote the Norfolk *Journal and Guide*, "is the first American—so far as our recollection goes—to assert that one or more American Negroes have committed treason. He has cast a shadow over the proud record of his race, a thing which he will find extremely difficult to substantiate, and for which he will be shunned by millions who have heretofore admired and respected him."[63] T. J. Sellers of the Baltimore *Afro-American* announced "The Passing of Dean Pickens." Sellers, as a youth, remembered Pickens as a fiery, uncompromising race leader.

> I sat wild-eyed while still in knee pants and heard him thunder out the kind of democracy that the race expected. No one ever talked or popped gum when Dean spoke. Every ear listened in those days as he hammered home the things colored boys were dying for in World War I. . . . Some disciples caught that gospel and learned to preach it earnestly. . . .
>
> Maybe these men and women are among the "traitors" mentioned in the Dean's classic letter to a Richmond daily paper a few days ago. They are perhaps counted among the "silly" ones reported by the former field agent of the NAACP.
>
> But this is the ironic twist: all of this fury came from the former prophet because his converts were sold on his basic philosophy! This was the pay dished out by the Dean to those who brought his work home.[64]

Two weeks later the NAACP board, having received numerous complaints about Pickens's article, met to consider what action they should take. The board had faced a similar situation in 1934, when W. E. B. Du Bois, then the *Crisis* editor, had feuded with Walter White and members of the board, criticized the direction the organization was taking, and publicly disagreed with the Association's antisegregation policy. Although the two cases had common elements, there were several important differences.

While Pickens advocated acceptance of a segregated army as a temporary expedient, Du Bois had wanted blacks to embrace segregation in all its forms and to turn it to their own advantage. His scheme, born of the depression and the black experience, was a mixture of ideas borrowed from Booker T. Washington, Marcus Garvey, and Karl Marx. In his view, in order to compete with the dominant white society, blacks must adopt economic nationalism, based on manufacturing and consumer cooperatives, which would provide economic self-sufficiency and inculcate racial pride and identification as a collectively exploited class.[65] Another difference in the two cases was that Pickens had criticized specific NAACP policies but not its entire program, while Du Bois, by 1934, had described the NAACP as being "without a program, without effective organization, without executive officers, who have either the ability or disposition to guide the [Association] in the right direction." Finally, although Pickens had privately criticized White, Du Bois had done so in print, even suggesting that White was more comfortable with white men than with blacks.[66]

When a break between Du Bois and the Association seemed inevitable, Pickens had tried, unsuccessfully, to mediate their differences and "to reconstruct a united front."[67] Several board members had wanted to fire Du Bois, but Pickens had cautioned against such action, arguing that, since Du Bois would voluntarily retire "before many moons, I wish we could be spared the shock of retiring an officer in a contentious atmosphere or in strife." "There are many," he concluded, "who will take advantage of us in such a case."[68] The board had agreed and, in accepting Du Bois's resignation "with deepest regret," had paid tribute to his contributions to the Association and the race. Although the board had not "always seen eye to eye with him," such differences "had in no way interfered with his usefulness, but rather the contrary." "A mere yes-man," the board wrote, "could not have attracted the attention of the world, could not even have stimulated the Board itself to further study of various important problems. We shall be the poorer for his loss."[69]

When Pickens's case came before the board, however, he did not receive such consideration and deference. The board could have ignored Pickens's letter to Dabney or mildly censured him for his unfortunate choice of words. But several members argued that "numerous acts and statements by Mr. Pickens made it impossible for him to continue as a member of the staff." Since his leave was due to expire in two weeks, the board could have denied renewal and asked for his resignation. Rejecting this option, James Robinson said, "Any attempt to have Pickens resign would be used by him as he wishes." Robinson preferred "standing by the membership of the Association which does not want compromise on fundamental issues." Judge Hastie "strongly opposed" a suggestion that the board announce that Pickens was being replaced because his duties with the Treasury Department left important branch work unattended. On Hastie's motion, the board voted, "That the status of Mr. Pickens as Director of Branches of the NAACP is hereby terminated on June 15, 1942, the date of expiration of his present leave of absence."[70] There were no regrets, no tributes, no statements praising his more than thirty years' service with the Association.

The following week White dispatched two letters to Pickens. In one he formally announced the board's decision; in the other he expressed "very keen regret that increasing differences of opinion between yourself and the Association had necessitated this step." "You and I have disagreed from time to time," he added, "but then, now and in the future I have been and always will be certain that these differences were of the head and not of the heart."[71] Pickens did not appeal the board's action and, in his initial response to White, he seemed resigned, almost relieved, that the break had come. "Thanks for the good will which breathes through your letter," he replied. "There is much work ahead for all of us now. Let us go forward and cooperate and try to do this biggest job in the history of our country: defending our own country and trying to uphold democracy and freedom everywhere in the world." However, when he read the board meeting minutes summarizing his alleged misbehavior, Pickens sent off another letter to White, rejecting as "billingsgate" the charges against him. "It is as bad a lot of false statements and slur and slander," he wrote, "as my eyes have ever lit upon."[72]

Pickens was convinced that his dismissal was the culmination of a carefully executed campaign by White. "Walter and I," he had written to John Haynes Holmes, "have worked in the NAACP together for twenty-two years and some weeks, and for twenty-two years of that time he has done all in his mortal power to destroy or hurt me in some way."[73]

Some observers outside the Association drew the same conclusion. "Once every decade or so," wrote the editor of the Norfolk *Journal and Guide,* "some one connected with the official family of the NAACP becomes disgusted with the leadership of the Association and throws in the towel. A few years ago the celebrated Dr. Du Bois . . . was fed up with Walter White, and that is what is wrong with Mr. Pickens, who White tried to toss out of the NAACP line-up a month or so ago."[74]

White had several reasons for wanting to remove Pickens from his executive position. Because of their differences in age, background, personalities, attitude toward organizational work, political philosophy, and party preference, the two men had never achieved harmony in their work. Pickens, outspoken and impulsive, had made many friends for the NAACP, but he also had antagonized a number of influential black leaders. White, who had greater public self-restraint, had alienated many of his co-workers, but had generally avoided controversy with individuals and groups outside the Association. After the attempt to oust White in 1931 had failed, he and Pickens had established an uneasy truce. But by 1940, because of the events at the NAACP annual meeting, the conflict over Pickens's participation in the Willkie campaign, and his advocacy of American intervention in the war, they had resumed hostilities. White also had become more firmly convinced that Pickens was a liability to the Associaton as a fund-raiser, administrator, and branch director. White wanted to modernize the organization and make it a more effective instrument for political action. Pickens, who admitted that he could not adjust readily to new methods, did not fit into White's plans.

One week after Pickens had joined the Treasury Department, on leave from the NAACP, White had written to him about his plans for renovating the Association's branch structure. Rejecting some ideas that Pickens had offered, he suggested instead that a "fresh and critical examination of every phase" of branch work was needed. "It may mean the throwing overboard of a lot of practices of the past," he added, "and the substitution of new ways of doing the job." "Critical years are ahead of us," he concluded. "Unless we can change our machinery to meet these changing conditions, the Association will decline in influence no matter how many court victories we win or how much is done by the national office."[75] White's implication was clear. The Association needed a branch director who was a skilled, energetic administrator, not a spell-binding, inspirational orator of the old school. Even if Pickens had not written those ill-fated letters to the New York *Amsterdam News* and the Richmond (Va.) *Times-Dispatch*, he, in White's view, would not have been entitled any longer to a place among the NAACP leadership.

Some observers felt that the NAACP was justified in dismissing

Pickens and that he, as reflected in his "traitor" statement, had lost touch, not only with the NAACP, but with the mood of the Negro masses. T. J. Sellers of the Baltimore *Afro-American*, who thought that Pickens had "given up the ghost" as a race leader, wrote, "I don't think he [Pickens] has the right to tell white folks that he knows the colored masses, because I don't think the Dean knows the mass mind of 1942."[76] Yet, although Pickens did not know the Negro's "mass mind," neither did Sellers or anyone else. Many black leaders, covering the whole political spectrum from conservatives to communists, supported Pickens's position on the segregation issue.[77] Therefore, in their disagreement on the segregation issue, Pickens and White had faced a classic Negro dilemma—when to compromise principle in exchange for real or potential racial gains. Both were lifelong integrationists but, in this instance, Pickens was willing to compromise because of what he considered the overriding importance of the war and his hope that blacks would be more readily integrated into a peacetime army. On this issue White held the line against segregation, but, over the years, he had made numerous compromises with racial injustice. While Pickens had consistently opposed President Roosevelt for failing to support an antilynching bill and for a generally unimpressive record on civil rights, White had urged blacks to vote for him. White, furthermore, also had compromised on the question of segregation in the armed forces. In 1941, for example, he worked with A. Philip Randolph in organizing a massive Negro march on Washington, whose twofold purpose was a demand for desegregation of the armed forces and an end to discrimination in industries holding government contracts. When Roosevelt issued an executive order purportedly banning discriminatory hiring practices in war-related industries, Randolph, with White's concurrence, called off the march. Since Roosevelt's order said nothing about military segregation, some blacks accused Randolph and White of selling out the race.[78] For White, a Fair Employment Practices Commission, established under Roosevelt's executive order, was a major victory. Both White and Pickens were willing to accept partial victories against racial injustice. They believed a mixture of protest and accommodation was required to break down the walls of discrimination and segregation.

9
THE LAST BATTLE, 1943–1954

> One group is trying to cut my throat for being too loyal, while the other wants to cut my throat for not being loyal enough. So where am I?
>
> —Pickens, 12 February 1943

After a long and often stormy career, first as an educator and later with the NAACP, William Pickens found at the Treasury Department a congenial atmosphere, appreciative supervisors, and work well-suited to his talents. His assignment was not only to persuade Negroes to buy savings bonds, but also "to sell them the United States of America."¹ This he did with great enthusiasm and considerable effectiveness. Following his dismissal as an NAACP officer, his years with the Treasury, except for one brief and painful encounter with the House Committee on Un-American Activities (HUAC), were free from controversy. "For the first time," he wrote shortly before retiring, "I am working with colleagues and under directors who do not want to get rid of me."² In his last years, Pickens, in part because of his work with the Treasury Department, lost some of his aggressiveness as a black activist and, in some ways, adopted an attitude on the race question not unlike that of the late Booker T. Washington.

The Treasury Department was pleased when Pickens joined its staff, but Representative Martin Dies (D-Tex.), chairman of the HUAC, was convinced that he was a Communist. When Pickens first joined the Treasury Department in 1941, Dies, an indefatigable crusader against Communist subversion, had challenged his fitness, citing the radical and Communist-front organizations with which Pickens, from 1927 onward, had been associated. The FBI and the Secret Service, however, investigated Pickens's record and found no cause to consider him a subversive. "The FBI looked me up from the cradle up"; Pickens wrote to John Haynes Holmes, "they inquired of my acquaintances everywhere and got the most marvellous and enthusiastic reports."³

Martin Dies's record for unearthing disloyal government employees was poor. In 1942 he had submitted to Attorney General Francis Biddle a list of more than one thousand alleged subversives. Biddle, after an investigation, stated that in nearly all cases the charges were "unfounded and . . . should never have been submitted for investigation in the first instance." Membership in so-called front organizations, Biddle argued, comprised the bulk of Dies's evidence and was "thoroughly unsatisfactory" as an objective test for disloyalty.[4] Undaunted, Dies, on 1 February 1943, read to the House another list of alleged subversives. Pickens's name was among thirty-nine "irresponsible, unrepresentative, crackpot, radical bureaucrats," who, Dies insisted, should be purged from government payrolls. Among others on his list were Gardner Jackson, an economist with the Department of Agriculture; Robert Morss Lovett, government secretary of the Virgin Islands; David Saposs, an economist with the War Production Board; and Mary McLeod Bethune of the National Youth Administration. Bethune, the only other Negro listed by Dies, was an influential member of the "Black Cabinet" and one of the best-known and most highly respected black women in the nation. Dies's evidence against her was typical. She had been "publicly and prominently affiliated" with four organizations that the attorney general had branded as subversive—the American League for Peace and Democracy, the American Youth Congress, the National Negro Congress, and the Washington Committee for Democratic Action. Dies's "case" against Pickens was based on his writings for the *Daily Worker and New Masses;* his association with known Communists, such as Earl Browder and Elizabeth Gurley Flynn; and his vice-chairmanship of the American League Against War and Fascism, his support for the Greater New York Emergency Conference on Inalienable Rights, and his speech before the United Congress Against War, all of which the Justice Department had ruled to be subversive.[5]

Although some of the thirty-nine accused were in fact Communists, most were liberals or Socialists who had joined these organizations because they opposed war, colonialism, economic exploitation, or racial discrimination. Many of them, including Pickens and Bethune, had left organizations that became Communist fronts before they were placed on the attorney general's list.[6]

Dies persisted in labeling these people subversive for three reasons: he was convinced that many of them were part of a "united front of communists, crackpots and socialists" threatening to undermine the nation's security; he wanted to embarrass the Roosevelt administration, which, in his view, was leading the country toward "bureaucratic and centralized government and away from the original concept of our fathers"; and, finally, with a vote imminent on extending the life of his committee, he wanted to convince the House of its value in ferreting out subversives. "I could stand here for day in and day out," Dies told the House, "and read you the records of men who have no place in our Government, who have gone on record against the kind of thing that the people in your district and my district believe in with all their hearts and with all their minds."[7] Since the executive branch refused to weed out the disloyal elements, he concluded, Congress had to remedy the situation. Congress should say to the administration, "If you do not get rid of these people, we will refuse to appropriate money for their salaries."[8]

Four days later Joe Hendricks (D-Fla.), acting on Dies's suggestion, added to a major Treasury Department appropriation bill an amendment that would prohibit the use of any funds allocated to pay the salaries of any of the accused government employees. Since the administration had shifted employees who came under fire from one department to another, Hendricks promised, if the amendment was adopted, to offer it on every appropriation bill that comes before the House. "Then," he added, "there will be no place for these men to hedge hop." He first focused attention on Pickens, who was the only Treasury Department employee on Dies's list. He quoted from a speech at a meeting of the United States Congress Against War in 1933 at which Pickens said, "To take the profit motive out of war, we must take the class-profit opportunities out of our economic system."[9] "Does that," Hendricks asked, "sound like the capitalistic system or communism?" Pickens's alleged affiliation with several Communist-front organizations was sufficient proof for Hendricks that he was unfit for government service. "If Pickens is worth $4600 [actually $5600] to the Government," he concluded, "he is intelligent enough to know when he is in the wrong sort of company."[10]

Several congressmen were appalled by Hendricks's attempt to condemn Pickens and the other accused government employees on such evidence and without giving them an opportunity to answer the charges. "I do not want to be a party to the crucifying of persons," said Geroge Bender (R-Ohio), "without giving them a proper hearing. I do not like that sort of thing; it is not American and it is not tolerant." Bender pointed out that Pickens, whom he identified as "secretary" of the NAACP, had been given "a clean bill of health" by the Secret Service and the FBI. "How about Mary Bethune," he asked, "whose name also appears on the purge list? She is a prominent colored lady who has done a great deal for her people. I do not want to vote for an amendment which includes her name as an undesirable citizen."[11]

Louis Ludlow (R-Ind.) agreed with Bender. Pickens "should not be thrown off the rolls in this off-handed way," he argued, "when we are the judge, jury and the executioner." He read into the record a letter from Harold N. Graves, director of the Treasury's Savings Division, in which he attested to Pickens's effectiveness and his loyalty. Graves wrote:

> Mr. Pickens has performed [his] duties to the entire satisfaction of this Department. He has been diligent and successful in his work, and he and his small group have done much to bring about an understanding of the war-savings program on the part of the colored people and a steadily increasing participation by them in that program. In the period of his employment by this Department, nothing has transpired which would suggest that he is anything but a patriotic American, completely loyal to the traditions of the country and to its established form of government. . . . The Department has long been aware of the charges made by the Dies Committee regarding, Mr. Pickens. It will be appropriate to say that we are convinced that they are without any substantial foundation.

When the House seemed to be reluctant to pass hasty judgment on thirty-nine individuals, Hendricks dropped all but Pickens's name from his amendment to the Treasury Department appropriations bill. Since none of the other alleged subversives were Treasury employees, they would not in any case have been affected directly by the amendment. As Ludlow put it, "It all simmers down to one question: and that is whether one individual named William Pickens should be dispossessed of his job in the Treasury Department."[12] Despite appeals from several other members that Pickens was being denied due process, the House voted 163 to 111 to cut off funds for his salary.[13]

Pickens's colleagues in the Treasury Department, especially his immediate supervisor James Houghteling, spent the weekend calling on friends in the House to reopen the case. Houghteling, the son-in-law of Frederick Delano, the president's uncle, and former editor of the Chicago *Daily News,* knew several House members personally and was a lifelong friend of Representative Charles S. Dewey (R-Ill.).[14] Two other factors worked in Pickens's favor. First, many congressmen felt that he had been victimized by an unconstitutional device—a bill of attainder. Second, since the only one of the thirty-nine alleged subversives the House had acted against was a Negro, leaders of both parties feared that blacks would misconstrue the vote as racially motivated. This, they felt, would undermine Negroes' morale and diminish their support for the war effort. When the House reconvened, Harold Knutson (R-Minn.) made his point. If the House condemned a Negro, Knutson argued, and "white-washed" similar activities by thirty-seven whites, "that is almost lynch law. It is what is termed shotgun justice out in my country."[15]

Hendricks replied that Pickens "had been singled out because he was the only one that was actually and directly affected by the bill." Race was not a factor, Hendricks asserted, since he had not known that Pickens was a Negro. As proof, he claimed that he had several times referred to Pickens as "mister." "Any man coming from the South," he added, "knows that a Southerner does not refer to a colored man as 'mister!' "[16] In fact, although he had mentioned Pickens's name a dozen times, Hendricks had never referred to him as "mister." Most House members had never heard of Pickens, but, during the debate, at least two—Bender and Ludlow—had referred to his race. Furthermore, it is surprising that a southern politician had never heard of the NAACP field secretary, who had toured the South, including Florida, for more than twenty years. With forces in both parties anxious for a reversal of the vote, Hendricks, it seems, was trying to prevent that move by demonstrating that race had not been a factor in the action against Pickens.

Martin Dies also denied that Pickens had been singled out because of his race. After paying "sincere tribute to the millions of loyal, patriotic colored people," he elaborated on his previous testimony against Pickens, citing twenty-one organizations on the attorney general's list with which Pickens had been affiliated. "I have the record here," he stated, "not a record based upon what anybody said of him, but a record which he himself made, a record no one can dispute." "It would be hard to find a man anywhere in the United States," Dies concluded, "whose extensive affiliations with Communist-front organizations were of a more serious nature than those of William Pickens." The organizations Dies added to his original list included the League Against Colonial Oppression, the International Labor Defense, the League Against Imperialism, the Prisoner's Relief Fund, and the Medical Bureau and North American Committee to Aid Spanish Democracy.[17]

The one Negro member of the House, William L. Dawson (D-Ill.), had not yet spoken. Dawson, who had been elected only the previous fall and had never addressed the House, chose an appropriate time to deliver his maiden speech. Dawson, who had known Pickens for forty years, was convinced that he was not a Communist nor had "knowingly" affiliated himself with a Communist organization. As the only black man in the chamber, Dawson felt that he could best explain to the members why Pickens, whose voice always had "been heard in defense of the high ideals of this country," would associate with organizations that subsequently proved to be subversive. Dawson said:

> I wish I could command words well enough to convey to you something of the psychology of an underprivileged people, something of the psychology of a people who are told they have every right in fact, but who know they do not have those rights in actuality. I wish you could envision in your minds how we struggle wherever we can to make the Constitution and our democracy a living reality. I know something about communism; I know how the Communists have tried to infiltrate among our people, playing upon the ills we have suffered; . . . and I know how often they did not come to us under the name of Communists, but came with loud-sounding names, talking of freedom, talking of democracy, and talking of inalienable rights, things that are dear to the heart of every American, be he white or black. . . . You refer back to 1927; that is a long time ago. Many names might be found on the rolls of some organization that has since been deemed a subversive organization.

Dawson pointed to the effective work Pickens had done as a War Bonds salesman and, without specific reference to the NAACP, to the personal sacrifice he had made in putting the war effort before everything else. "We know," he said,

> that William Pickens has been the means of going up and down the length and breadth of this country teaching Americanism. . . . He was for the preservation of America above all domestic problems, and for that reason he was deserted by many of those who at one time had been associated with him. . . . William Pickens is a true American, and I state that with all the integrity of a man who would fight and die for America today.[18]

Dawson's speech had no effect on John E. Rankin (D-Miss.), who in 1945 would succeed Dies as chairman of the HUAC. "I am convinced," Rankin asserted, "that this Negro, William Pickens, . . . is a Communist. I voted to strike him off when I thought he was a white man, and I shall certainly not vote to put him back because he is a Negro."[19] Dies, aware that he and his committee had many critics in the House, feared that they would use the race issue to win a reversal of the vote on Pickens, which, in effect, would reflect the House's lack of confidence in his committee's usefulness. Pickens, he argued, was "immaterial in so far as the real issue is concerned." The basic question, he insisted, was whether individuals were free to undermine constitutional government and national security. "We are asked to send our boys to the trenches," Dies said, "and fight in defense of our constitutional form of government. Yet in the government itself are men who over a long period of time have been identified with movements and organizations that are opposed to our form of government and are seeking to destroy it."[20]

At this point the leaders of both parties intervened. Majority Leader John McCormack (D-Mass.), who had not yet participated in the debate, reminded the House that the Constitution provided for a resolution of the conflict between national security and individual freedom. He considered Hendricks's amendment "unwise," because "one of the basic considerations of our democratic form of government is to give a man an opportunity to be heard when he is accused." McCormack suggested that Pickens's case, as well as those of the others on Dies's list, should be presented to a special subcommittee, which, after thorough investigation, would make recommendations for further action by the House.[21]

The next day, 9 February, Adolph J. Sabath (D-Ill.), "Dean" of the House, introduced such a measure.[22] According to Sabath's resolution, a special subcommittee of the Committee on Appropriations would examine and take testimony on the charges against government employees accused of being unfit for service "by reason of their present association or membership, or past association or membership in or with organizations whose aims, or purposes are or have been subversive to the Government of the United States." Although the resolution would take some power away from the Dies committee, making it more of an investigatory body and less a judicial one, Sabath's measure still could penalize individuals, including Pickens, who had "past association" with organizations later branded as subversive. Nevertheless, many representatives thought the resolution a considerable improvement over Hendricks's "lynch law."

Minority leader Joseph Martin (R-Mass.) indicated that the measure had bipartisan support. He reminded his colleagues, however, that, since they had voted to cut off Pickens's salary, the

Sabath resolution would not apply to him. Martin then returned to the race question. "Certainly it would be unfortunate for the war effort," he argued, "and for our own home economy, if we proceeded in a way to make any large part of our population believe we were discriminating against a man because of his race or color." He suggested that the House rescind Hendricks's amendment so that Pickens's case also could be heard by the special subcommittee.[23]

Southern Democrats Alfred L. Bulwinkle of North Carolina, and William M. Colmer of Mississippi, accused Martin and the Republicans of "playing politics" and switching sides in order to win Negro votes in the next presidential election.[24] Colmer asserted that the nation, as indicated by the 1942 congressional elections, had hoped that a Republican-conservative Democratic coalition would rid the government of "subversive influences." "But," Colmer asked, "what do we find? We find politics as usual. . . . Somebody is playing to the Negro vote." He quoted another member as saying: "We voted the man Pickens off the pay roll on the theory that he was a 'red.' Then we found out that he was black and proceeded to place him back on the pay roll. Evidently that makes us yellow."[25]

Jack Nichols (D-Okla.), like a number of his colleagues had little patience with due-process procedures.

> Pickens stands convicted of enough to warrant me in saying that he has no business on the Government pay roll. . . . Talk to me about a man having a day in court when he has a record from 1933 to 1940 that no one has disputed. Tell me that he should be granted justice. He stands convicted today. . . . If he is a Government employee, that you and I have reason even to suspect his loyalty to his Government, he should be kicked off the pay roll first and tried later.[26]

The debate on Pickens, which had taken the better part of four days, centered on two questions: the constitutionality of the House's action against him; and the effect that action might have on the Negro community. Of the two issues, the House was concerned more about the political implications of the racial question. Party leaders McCormack and Martin had intervened only after they learned that Pickens was black. With their support, the House, by a voice vote, passed Sabath's resolution establishing a subcommittee to deal with charges of disloyalty against government employees. Then, reversing its decision on Hendricks's amendment, the House voted 267 to 136 to send

Pickens's case along with the others to the newly created subcommittee.[27]

During the House debate, Pickens, under advice from his superiors at the Treasury Department, had made no public statement. At first he was "unapprehensive of the seriousness of the situation,"[28] He was puzzled that Dies should accuse him of being a Communist inasmuch as he had been cleared by the FBI, repeatedly branded by the Communists as a lackey of the capitalists, and had broken with the NAACP in order to serve the war effort. Immediately after the House vote rescinding the Hendricks amendment, Pickens was quoted as saying: "One group is trying to cut my throat for being too loyal, while the other wants to cut my throat for not being loyal enough. So where am I?"[29] However, once he recognized the seriousness of his predicament, Pickens, anticipating a call by the special Appropriations Subcommittee, headed by John H. Kerr (D-N.C.), prepared a defense of his past record. He dealt point by point with each of the charges in Dies's indictment, but omitted any reference to his personal correspondence with self-proclaimed Communists such as Robert Minor and Lovett Fort-Whiteman. He denied any personal contact with Earl Browder or Elizabeth Gurley Flynn other than sharing public platforms with them, and pointed out that in 1940, as a member of the National Committee of the American Civil Liberties Union, he had voted with the majority to expel Flynn from the organization.[30] He explained that he had terminated membership in any organization, such as the International Labor Defense and the League Against War and Fascism, when it proved to be a Communist front. In every instance his "principal interest was to convey the program of the Association to whomever would receive it." He had supported the Spanish Loyalist cause, not because it was "a Communist enterprise," but because "it was a fight of democracy against a Fascist regime." As a contributing editor of the Associated Negro Press (ANP) since 1919 he had had access to scores of Negro newspapers that published his material. "I submit," he concluded, "that any examination of this material will fail to disclose any advocacy of Communism."[31]

But Pickens never read his statement to Kerr's committee, for he was never called to testify before it. Without explanation, the charges against him were dropped, and he was permitted, without further disturbance, to continue his work at the Treasury Department. Had he been called by Kerr's committee, he might have suffered the same fate as Robert Morss Lovett, another government employee on Dies's list of subversives. Lovett had never been a Communist but, like Pickens, had been associated with many liberal, radical, and Communist-front organizations. Kerr's committee recommended his dismissal as government secretary of the Virgin Islands, and Interior Secretary Ickes, with great reluctance, asked for his resignation. The Supreme Court subsequently ruled that Congress had acted unconstitutionally against Lovett, but by then he had left the government.[32] If, as it seems, Pickens had been spared because he was a Negro, it was one of the few times in his life that his race had worked to his advantage. He was more fortunate than Lovett because he appeared as a potential victim, not only of the "red-baiting" Dies Committee, but of racial prejudice. At a time when the country was at war with Nazi Germany, which practiced the most virulent form of racism, his dismissal might have been a national embarrassment.

During his brief encounter with the Dies Committee many prominent figures, both black and white, came to Pickens's defense. The *New Republic,* the *Nation,* and the *New York Times,* published editorials in his behalf. "This attempt to crucify William Pickens," wrote Richmond (Va.) *Times-Dispatch* editor Virginius Dabney,

> is nothing surprising, in view of the Dies Committee's spotty record in the past. . . . For every genuine "Red" it has dug up, it has smeared another innocent person. . . . Dr. Pickens, the sort of level-headed and conservative Negro leader whom Dies and the whole House ought to admire, is the latest victim of the Texas congressman's blundering, blunderbuss technique.[33]

Harold Ickes condemned Dies's attempt to "crush the tiniest spark of liberalism or tolerance that may flicker before his bloodshot eyes."[34]

Besides Representative Dawson, Pickens received strong support from a number of blacks, including those in the leadership of the NAACP. His one-time adversary, R. R. Wright, Jr., a bishop of the African Methodist Episcopal Church, offered to testify at his own expense before Kerr's committee. Pickens had "more than once seriously disagreed" with him in the press and on public platforms, especially over religious fundamentalism, but Wright had never questioned his "Americanism." He pointed out that Pickens, who "had perhaps appeared before more audiences than any other man of his race," had been criticized often, but

Wright had never heard anyone accuse him of being a Communist. "The Negroes with whom I have talked," Wright concluded, "of all denominations, all political parties, all lines of business, labor, and professions, are agreed that the charge against Dr. Pickens is false. . . . There is practical unanimity in the fear that for some reason Dr. Pickens is being persecuted."[35]

The NAACP board declared the attack on Pickens to be typical of the "character assassination, professional lynching and intimidation of public officials" by the "warped minds" and "Gestapo" tactics of the Dies "clique." The "outrageous action" was a "direct assault" against American liberalism and all indiviuals who believed in minority rights. The Association pledged to oppose the reelection of every congressman who supported Hendricks's amendment and who would vote to extend the life of the Dies committee and its "evil work."[36] Nevertheless, the day after it passed Sabath's resolution and rescinded Hendricks's amendment, the House extended the life of the Dies committee for the duration of the Seventy-Eighth Congress by an overwhelming vote of 302 to 94.[37] The House, in Pickens's case, had responded from political expediency rather than concern for constitutional rights.

During his ordeal, Pickens was most gratified by the support he received from his colleagues in the Treasury Department. After a lifetime of conflict with superiors, first at Talladega, then at Morgan, and finally in the NAACP, he was deeply moved by the way the people at the Treasury rallied behind him. Harold Graves, in his letter to Representative Ludlow, had praised Pickens's work and defended his loyalty. Immediately following Dies's attack, Assistant Treasury Secretary Charles W. Adams had called Pickens into his office and told him: "I believe you. You're no damned Communist." "Those words," Pickens later wrote to Adams, "came from you so spontaneously and sincerely, that I can never forget them. Dozens of times I have repeated them inside me."[38] "When the enemy struck at us from Capitol Hill," Pickens wrote to his immediate supervisor, Houghteling, "never shall I lose the picture of you from my memory's eye, sitting at the telephone for several days, calling up, telling the truth, fighting." "Those were strenuous and treacherous hours for us," Pickens added, "and you were the captain of the ship that brought us through."[39] Although black men had defended Pickens, white men—Graves, Adams, Houghteling, and House leaders McCormack and Martin—had saved him.

The charges against him having been dropped, Pickens resumed his duties in the Treasury Department's Interracial Section. He had begun in 1941 with one secretary and one staff consultant, but by 1945 the section had been expanded to include ten staff members, fifteen dollar-a-year consultants, and "thousands of patriotic volunteer workers in every state of the Union."[40] He and Nell Hunter, former staff member of the National Youth Administration, handled most of the field work. Hunter dealt with black women's groups and Pickens concentrated on other Negro organizations, such as church conventions, fraternal orders, civil rights groups, business and professional groups, farmers' organizations, and workers in defense plants.[41] In 1943, for example, he spoke at 216 meetings before a total of approximately 200,000 black people and sold an estimated six million dollars worth of war bonds.[42] Although the Treasury Department did not keep separate records for bonds purchased by various ethnic and racial groups, the Interracial Section estimated that, by the end of the war, blacks had invested more than one billion dollars in war bonds.[43] "In proportion to his wealth and opportunities," Pickens wrote, "[the Negro] did very well indeed."[44]

Pickens believed that his section not only had helped finance the war effort, but had "done much to build and sustain the morale and to open the eyes of the colored population toward the community of interest which they hold with all Americans." "Perhaps," he added," this latter phase of the work is its most important phase."[45] To accomplish this, Pickens, in his speeches, expressed for him an uncharacteristically moderate view on the race problem, emphasizing the improvement in the Negro's status as well as the potential for future gains.

> We repeat what we have said a thousand times: This is no perfect country. This is just the best country and we are luckily in it. It is ours,—we want to keep it. If we lose it now, we could not improve it. If we defend it now, we have all the time that is ahead of us to work for its improvement.[46]

Some Negroes were not particularly upset by reports that the Axis powers, especially the nonwhite Japanese, were killing white American soldiers.[47] In his speeches, Pickens often dealt with this attitude. He would say, "If the United States should lose this war, our white people would catch hell." When his black audience "got through laughing and chuckling," he would add, "And if the United States should lose this war, our black people would catch two hells—hell from without and hell from within."[48]

After the war Pickens remained with the Treasury Department and, despite a drastic reduction in his staff, continued to be an effective bonds salesman.[49] In peacetime, however, he offered Negroes somewhat different reasons for purchasing savings bonds. He stressed the need to fight postwar inflation, to continue "thrift habits" developed during the war, and, especially, to identify more closely with the national government which, in the past, blacks had found to be "remote, ambiguous and complex." "When you own U.S. Savings Bonds," he told black audiences, "you have the very real, the very tangible feeling of oneness, of belonging to something vast and important."[50] This was more than a sales "pitch." Pickens hoped that, when the promissory notes matured, the nation would repay blacks not only the monetary debt, but also redeem a moral debt, long deferred, by accepting them as equal members of society.

Pickens's success as director of the Interracial Division, especially his harmonious relations with Treasury Department colleagues, was something of a novel experience for him. After a lifetime of conflict and controversy, culminating in his sixtieth year with dismissal from his NAACP post and the traumatic episode with the Dies committee, he was deeply affected by the support, respect, and praise he received at the Treasury. For example, Houghteling, his former supervisor, had written to him:

> I am convinced that no one else could have accomplished the tremendously beneficial results which you have obtained in bringing the patriotic and constructive message of the U.S. Savings Bonds Program to the entire colored population of this country. You have shown superb patience and Christian fortitude in facing and overcoming many obstacles.[51]

When he retired from the Treasury Department in December 1950, on the eve of his seventieth birthday, Pickens, at a testimonial dinner in his honor, received a book containing letters of appreciation from his former supervisors, including ex-secretaries of the treasury Fred M. Vinson and Henry Morgenthau, Jr., and the incumbent secretary, John W. Snyder. He also was warmly praised by his immediate supervisor, Vernon L. Clark, who, in 1946, had replaced Houghteling as the Bonds Division's director. Clark was "deeply impressed" with Pickens's "devotion to duty and loyalty to the Savings Bonds Program," as well as his "outstanding record and reputation" with State Bonds directors and volunteer workers throughout the country.[52]

Pickens was very proud of his record with the Treasury Department. "We prize the fact," he wrote, "that we have learned how to work harmoniously with our Division's State leaders of all sections of the United States. That required tact, patience and some knowledge of our country and its people." "You will be interested to hear," he wrote to W. E. B. Du Bois shortly before retiring, "that nobody here wants me to leave, from the Secretary down to the associates in my immediate office and in the neighboring offices."[53]

One reason for Pickens's newly found tact and patience at the Treasury was that, in contrast with the NAACP home office, where he often felt unappreciated and unduly restricted in his work, he found colleagues who admired his work and had not interfered with it. Furthermore, during his years in the Interracial Division, because he was a civil service employee, Pickens had abandoned his political activity as well as his weekly contributions to the ANP, both of which had caused conflicts between himself and NAACP leaders. At the Treasury Pickens was also free of the personal animosities that existed in the NAACP. These intense rivalries were prevalent not only in the NAACP, but in most Negro organizations because, as Pickens noted, "the [less] numerous the opportunities facing a group, the [more] reason there is for rivalry, jealousy, envy, and even practical enmity among the members of that group."[54] Finally, as a bonds salesman stressing the positive side of race relations, he even won the approval of black conservatives who previously had considered him something of a rabble-rousing radical. For example, during the 1920s and 1930s, Pickens had clashed with Baptist clergymen on religious and political questions. But during the war, as a bonds salesman, he was a welcomed speaker at their annual conventions.

In the twilight of a career in which he had distinguished himself principally as a militant spokesman for Negro rights, Pickens, in his ten years at the Treasury, had become more accommodating in his attitude toward the race question. His more moderate position resulted, in part, from his overriding concern for winning the war and, in part, from the nature of the work itself. Had he returned to the NAACP after the war he might have resumed his more outspoken criticism of American treatment of blacks. But as chief bonds salesman to Negroes he continued to preach thrift, patience, and patriotism, stressing the progress blacks had made over the years rather than the distance still to be covered before full equality was achieved. In this and in other respects he had moved back toward the views of the late Booker T. Washington, with whom he had severed ties in 1910. For example, like Washington, he came to believe that the Negro had a future in the South, although in the 1920s and 1930s he had thought that the South was "the limbo of Hell."[55] During the war his attitude had begun to change, in part because southern whites no longer threatened to kill him, since he was selling bonds and patriotism instead of organizing NAACP branches and investigating lynchings. Furthermore, he had also learned, after twenty years in the North, that blacks also faced hostility, discrimination and, sometimes, death outside the South. His more benign attitude toward the South was also a product of the respect and friendship he received from southern white colleagues in the Treasury Department. "I found better friends," he wrote, "many of them Southerners of the deep South, in the Treasury, than I found in any other group of fellow-workers."[56] Therefore, by 1944, he believed, as had Washington, that, "Treated with patience and respectful forbearance by the outside world, the whites and colored people of the South will ultimately solve all their inter-racial problems in a way to keep them solved." "Outsiders can help if they are tactful," he added, "but they can only hurt if they be rash and do not consider, before they dip in, . . . that each section has something which is peculiar to it."[57]

Back in 1910 Pickens had joined with Du Bois and others in criticizing Washington for suggesting that American Negroes lived better than the downtrodden classes of other countries. Yet in 1951 Pickens agreed "without reservation" with George Schuyler who had written that the "most exploited" Negro in Mississippi was "better off" than "the citizen of Russia or her satellites" or the "impoverished" peasants of Latin America. "Stick by your guns; you are correct," Pickens wrote to Schuyler. "This country is not what many of us . . . want it to be, but, by the Eternal, it is the only great country . . . we have."[58]

As Washington revered President Theodore Roosevelt, so too did Pickens come to respect his distant cousin Franklin. He had strongly opposed Roosevelt when the latter was a peacetime president, but during the war he supported him as commander in chief of the armed forces. When Roosevelt was elected for a fourth term in 1944, Pickens wrote to him, "I congratulate the American people and I thank the commander-in-chief for his extraordinary leadership." To Houghteling he wrote, "When the near-future has done with the evidence, only the immortal Lincoln and George Washington will be in a class with this second Roosevelt."[59] Pickens's newly found admiration for Roosevelt was related directly to American military successes against the Axis powers. But he also may have been affected by the fact that, in October 1944, his daughter, Harriet Ida Pickens, was the first Negro woman to receive an officer's commission in the recently desegregated Navy Women's Auxiliary (WAVES).[60]

By 1950 Pickens was less critical of American society than at any time since his college days. This was due, in part, to his advanced age, the impact of World War II, and his feeling of acceptance at the Treasury Department. But he also sincerely believed, after forty years of active participation in the civil rights struggle, that the Negro's status, relative to that of 1915, was measurably improved. He had witnessed, since Washington's death in 1915, a massive migration of blacks from the South to all parts of the nation, and he had participated in the development of a vigorous, broadly based Negro protest movement. If nothing else had been achieved since 1915, the Negro had made himself more visible to whites and more of a national than a regional problem, one that the dominant white society no longer could ignore.

Although, in his last years, he no longer had a place in the civil rights movement, Pickens wanted to remain active after his retirement from the Treasury Department. But there were few opportunities for a man of his age and experience. "Since I left Yale University in 1904," he had written to Houghteling in 1945, "there has never been a minute of my life when I was not engaged in some honorable and useful work: The colleges, the NAACP, and the Government." He would have liked an ambassadorship and had suggested to Houghteling, who had close ties with the Roosevelt family, that, after the war, he could "represent the United States wherever it needs a Negro representative: in Liberia, Haiti, Central or South America." But Pickens dropped the idea when, in 1946, Houghteling left the Treasury.[61]

After retiring, Pickens planned to add "a half a dozen or so" chapters to his autobiography, *Bursting Bonds*, which he had written in 1923 and that had ended with his appointment as NAACP field secretary. However, when he had difficulty in finding a publisher, he abandoned the project.[62] Nevertheless, he was too vigorous a man to remain totally inactive and, in his last years, he worked part-time as consultant to the Treasury Department, and did a good deal of traveling as well as some writing and lecturing.

Pickens was still remembered as a public speaker, and, in 1951, he was invited to participate in Morgan State College's (now Morgan State University) Founder Day's program. That year he also represented another of his former schools, Talladega College, at Stevens Institute's (New Jersey) installation of a new president. In 1953 at the Cooper Union Forum in New York he chaired a panel discussion commemorating the ninety-third anniversary of Abraham Lincoln's famous address there.[63]

Pickens, who loved to travel, spent his last summers vacationing with his wife in Europe and Latin America. In 1952 they went on a Mediterranean cruise that Pickens described in serial form for the *Amsterdam-Star News*. The following summer they toured Egypt and Israel. In 1954 they visited South America and the Caribbean islands, but, on their way home on the S.S. *Mauretania*, just off Kingston, Jamaica, Pickens suffered a heart attack and died. On 6 April 1954 the seventy-three-year-old race leader was buried at sea.[64] In reporting his death the Pittsburgh *Courier* wrote, "While he has been active since retiring from the Treasury Department, his intelligent and faithful labor for the full emancipation of the Negro will never be forgotten."[65]

Pickens will be best remembered for his work with the NAACP. Although some within the Association's hierarchy, especially White, thought that he hindered the organization more than he helped it, many other black leaders agreed with A. Philip Randolph that Pickens was "quite a productive and creative force in the NAACP."[66] Although Pickens's contributions to the Association were less spectacular than Du Bois's, Johnson's, or White's, they were no less important. Between 1920 and 1940 he recruited more members, organized more branches, and helped to keep them functioning, and publicized the Association's activities more than any other NAACP officer. He also played a major role in broadening the Association's activities to include political activism and international affairs. The Association never succeeded in appealing to large numbers of the black masses, but Pickens was more successful in appealing to those masses than any other NAACP official. In 1940 George Schuyler wrote of him, "He has always been able to effectively reach the masses in a far more successful manner than many of his contemporaries." Schuyler thought that Pickens was popular with the masses because he was "a man of the people" rather than a "self-conscious scholar."[67]

Although White, in his eulogy, called him "a brilliant scholar," Pickens, by becoming a race man, had given up the possibility of developing along those lines. Pickens's writing, like his public speaking, had wit, irony, drama, and passion. But, since he neither had the time nor the training to develop his interests in history, economics, and literature, his literary style, although effective, was unpolished, and his ideas, although clearly expressed, were, for the most part, derivative. As Pickens himself wrote, "No part of America offers a fair field for the fullest development of the genius of a black man."[68]

By becoming a race man, who, as one observer wrote, "feared no man and risked death more than once in behalf of justice and opportunity for Negroes,"[69] Pickens expressed his creativity through his oratory. A. Philip Randolph, himself an accomplished public speaker, called him an "exceptionally brilliant orator." White thought him to be "one of the most skillful orators America has produced"; his old friend and colleague John Haynes Holmes compared him "in his eloquence" with Frederick Douglass and Booker T. Washington. The Negro historian William Brewer even suggested that Pickens "equalled or surpassed Frederick Douglass as the most powerful Negro spokesman that has appeared in America."[70] Although Pickens was not the most "powerful," he was the most popular Negro orator during the years between Washington's death and the emergence in the 1950s of Martin Luther King, Jr. He addressed thousands of whites and probably more black audiences than any of his contemporaries. Through his gift for rhetoric, a gift that had brought him from the swamplands of Arkansas to Talladega College and, later to Yale, the NAACP, and the nation's Capitol, Pickens tried to persuade blacks to demand their rights and to persuade whites to accept blacks as equals.

Pickens consciously borrowed his major theme—the interrelated destiny of the two races—from Washington. He often quoted Washington's line, "One man cannot hold another down in the ditch without staying down in the ditch with him."[71] This idea was central to Pickens's philosophy and he expressed it often and with great eloquence. "We may write all the creeds we please," he wrote in 1926, "but ultimately the issue of the black man's struggle for salvation in our midst will either nourish or dry up the roots of our faith in the Brotherhood of Man. This is our test, and by the test . . . we must succeed or fail."[72] He believed that the race problem presented the greatest challenge to

American democracy, but he was convinced, especially in his last years, that the nation ultimately would pass the test.

A school boy of fifteen when the Supreme Court, in *Plessy v. Ferguson* (1896), announced the separate-but-equal doctrine, Pickens died one month before the Court, in *Brown v. Topeka Board of Education* (1954), overturned that decision. However, he anticipated the reversal of the doctrine as early as 1938, when the Court, in *Missouri ex. rel. Gaines v. Canada*, first clearly challenged segregation in education. In Pickens's view, the Court had indicated that "in America equality has priority over . . . separation." "We have not attained democracy" by this decision, he wrote, "but for 150 years we have been pursuing it. We solved the problem of slavery and we will solve the problems of freedom."[73]

Notes

Chapter 1. Up from Washington, 1881–1914

1. William Pickens, *The Heir of Slaves: An Autobiography* (Boston: Pilgrim Press, 1911), 125–26. Most of the material on Pickens's early life was taken from this work. Pickens to Booker T. Washington, 13 April 1903, Box 271, Booker T. Washington Papers (Manuscript Division, Library of Congress); hereafter cited as Washington Papers.

2. Pickens, "Hayti," *Yale Literary Magazine* 68 (April 1903): 236–37. His essay also appeared in *Voice of the Negro*, a black monthly journal, along with three other articles on Haiti by black writers. All were critical of black Haitian leadership, but only Pickens advocated American intervention. For example, the first black minister to Haiti (appointed in 1869), Ebenezer D. C. Bassett, wrote: "Should Haiti . . . be annexed to the United States? . . . Why, no, no! Let Haiti alone; let her alone to work out her mission for the children of Africa in the New World and to fulfill her destiny among the Nations of the Earth." "Should Haiti Be Annexed to the United States?" *Voice of the Negro* 1 (May 1904): 198.

3. William Monroe Trotter's uncompromising attitude on the race question was reflected in the *Guardian*'s motto: For Every Right With All Thy Might. For a biography of Trotter, see Stephen R. Fox, *The Guardian of Boston: William Monroe Trotter* (New York: Atheneum, 1970).

4. *Guardian* (Boston), 9 May 1903.

5. Ibid., 11 April 1903.

6. Ibid., 9 May 1903.

7. Ibid., 23 May 1903. Trotter was capable of "personal, vituperative, and occasionally vicious" attacks against those with whom he disagreed. See Fox, *Guardian of Boston*, 39–41, passim.

8. The best account of the "Boston Riot" is Fox, *Guardian of Boston*, 51–57. The charges against Maud Trotter were dropped. See also *New York Times*, 31 July, 1903; *Afro-American Ledger* (Baltimore), 31 July 1903; Elliott Rudwick, *W. E. B. Du Bois: Propagandist of the Negro Protest* (1960; reprint ed., New York: Atheneum, 1969), 72–74, Louis R. Harlan, *Booker T. Washington: The Wizard of Tuskegee, 1901–1915* (New York: Oxford University Press, 1983), 54–56.

9. Although George Washington Forbes was with Trotter in the church, he was not arrested. For additional material on Forbes, see Fox, *Guardian of Boston*, 51, 56, passim.

10. Wilford H. Smith to Washington, 31 July 1903, Box 277, Washington Papers.

11. Smith to John D. Converse, 2 September 1903, Box 277; Smith to Emmett J. Scott, 6 September 1903, Box 266; Converse to Smith, 11 September 1903, Box 277; Smith to Washington, 12 September 1903, Box 277, Washington Papers.

12. Rudwick, *W. E. B. Du Bois*, 76f. 66; Fox, *Guardian of Boston*, 69.
13. Washington to Smith, 4 November 1903, Box 277; Washington to R. W. Thompson, 12 November 1903, Box 279; Scott to Washington, 23 November 1903, Box 274, Washington Papers; Fox, *Guardian of Boston*, 69.
14. Pickens to Washington, 8 November 1903, Box 275, Washington Papers.
15. See Pickens to Washington, 1 August 1903, Box 271; Pickens to Washington, 15, 26 January 1904, 3 February 1904; Washington to Pickens, 11 December 1903, 21 January 1904, Box 684; Pickens to Washington, 8 November, 4 December 1903; Washington to Pickens, 11 December 1903, Box 275; Anson Phelps Stokes to Washington, 19 December 1903, Box 272, Washington Papers.
16. Pickens, *Heir of Slaves*, 3–14.
17. See photographs of Pickens among his papers at the Schomburg Collection, New York Public Library.
18. Pickens, *Heir of Slaves*, 10.
19. Pickens, "What I Owe to My Father," Manuscript, 1931, Folder 34, Box 8, Pickens Papers (Schomburg Collection, New York Public Library); hereafter cited as Pickens Papers.
20. Pickens, *Heir of Slaves*, 26.
21. Ibid., 22–24.
22. Ibid., 40.
23. Ibid., 57.
24. Ibid., 55.
25. Ibid., 75–82.
26. Ibid., 90–98. Pickens's description of the events leading to his admission to Talladega closely parallels Washington's trek from the mines of Malden, West Virginia, to Hampton Institute. See Washington, *Up from Slavery: An Autobiography* (London: Alexander Moring, 1902), 46–51. The style, tone, and even the title of Pickens's autobiography are reminiscent of Washington's book.
27. Besides Talladega, the American Missionary Association (AMA) established some of the best Negro colleges, including Atlanta University, Fisk University, Tougaloo College, and Hampton Institute. See August Meier and Elliott M. Rudwick, eds., *From Plantation to Ghetto: An Interpretative History of American Negroes* (1966; reprint ed., New York: American Century Series, 1968), 143.
28. Pickens, *Heir of Slaves*, 99.
29. Ibid., 102.
30. Ibid., 104.
31. Pickens, "Negro Evolution," Talladega College pamphlet, 1900, copy in the Schomburg Collection, New York Public Library.
32. Pickens, *Heir of Slaves*, 105.
33. Ibid., 109–10.
34. Ibid., 104–5.
35. Ibid., 112.
36. Ibid., 118, 132–39; Judith A. Schiff, Chief Reference Specialist, Manuscripts and Archives, Yale University Library to the writer, 12 February 1970.
37. Pickens, *The New Negro: His Political, Civil and Mental Status and Related Essays* (New York: The Neale Publishing Co., 1916), 188.
38. Washington to Pickens, 21 January 1904, Box 684, Washington Papers.
39. Quoted in Pickens to Washington, 3 February 1904, Box 684, Washington Papers.
40. Ibid.
41. Pickens, *Bursting Bonds* (Boston: Jordan and More Press, 1923), 140.

This volume duplicates the first eight chapters of *Heir of Slaves*, but adds three chapters, taking Pickens's life up to 1920.

42. Pickens, "What Talladega Is Doing for the Negro," *Missionary Review of the World* 28 (June 1905); 436–37.

43. Pickens, *Bursting Bonds*, 151.

44. Ibid.

45. Rudwick, *W. E. B. Du Bois*, 94–97; Francis L. Broderick, *W. E. B. Du Bois: Negro Leader in a Time of Crisis* (reprint ed., Stanford: Stanford University Press, 1959), 75–76; *Outlook*, 80 (29 July 1905): 795; Louis Harlan, "Booker T. Washington and the Politics of Accommodation," in John Hope Franklin and August Meier, eds., *Black Leaders of the Twentieth Century* (Urbana: University of Illinois Press, 1982), 7.

46. *Afro-American-Ledger* (Baltimore); 29 July 1905.

47. Ibid., 15 July 1905.

48. Rudwick, *W. E. B. Du Bois*, 98–103; Harlan, "Booker T. Washington," 13.

49. Pickens, *Bursting Bonds*, 151.

50. Charles Crowe, "Racial Massacre in Atlanta, September 22, 1906," *Journal of Negro History* 54 (April 1969). 157–158, 166–168; James A. Tinsley, "Roosevelt, Foraker and the Brownsville Affray," *Journal of Negro History* 41 (January 1956); 46–49; Franklin, *From Slavery to Freedom: A History of Negro Americans*; 3rd ed. rev. (New York; Knopf, 1967), 441–42; Rudwick, *W. E. B. Du Bois*, 107, 109; Meier and Rudwick, *From Plantation to Ghetto*, 164–165; C. Vann Woodward, *The Strange Career of Jim Crow*, (2d ed. rev. 1955, reprint ed., New York: Oxford University Press, 1966), 44, passim.

51. Meier, "Booker T. Washington and the Rise of the NAACP," *Crisis* 61 (February 1954): 76.

52. Pickens, "Southern Negro in a Northern University," *Voice of the Negro* 2 (April 1905); 234. By September 1905, J. Max Barber included the twenty-four-year-old Pickens along with Du Bois, Kelly Miller of Howard University, and John Hope of Atlanta Baptist (later Morehouse) College among black educators "able to state the Negro's cause before the bar of public thought." *Voice of the Negro* 2 (September 1905): 647.

53. Pickens, "Social Equality, *Voice of the Negro* 3 (January 1906); 27.

54. Pickens, "Choose!" *Voice of the Negro* 3 (June 1906); 404.

55. Ibid., 405–6.

56. Ibid., 407.

57. Pickens, "Negro Public Education in Alabama," *Voice of the Negro* 3 (September 1906); 643. "Require just as much of the Negro," Pickens wrote immediately following the Atlanta riot, "as you would require of any man. And I dare you, Caucasian, giant of a hundred generations and lord of a hundred lands, I double dare you to run the race of the next century with the 'black man of America' after granting him, not patronage and pity, but only EQUALITY OF OPPORTUNITY." Pickens, "The Educational Condition of the Negro in Cities," *Voice of the Negro* 3 (October 1906): 430.

58. Pickens, *New Negro*, 173.

59. Ibid.

60. Washington to James W. Cooper, 20 June 1908, Box 367, Washington Papers.

61. Ibid.

62. Cooper to Washington, 30 June 1908, Box 367, Washington Papers.

63. Charles Flint Kellogg, *NAACP: A History of the National Association*

for the Advancement of Colored Peoples, 1901–1920 (Baltimore: Johns Hopkins Press, 1967), vol. 1, 26; Rudwick, *W. E. B. Du Bois*, 120.

64. Platform of the National Negro Committee, 1909, Box A-3, NAACP Papers (Manuscript Division, Library of Congress); hereafter cited as NAACP Papers.

65. Ibid.

66. Kellogg, *NAACP*, 41.

67. Ibid., 48f. 7.

68. Herbert Aptheker, ed., *A Documentary History of the Negro People in the United States* (New York: Citadel Press, 1951), 885. Among the other twenty-three black radicals who signed the "Appeal" were Barber, Trotter, Waldron, and Archibald Grimké: see Louis R. Harlan, *Booker T. Washington: The Wizard of Tuskegee, 1901–1915* (New York: Oxford University Press, 1983), 368–70.

69. A. F. Beard to Pickens, 11 December 1913; Pickens to Beard, 9 October, 13 December 1913, Box 1, Pickens Papers.

70. *Buchanan v. Warley*, 245 U.S. 60 (1917). See Albert P. Blaustein and Robert L. Zangrando, (eds.) *Civil Rights and the American Negro: A Documentary History* (New York: Washington Square Press; 1968), 388.

71. Pickens to Joel E. Spingarn, 16 December 1917, Joel E. Spingarn Papers (Moorland-Spingarn Collection, Howard University Library, Washington, D.C.). Langston Hughes, *Fight for Freedom: The Story of the NAACP* (New York: Norton; 1962), 30.

72. *The Survey* 32 (30 May 1914): 234; *Crisis* 8 (June 1914); 87 (July 1914): 121, 125.

73. Pickens, "Utica," *Independent* 72 (22 February 1912): 407.

74. Pickens, *Bursting Bonds*, 142–43.

75. Ibid., 145.

76. Ibid., 149.

77. A. F. Beard to Pickens, 29 April 1914, Box 1, Pickens Papers. A similar student demonstration had occurred at Shaw University in Raleigh, North Carolina. "For manhood, righteousness and a square deal 250 young men went on strike a week ago." Reverend P. R. DeBerry to Pickens, 10 January 1914, Box 1, Pickens Papers. The Talladega student strike of 1914 foreshadowed a number of black college protests in the 1920s. See Raymond Wolters, *The New Negro on Campus: Black College Rebellions of the 1920s* (Princeton: Princeton University Press, 1975), 276, 341.

78. H. L. McElderry to Pickens, 1 April 1914, Box 1, Pickens Papers.

79. Pickens to McElderry, 1 April 1914, Box 1, Pickens Papers.

80. J. M. P. Metcalf to Washington, 6 August 1915, Box 510, Washington Papers.

81. Washington to Metcalf, 15 August 1914, Box 510, Washington Papers.

82. Pickens to H. H. Proctor, 14 January 1915, Box 1, Pickens Papers.

83. Pickens, *Bursting Bonds*, 165.

84. Manuscript of a speech Pickens delivered in Philadelphia on 1 April 1934, Box 9, Pickens Papers.

Chapter 2. "The New Negro," 1914–1919

1. Pickens, *Bursting Bonds*, 166–68.

2. "Biographies," *History of the Class of 1904* 4 (1929): 248, copy in Yale University Library.

3. Ibid., 169.

4. *New York Times*, 23 October, 17 December 1913; 13 May, 8 August, 12 December 1914. One of the major race riots during the "Red Summer" of 1919 occurred in Longview, Texas, about twenty miles from Marshall. See Arthur I. Waskow, *From Riot to Sit-In, 1919 and the 1960s* (1966; reprint ed., Garden City: Anchor, 1967), 16–20.

5. Pickens, *Bursting Bonds*, 198.

6. Ibid., 178–188.

7. Ibid., 199–203.

8. J. F. Marsh to William Feagin, 25 March 1915; Feagin to Booker T. Washington, 27 March 1915; Marsh to Washington, 6 April 1915, Box 939, Washington Papers.

9. M. W. Dogan, in a letter to Emmett J. Scott, suggested that he forced Pickens to leave Wiley because Washington and Scott wanted it. See Harlan, *Booker T. Washington*, 467fn.96.

10. Andrew B. Humphrey to Pickens, 19 April 1915; Pickens to Humphrey, 22 April 1915, Box 1, Pickens Papers.

11. J. W. Bowen to Pickens, 11 December 1914, 20 March, 4 May, 14 June 1915; Pickens to Bowen, 16 December 1914, 26 February 1915, Box 1, Pickens Papers. Morgan College is now Morgan State University.

12. Dogan to Pickens, 19 June 1916, Box 1, Pickens Papers.

13. Pickens to Channing H. Tobias, 18 June 1915, Box 1, Pickens Papers.

14. Pickens to Joel E. Spingarn, 22 July 1916, Joel E. Spingarn Papers.

15. W. E. B. Du Bois, *The Amenia Conference: An Historic Gathering* (Amenia, N.Y.: 1925), 9, copy of this pamphlet is in the Schomburg Collection, New York Public Library.

16. Ibid., 12.

17. Program of the Amenia Conference, 24–26 August 1916, Box C–229, NAACP Papers. Pickens joined R. R. Wright and Robert E. Jones, editor of the *Christian Advocate*, in a panel discussion called "Practical Paths." Other panels discussed "Education and Industry," "The Negro in Politics," "A Working Program for the Future," and "Social Discrimination."

18. Pickens was interested in American history, especially those topics related to racial questions. He was a member of the American Negro Academy, a selective and scholarly society, and at its nineteenth annual meeting, in December 1915, he read a paper on "The Status of the Free Negro from 1860 to 1870." *Occasional Papers of the American Negro Academy* 18 (1916); 64–70.

19. "Pickens was as homely as a mud hen," wrote Roy Wilkins of the NAACP, "but beautiful to watch in action. He could be by turns witty, sarcastic and moving." Wilkins, *Standing Fast: The Autobiography of Roy Wilkins* (New York: Viking, 1981), 98.

20. Du Bois, *Amenia Conference*, 12–16.

21. Ibid., 17.

22. Pickens, *The New Negro*, 149.

23. Ibid., 45.

24. Ibid., 176.

25. Ibid., 187.

26. Ibid., 43.

27. Ibid., 59–60.

28. Although the concept of the "New Negro" is often associated with the post–World War I Harlem literary "Renaissance," Meier, in *Negro Thought in America, 1880–1915: Racial Ideologies in the Age of Booker T. Washington* (1963; reprint ed., Ann Arbor: University of Michigan Press, 1968), 258, has

shown that for at least two decades prior to the war, blacks were discussing the emergence of a "self-respecting, educated, progressive, race-proud, self-dependent" Negro.

29. Pickens, *New Negro*, 239.
30. Ibid., 43.
31. For a brief discussion of separatist schemes during this period, such as "Chief" Sam's and Arthur Anderson's, see Meier, *Negro Thought in America, 1880–1915*, 272–73.
32. Pickens, *New Negro*, 161–162.
33. Ibid., 49.
34. Ibid., 172.
35. Ibid., 64.
36. Ibid., 219.
37. Ibid., 33.
38. Pickens, *The Negro in Light of the Great War* (Baltimore: Morgan College Press, 1918), 2; copy of this eight-page pamphlet is in the Schomburg Collection, New York Public Library.
39. Scott, *The American Negro in the World War* (Chicago: Homewood Press, 1919), 66, passim; Franklin, *From Slavery to Freedom*, 455–56; Benjamin Quarles, *The Negro in the Making of America* (New York: Macmillan, Collier, 1964), 180–81; Kellogg, *NAACP*, 256–66.
40. Pickens, *Bursting Bonds*, 216.
41. Quarles, *Negro in the Making of America*, 182.
42. Scott, *Negro in the World War*, 92, passim; Du Bois to Secretary of War Newton D. Baker, 1 October 1917, minutes of the Board of Directors meeting, 19 October 1917, Box A–1, NAACP Papers.
43. Dogan to Pickens, 27 August 1917, Box 1, Pickens Papers.
44. Scott, *Negro in the World War*, 92; Daniel R. Beaver, *Newton D. Baker and the American War Effort 1917–1919* (Lincoln: University of Nebraska Press, 1966), 227; an NAACP investigator blamed the riot on the "habitual brutality of the white police," quoted in Kellogg, *NAACP*, 261. See also Bernard C. Nalty, *Strength for the Fight? A History of Black Americans in the Military* (New York: Free Press, 1986), 102–6.
45. Scott, *Negro in the World War*, 82, passim; Beaver, *Newton D. Baker*, 225; Franklin, *From Slavery to Freedom*, 455.
46. Pickens to Spingarn, 27 February, 12, 28 March, 9, 13 April 1917, Joel E. Spingarn Papers; Kellogg, *NAACP*, 254; Scott, *Negro in the World War*, 83; Beaver, *Newton D. Baker*, 225. Du Bois was one of the few editors who supported Spingarn and Pickens, See *The Crisis* 13 (April 1917): 270–71.
47. Pickens, *Bursting Bonds*, 217–18; Pickens to Spingarn, 27 February 1917, quoted in Kellogg, *NAACP*, 254.
48. Scott, *Negro in the World War*, 85. "One of the best services ever rendered the American Negro," Pickens wrote to Joel E. Spingarn, "was your timely and vigorous work to secure training for these colored officers." Pickens to Spingarn, 13 November 1917, Spingarn Papers.
49. Kellogg, *NAACP*, 255–56; Scott, *Negro in the World War*, 87.
50. Scott, *Negro in the World War*, 89–90. On 15 October 1917, 639 black officers received their commissions.
51. Pickens, "The New Year (1918)," manuscript, 1 January 1918, Box 7, Pickens Papers.
52. F. H. Miller to Pickens, 15 March 1918; Pickens to Miller, 20 March 1918, Box 1, Pickens Papers.
53. Du Bois, *The Crisis* 16 (July 1918): 111.

54. See Du Bois's editorials in *The Crisis* 13 (April 1917): 270–71; 14 (July 1917): 131; 16 (June 1918): 60; 16 (July 1918): 111.
55. Scott to Pickens, 6 July 1918, Box 1, Pickens Papers.
56. Ibid.
57. Copy of a manuscript of a speech delivered 30 May 1918 in the Pickens Vertical File (Schomburg Collection, New York Public Library); hereafter cited as Pickens Vertical File.
58. Du Bois, *The Crisis* 16 (June 1918): 60.
59. Scott, *Negro in the World War*, 458.
60. Scott, *Negro in the World War*, 355–73; Franklin, *From Slavery to Freedom*, 461–71.
61. Pickens, *Negro in Light of the Great War*, 4.
62. The best account of the race riots of 1919 is Waskow, *From Riot to Sit-In*. See also Kellogg, *NAACP*, 235–44.
63. *Crisis* 19 (March 1920): 243.

Chapter 3. The Field Secretary and "The Emperor of Africa," 1919–1927

1. John O. Spencer to Pickens, 20 May 1916, Box 1, Pickens Papers.
2. Spencer to Pickens, 10 March, 2 November 1917; Pickens to Spencer, 30 October, 5 November 1917, Box 1, Pickens Papers.
3. D. Stuart Dodge to Pickens, 26 December 1917; William H. Baldwin to Pickens, 16 December 1917; L. Hollingworth Wood to Pickens, 2 January 1918; Pickens to Wood, 7 January 1918, Box 1, Pickens Papers.
4. Dr. E. P. Roberts to Pickens, 21 December 1917, Box 1, Pickens Papers.
5. Eugene Kinckle Jones to Pickens, 12 December 1917, 7 January 1918, Box 1, Pickens Papers.
6. Pickens to Spencer, 7, 15 January 1918; Spencer to Pickens, 17, 20 January 1918, Box 1, Pickens Papers.
7. Pickens to Spencer, 27 September 1918, Box 12, Pickens Papers.
8. Pickens to Sarah Breedlove (Mme C. J.) Walker, n.d., Box 1, Pickens Papers.
9. Pickens, "The 'Chauvinism of Minorities' and of Benjamin Stolberg," manuscript, 1937, Box C-429, NAACP Papers, published as "Retort to Negro Snobbery," *Crisis* 44 (December 1937): 338.
10. Pickens received fifty dollars and expenses for each of his NAACP assignments. Pickens to F. E. Young, 12 August 1919, Box 1, Pickens Papers.
11. May Childs Nerney to Pickens, 19 December 1914, Box 1, Pickens Papers; minutes of the NAACP Board of Directors meeting, 5 January 1915, Box A-2, NAACP Papers.
12. *The Crisis* 9 (January 1915): 18, 39 (June 1919): 92; *New York Times*, 7 May 1919; James Weldon Johnson, *Along This Way* (New York: Viking, 1933), 330.
13. Hughes, *Fight for Freedom*; 30; *The Congregationalist and Advance* (Boston), n.d., copy in Box 7, Pickens Papers. Pickens's effectiveness before all kinds of audiences, white and black, was corroborated in interviews with his contemporaries: Roy Wilkins, Ralph Bunche, and Henry Lee Moon, New York, December 1969. "Dr. Pickens was an exceptionally brilliant orator." A. Philip Randolph to the writer, 30 December 1969.
14. Pickens to J. W. Youngblood, 25 November 1918; James Weldon Johnson to Pickens, 17 September 1919; J. E. McCall to Pickens, 22 September 1919, Box

1, Pickens Papers. Many of Pickens's syndicated columns for the period 1919 to 1941 are deposited in Pickens Papers and have been a major source for this study.

15. Vishnu V. Oak, *The Negro Newspaper* (Yellow Springs, Ohio: Antioch Press, 1948), 99–101, 108; Frederick G. Detweiler, *The Negro Press in the United States* (Chicago: University of Chicago Press, 1922), 28–29; Maxwell R. Brooks, *The Negro Press Re-Examined: Political Content of Leading Negro Newspapers* (Boston: Christopher Publishing House, 1959), 82–83; Roi Ottley, *New World A-Coming: Inside Black America* (Boston: Houghton Mifflin, 1943), 276; Franklin, *From Slavery to Freedom*, 563; ANP Contributing Editor Percival Prattis to Y. Hikida, 26 April 1934, copy in Box 2, Pickens Papers.

16. G. James Fleming, "The Negro Press," manuscript, quoted in Gunnar Myrdal, *The American Dilemma: The Negro Problem and Modern Democracy* (New York: Harper, 1944), 2:1424 n.30.

17. Pickens to Mary Ovington, 28 October 1933, Box C–72, NAACP Papers.

18. Spingarn to Royal Nash, quoted in Kellogg, *NAACP*, 134. August Meier called Johnson's appointment "an ironic master stroke." Meier, "Booker T. Washington and the Rise of the NAACP," *Crisis* 61 (February 1954): 123. See also the minutes of the NAACP Board of Directors meeting, 11 December 1916, Box A–1, NAACP Papers.

19. John R. Shillady to Pickens, 12 January 1920; Spencer to Pickens, 26 June 1920, Box 1, Pickens Papers.

20. *The Crisis* 19 (March 1920): 241, 250.

21. Ibid., 241.

22. Kellogg, *NAACP*, 291; Wilson Record, "Negro Intellectual Leadership in the National Association for the Advancement of Colored People, 1910–1940," *Phylon* 17 (4th quarter, 1956): 382–83. See especially Elliott Rudwick and August Meier, "The Rise of the Black Secretariat in the NAACP, 1909–1935," in Meier and Rudwick, *Along the Color Line: Explorations in the Black Experience* (Urbana: University of Illinois Press, 1976), 94–127.

23. *The Crisis* 19 (March 1920): 240–241.

24. Minutes of the NAACP Board of Directors meeting, 5 January 1920, Box A–2, NAACP Papers; Pickens to NAACP Board Vice President Arthur B. Spingarn, 16 November 1920, Arthur Spingarn Papers.

25. For example, the Pilgrim Press paid Pickens $125 and 10 percent of all sales for his first autobiography, *Heir of Slaves*. Pickens paid the Neale Publishing Co. for the first edition of *The New* Negro, but he received 50 percent of the net profit from all future editions. Pickens to Joel E. Spingarn, 17 January, 10 February 1916, Spingarn Papers.

26. Flora Avery (not related to the author) of Galesburg, Illinois, was active in the Congregational Church's American Missionary Association. She often visited Talladega College (an AMA school) while Pickens was teaching there and she was very fond of him and his wife. Mrs. Avery died on 8 March 1925. See Mrs. John J. (Flora E.) Avery to M. P. Shawkey, 13 April 1914, copy in Box 1, Pickens Papers; also see Pickens-Avery correspondence in Box 2 and 7, Pickens Papers.

27. See Pickens to his son William, Jr., 16 September 1938, Box 3, 5 March 1946, Box 6, Pickens Papers. The source of Mrs. Pickens's money remains a mystery. One informant who grew up with her suggests that it was an inheritance from a prominent white man in Meridian, Mississippi, who was her natural father.

28. Roy Wilkins, in an interview with the author, described Pickens as a

"penny-pincher." Much of Pickens's personal correspondence supports this view.

29. Gilbert Osofsky, *Harlem: The Making of a Ghetto* (1963; reprinted; New York: Harper, 1968), 120; Pickens to Arthur Spingarn, 16 November 1920, Arthur Spingarn Papers.

30. Ibid.

31. George S. Schuyler, *Black and Conservative: The Autobiography of George S. Schuyler* (New Rochelle: Arlington House, 1966), 142–43.

32. Interview with Harriet Ida Pickens. See also Ottley, *The Lonely Warrior: The Life and Times of Robert S. Abbott* (Chicago: Henry Regnery, 1955), 229.

33. Interviews with Harriet Ida Pickens and Lemuel Foster; Schuyler, *Black and Conservative*, 212–13; see also Mrs. Pickens's obituary in the *New York Times*, 11 January 1955.

34. "Biographies," *History of the Class of 1904* 4 (1929): 248, copy in Yale University Library.

35. Harriet Ida Pickens, who died in 1969, had the most interesting and successful career. During the New Deal she was an administrator in the Works Progress Administration in New York. During World War II she was the first black woman commissioned officer in the WAVES. After the war, she worked for the Harlem Tuberculosis and Health Association until 1961, when she joined the staff of the New York City Commission on Human Rights. In 1963 she became the head of the Community Action Division of that commission, a post she held until her death of a stroke at age sixty. For an interview with Harriet Ida Pickens, see also *New York Times*, 30 December 1969.

36. Pickens to Joel E. Spingarn, 21 December 1920, Box C–71, NAACP Papers.

37. Minutes of the NAACP Board of Directors meeting, 10 January 1921, Box A–2, NAACP Papers. Hunton, who was also a champion of women's suffrage, had been an active NAACP member for several years, and, in 1919, she was one of the Association's representatives in Paris attending the Pan-African Congress. Franklin, *From Slavery to Freedom*, 468; Kellogg, *NAACP*, 283.

38. Pickens to Mary White Ovington, 14 June 1921, Box C–71, NAACP Papers.

39. Du Bois to Pickens, 28 March 1921, Box 1, Pickens Papers.

40. For a discussion of clashes between Du Bois and Oswald Garrison Villard, Joel E. Spingarn, and other board members, see Kellogg, *NAACP*, 93–104, 107–109, passim. Kellogg writes, "Throughout his career Du Bois found it almost impossible to work closely with his fellowmen, black or white." Du Bois, in *The Autobiography of W. E. B. Du Bois* (New York: International Publishers, 1968), 258, admitted that he lacked a "friendliness of approach," "adaptability," and a deep "knowledge of human nature." "What I had was knowledge of the Negro problem, an ability to express my thoughts clearly, and a logical method of thought."

41. Pickens to Du Bois, 12 April 1921, Box 1, Pickens Papers.

42. The best studies of Garvey are Edmond David Cronon, *Black Moses: The Story of Marcus Garvey and the Universal Negro Improvement Association* (1955; reprint ed., Madison: University of Wisconsin Press, 1968); Judith Stein, *The World of Marcus Garvey: Race and Class in Modern Society* (Baton Rouge: Louisiana State University Press, 1986). See also Tony Martin, *Race First: The Ideological and Organizational Struggles of Marcus Garvey and the Universal Negro Improvement Association* (Westport, Conn.: Greenwood Press, 1976);

John H. Clarke, ed. *Marcus Garvey and the Vision of Africa* (New York: Vintage, 1974); Lawrence W. Levine, "Marcus Garvey and the Politics of Revitalization," in Franklin and Meier, eds. *Black Leaders of the Twentieth Century*, 105–38.

43. Prior to 1921, few black leaders openly criticized Garvey. Among those who did raise serious questions about the UNIA were Cyril V. Briggs, editor of the *Crusader*, and Robert S. Abbott, publisher and editor of the influential *Defender* (Chicago). See Cronon, *Black Moses*, 75.

44. *The Crisis* 21 (December 1920): 58.

45. Ibid. (January 1921): 115.

46. Ibid., 114.

47. Ibid., 115.

48. Pickens to Garvey, 12 September 1921, Box 1, Pickens Papers. The "traitors" to whom he refers were UNIA officers, such as Edgar M. Gray, Richard E. Warner, Orlando M. Thompson, and Elie Garcia, who, unlike Garvey, probably pocketed some of the organization's funds. See Cronon, *Black Moses*, 78–79.

49. Pickens to the NAACP Board of Directors, 17 September 1921, Box 1, Pickens Papers.

50. Pickens to Joel E. Spingarn, 25 September 1921; Pickens to James Weldon Johnson, 8 October 1921, Box C–71, NAACP Papers. Minutes of the NAACP board meeting, 10 October 1921, Box A–2, NAACP Papers.

51. Pickens to Ernest Gruening and Norman Thomas (coeditors of the *Nation*), 11 October 1921, Box 1, Pickens Papers.

52. Although written in September or early October, the article was not published until December 1921. The original text appeared in Garvey's *Negro World* on 17 December and has been quoted herein. An edited version appeared in the *Nation* 113 (28 December 1921): 750–51.

53. *Negro World*, 17 December 1921.

54. *Black Dispatch* Oklahoma City, 22 December 1921.

55. Pickens to Dr. H. Claude Hudson, 4 June 1922, Box, 1, Pickens Papers.

56. Cronon, *Black Moses*, 84–85, 97–98; Stein, *World of Marcus Garvey*, 152–54; Ottley, *New World A-Coming*, 79; Levine, "Garvey," 127–28.

57. *Negro World*, 21 January 1922.

58. James W. Johnson to Garvey, 20 January 1922, Box C–304, NAACP Papers.

59. Garvey to Johnson, 21 January 1922, Box C–304, NAACP Papers.

60. Du Bois, "Back to Africa," *The Century* 105 (February 1923): 547.

61. *New York Times*, 10 July 1922.

62. Amy Jacques-Garvey, *Philosophy and Opinions of Marcus Garvey* (New York: Atheneum, 1969), vol. 2, 71.

63. Cronon, *Black Moses*, 189–90; Stein, *World of Marcus Garvey*, 158–61; Ottley, *New World A-Coming*, 74.

64. Pickens, "The Puzzle: Find the Liar," manuscript, n.d., Box C–304, NAACP Papers.

65. Pickens to Garvey, 24 July 1922, Box C–304, NAACP Papers. Another copy of the letter is in Box 1, Pickens Papers. The letter was published in the *Public Journal* (Philadelphia), 29 July 1922.

66. Pickens memorandum of the "Friends of Negro Freedom" meeting, at the Shuffle Inn, 6 August 1922, Box 7, Pickens Papers.

67. *Negro World*, 7 August 1922.

68. Pickens to Johnson, 14 September 1922, Box C–71, NAACP Papers.

69. "Committee of Eight" To Attorney General Harry M. Daugherty, 15 January 1923, Box C–304, NAACP Papers. See Stein, *World of Marcus Garvey*, 165–68.
70. Ibid. The "Eight" also included John E. Nail, Julia P. Coleman, Harry Pace, Robert Abbott, and George W. Harris.
71. Pickens, "Weekly Editorial," The *Public Journal* (Philadelphia), n.d., Box 1, Pickens Papers.
72. *Negro World*, 6 February 1923, reprinted in Jacques-Garvey, *Philosophy and Opinions*, vol. 2, 308.
73. Ibid., 307.
74. *Defender* (Chicago), 26 April 1924, quoted in Cronon, *Black Moses*, 194.
75. Cronon, *Black Moses*, 113–18.
76. Pickens, "The Emperor of Africa: The Psychology of Garveyism," *Forum* 70 (23 August 1923): 1791.
77. Pickens, "Garvey's Last Stand," manuscript, n.d., Box 7, Pickens Papers.
78. Pickens, "The Emperor of Africa," 1791.
79. Ibid., 1792.
80. Du Bois, "Back to Africa," 544.
81. *The Messenger* 5 (March 1923): 645.
82. W. A. Domingo, letter to the editor, *The Messenger* 5 (March 1923): 639–40. For a discussion of West Indian influence in Garvey's movement, see Harold Cruse, *The Crisis of the Negro Intellectual* (New York: Morrow, 1967), 115–29. Cruse has a strong anti-West Indian bias and offers no evidence to support his contention that the UNIA was "predominantly West Indian."
83. Ibid.
84. Domingo to Du Bois, 24 August 1922, Box C–304, NAACP Papers.
85. Cronon, *Black Moses*, 224.
86. Ibid., 135–36.
87. Pickens, letter to the editor, *New Republic* 52 (31 August 1927): 46–47.
88. *New York Times*, 3 December 1927.
89. Cronon, *Black Moses*, 168, passim.
90. Pickens, "The Emperor of Africa," 1792.

Chapter 4. The Reluctant Republican, 1920–1928

1. Pickens, "Political Parties and the Negro," *The Messenger* 5 (March 1923): 625.
2. Pickens, manuscript of a speech delivered before the National Conference of Social Work, Toronto, 26 June 1924, Box 7, Pickens Papers.
3. Minutes of the NAACP Board of Directors meeting, 9 February 1920, Box A–2, NAACP Papers.
4. For a detailed discussion of U.S. involvement in Haitian affairs, see Arthur C. Millspaugh, *Haiti under American Control, 1915–1930* (Boston: World Peace Foundation, 1931); Ludwell Lee Montague, *Haiti and the United States, 1714–1938*, 2d ed., New York: Russell & Russell, 1966); Kellogg, *NAACP*, 284–86; Paul H. Douglas, "Political History of the Occupation," in Emily Greene Balch, ed., *Occupied Haiti* (New York: The Writers Publishing Co., 1927). For NAACP interest in Haiti, see the minutes of NAACP Board of Directors meetings for 11 October 1915, 11 March, 9 September 1918, 13 January 1919, 9 March, 6 November 1920, 14 February, 14 March 1921, Boxes A–1 and A–2, NAACP Papers.

5. Minutes of NAACP board meeting, 13 September 1920, A–2, NAACP Papers. See Richard B. Sherman, *The Republican Party and Black America: From McKinley to Hoover, 1896–1933* (Charlottesville: University of Virginia Press, 1973), 13.

6. Richard B. Sherman, "The Harding Administration and the Negro: An Opportunity Lost," *Journal of Negro History* 49 (July 1964): 151.

7. Pickens, "Harding-Regular Republican," in *Public Journal* (Philadelphia), 3 June 1922.

8. *St. Louis Argus*, 1 December 1922. After his first State of the Union message, Harding "never again pressed Congress for legislation desired by Negroes." Sherman, "Harding Administration and the Negro," 157.

9. Pickens, "Harding-Coolidge," Associated Negro Press (ANP) release, n.d., Box 7, Pickens Papers.

10. *Public Journal* (Philadelphia), n.d., Box 7, Pickens Papers.

11. *Crisis* 26 (October 1923): 248.

12. See John L. Blair, "A Time for Parting: The Negro During the Coolidge Years," *Journal of American Studies* 3 (December 1969): 177–99.

13. *Crisis* 28 (July 1924): 104.

14. Pickens, "Political Parties and the Negro."

15. See Kenneth C. Mac Kay, *The Progressive Movement of 1924* (New York: Columbia University Press, 1947), 148, passim; Russel B. Nye, *Midwestern Progressive Politics : An Historical Study of Its Origins and Development, 1870–1958* (1959; reprint ed., New York: Harper, 1959), 300, 309; David Burner, *The Politics of Provincialism: The Democratic Party in Transition, 1918–1932* (New York: Knopf, 1968) 128–29.

16. Minutes of the NAACP board meeting, 14 April 1924, Box A–2, NAACP Papers.

17. Minutes of the NAACP board meeting, 14 April 1924, Box A–2, NAACP Papers.

18. *Courier* (Pittsburgh), 5 July 1924.

19. A copy of the NAACP's Philadelphia statement was sent to the Conference for Progressive Political Action (CPPA) and it was reprinted in the *Crisis* 28 (August 1924): 151–152. See Kenneth T. Jackson, *The Ku Klux Klan in the City, 1915–1930* (New York: Oxford University Press, 1967), 22–26.

20. Minutes of the NAACP board meeting, 14 July 1924, A–2, NAACP Papers.

21. Ibid.

22. Ibid.

23. *New York Times*, 5 July 1924.

24. Oswald G. Villard, "An Honest Convention," *Nation* 119 (16 July 1924): 63.

25. *New York Times*, 5 July 1924.

26. Mac Kay, *Progressive Movement of 1924*, 143–48; *Crisis* 28 (July 1924): 104.

27. Minutes of the NAACP board meeting, 14 July 1924, A–2, NAACP Papers. Mac Kay suggests there were a few other Negroes at the convention (p. 121), but Villard, who attended the sessions, wrote, "Only one colored man sat in the large audience," "An Honest Convention," 63.

28. Pickens, "Progressive Political Action," *Crisis* 28 (September 1924): 211.

29. Minutes of the NAACP board meeting, 14 July 1924, Box A–2, NAACP

Papers. Norman Thomas was the Socialist candidate for governor of New York.

30. *New York Times*, 5 July 1924.

31. Minutes of the NAACP board meeting, 14 July 1924, Box A–2, NAACP Papers.

32. Ibid. The CPPA leaders permitted other resolutions to be presented from the floor, including independence for the Philippines, the Irish question, and opposition to exploitation in Haiti, Santo Domingo, and Nicaragua, Mac Kay, Progressive Movement of 1924, 121.

33. *The New York Times*, 6 July 1924, mistakenly reported Pickens's address as a seconding speech for La Follette's nomination. Mac Kay, *Progressive Movement of 1924* 121, committed the same error.

34. Robert Littell, "La Follette for President!" *New Republic* 39 (16 July 1924): 201–2.

35. Ibid.

36. Minutes of the NAACP board meeting, 14 July 1924, A–2, NAACP Papers.

37. Pickens, "Progressive Political Action."

38. "How Shall We Vote: A Symposium," *Crisis* 29 (November 1924): 32.

39. Ibid.

40. *Courier* (Pittsburgh), 17 July 1924.

41. "How Shall We Vote," 33.

42. Ibid., 32.

43. Ibid., 33. Du Bois's last reference was to John W. Davis and his running mate, Nebraska's governor, Charles Bryan, brother of William Jennings Bryan.

44. Pickens, "Progressive Political Action."

45. Mac Kay, *Progressive Movement of 1924*, 218. Pickens even considered running for Congress in Manhattan's Twenty-first District as a Progressive, but he withdrew when the Republicans nominated a Negro, Dr. Charles Roberts, for the same office. *News* (New York), 30 August 1924.

46. Pickens, "Dawes Whitewashes the Klan," ANP release, n.d., Box 7, Pickens Papers. Ironically, Dawes's statement was made as part of what was otherwise a repudiation of the Klan. Norman Thomas agreed with Pickens and labeled Dawes's statement "a left-handed defense of the Klan." *New York Times*, 25 August 1924.

47. Pickens, "Negro Political Independence," ANP release, 6 October 1924, Box 7, Pickens Papers.

48. Pickens, "Progressive Political Action."

49. Mac Kay, *Progressive Movement of 1924*, 219–25; John D. Hicks, *The Republican Ascendancy, 1921–1923* (1960, reprint ed., New York: Harper, 1963), 102.

50. For example, Burner, *Politics of Provincialism*, 241, estimates that 4 percent of Chicago's black vote went to La Follette, while John M. Allswang, *A House for All Peoples: Ethnic Politics in Chicago, 1890–1936* (Lexington: University of Kentucky Press, 1971), 53, puts it at 10 percent.

51. Du Bois, *Crisis* 29 (December 1924): 55.

52. Mac Kay, *Progressive Movement of 1924*, 218.

53. Ibid. Franklin, in *From Slavery to Freedom*, 524, argues that in the 1924 election, "Negroes deserted the Republican Party in considerable numbers." Richard Sherman, in "The Harding Administration," 167, on the other hand, contends that "the rank and file of Negro voters remained true to their old party allegiance in 1924." Neither Du Bois, Mac Kay, Franklin, nor Sherman did a

systematic quantitative analysis of the Negro vote in 1924. Such an analysis might have shown that Negro voters began to desert the Republican party in 1924, rather than in the Hoover-Smith contest of 1928.

54. Sherman, "Harding Administration and the Negro," 165.

55. Cannon's letter was quoted in the minutes of the NAACP board meeting, 19 November 1924, Box A–2, NAACP Papers.

56. Perry Howard to Senator T. Coleman Du Pont and to Attorney General Harry Daugherty, 23 November 1922, quoted in an NAACP news release, 8 December 1922, Box A–2, NAACP Papers. Du Bois joined the Communist party at the end of a long life, but he generally shared Pickens's and Johnson's skepticism about the American Communist party's motives on the race issue. See Manning Marable, *W. E. B. Du Bois: Black Radical Democrat* (Boston: Twayne Publishers 1986), 157.

57. Kellogg, *NAACP*, 286–90.

58. Minutes of the NAACP board meeting, 10 May 1920, Box A–2, NAACP Papers. Emphasis added.

59. Pickens, letter to the editor of the *Public Ledger* (Philadelphia), n.d., Box 7, Pickens Papers. The accusation was made by Benjamin J. Davis of Georgia.

60. David A. Shannon, *The Socialist Party of America* (1955; reprint ed., Chicago: University of Chicago Press, 1967), 54–56.

61. LID *News-Bulletin*, July 1923, copy in Box 7, Pickens Papers.

62. Harry Laidler, head of the LID for many years, to the writer, 5 December 1969.

63. Pickens, "Progressive Political Action."

64. Several influential black newspapers supported Smith. The *Defender* (Chicago) supported a Democrat for the first time, albeit with little vigor. "If we have outlived our usefulness to the Republican party," read a *Defender* editorial on 20 October 1928, "there is a possibility that we can be of the same service to the opposition party. At any rate this is the only political move which we have not tried." The *Afro-American* (Baltimore), the *Journal and Guide* (Norfolk), the *Argus* (St. Louis), and the *News* (Louisville) endorsed Smith in similar fashion. Nevertheless, a majority of black newspapers, black leaders, and black voters remained in the Republican fold. See Henry Lee Moon, *Balance of Power: The Negro Vote*. (Garden City: Doubleday, 1949), 18, 106; Allswang, *House for All Peoples*, 53; Burner, *Politics of Provincialism*, 237.

65. Pickens, "The American Negro Vote in 1928," manuscript of an address delivered in Chicago, 14 October 1928, Box 8, Pickens Papers.

66. Walter White, *A Man Called White: The Autobiography of Walter White* (New York: Viking Press, 1948), 101.

67. Pickens, "Negro Vote in 1928."

68. Ibid.

69. Moon, in *Balance of Power*, 106, wrote of the 1928 election, "Democrats made deeper inroads on the Republicanism of Negro voters than in any previous national election." White, the first black NAACP national officer to join the Democrats, worked for Al Smith's campaign during a leave of absence from the Association. See Samuel O'Dell, "Blacks, the Democratic Party and the Election of 1928: A Mild Rejoinder," *Phylon* 48 (March 1987): 6.

70. Montague, *Haiti and the United States*, 276.

71. For a discussion of this appointment and the response of blacks to it, see chap. 5.

Chapter 5. The NAACP Comes of Age, 1920–1931

1. White, *Man Called White*, 111. For White's recollection of the Parker fight, see *Man Called White*, 104–14.
2. See White, *Man Called White*; and White, *How Far the Promised Land* (New York: The Viking Press, 1956); Nathaniel P. Tillman, Jr., "Walter Francis White: A Study in Interest Group Leadership," (Ph.D. diss., University of Wisconsin, 1961), deals with an attempt to purge White in 1950, but he ignores the 1931 attempt.
3. Interviews with William L. Patterson and Lemuel Foster, New York, December 1969. Foster, who was connected with the YMCA in the 1960s, knew Pickens at Talladega and, later, was his successor at the Treasury Department. Roy Wilkins and Henry Lee Moon of the NAACP denied that color distinction played a part in NAACP promotions or in the relationship between White and Pickens. Interviews with Wilkins and Moon, New York, December 1969.
4. J. Max Barber to Pickens, 18 June 1930, Box 1, Pickens Papers. Barber had been editor of the *Voice of the Negro*.
5. Interview with Wilkins.
6. Interview with Foster.
7. Pickens to the NAACP Board of Directors, 5 February 1923, Box C–71, NAACP Papers.
8. Mary W. Ovington, "The NAACP," *Journal of Negro History* 9 (April 1924): 116. The most famous example was the brutal beating inflicted upon white NAACP Secretary John R. Shillady, in Austin, Texas, in August, 1919. See Kellogg, *NAACP*, 239–41.
9. Pickens to the NAACP board, 1 June 1923, Box C–71, NAACP Papers.
10. Mulch, according to Pickens's informant, was a Chicago attorney who had gone to Shreveport to defend two Industrial Workers of the World organizers. He was seized from the lobby of a prominent hotel, severely beaten, and put on a train. Mulch had to get off at Dallas for medical attention. Unsigned letter to Pickens, 25 May 1922, Box 7, Pickens Papers.
11. Pickens, "Langston Hughes on 'Cowards and Churches,'" manuscript, ANP release, 22 August 1934, Box 7, Pickens Papers.
12. Pickens to Robert Bagnall, 9 March 1923; also see Pickens to the NAACP board, 1 June 1923, Box C–71, NAACP Papers.
13. Pickens, "Things No Body Believes: A Lesson in Religion," *Messenger* 5 (February 1923): 419.
14. Nannie H. Burroughs to Pickens, 12 March 1923, Box 1, Pickens Papers.
15. *Afro-American* (Baltimore), 16, 23 February 1923.
16. R. R. Wright, Jr., letter in the *Christian Recorder*, 1 May 1923.
17. Pickens to Mary Ovington, 8 March 1923, Box C–71, NAACP Papers.
18. Pickens to Ovington, 9 March 1923, Box C–71, NAACP Papers.
19. Pickens, "Intelligent Christianity: Not the Fear of Hell," *Messenger* 5 (April 1923): 668–69.
20. Pickens to Johnson, 20 September 1923; Pickens to Williams, 10 September 1923; Pickens to Johnson, 1 November 1924; Williams to Johnson, 1 November 1924, Box C–71, NAACP Papers.
21. Augusta Bird to Pickens, 2 April 1923, Box 1, Pickens Papers.
22. Pickens to Johnson, 14 November 1925; Johnson to Pickens, 19 November 1925, C–71, NAACP Papers.
23. Richetta Randolph to Pickens, 25 February 1927; Gladys Flynn to Johnson, 25 March 1927, Box C–71, NAACP Papers.

24. Pickens to Du Bois, 26 May 1929, Box 8; Pickens to Storey, 13 March 1928, Storey to Pickens, 6 March 1928, Box 1, Pickens Papers.

25. Bagnall to Pickens, 11 December 1929, Box 1, Pickens Papers. James Weldon Johnson had been granted leave to attend the Institute of Pacific Relations in Kyoto, Japan, minutes of the NAACP board meeting, 13 September 1929, Box A–2, NAACP Papers.

26. See the large file of heated exchanges between Pickens and Arnold in Pickens's file, 1930, Box C–71, NAACP Papers; also see Pickens to Arthur Spingarn, 28 May 1930, Arthur Spingarn Papers.

27. Pickens to White, 12 April 1930, Box C–71, NAACP Papers.

28. Richetta Randolph to Ovington, 9 May 1930, Box C–71, NAACP Papers.

29. Bagnall to Pickens, 5 April, 11 May 1930, Box 10, Pickens Papers.

30. Seligmann to Pickens, 21 May 1930, Box 10, Pickens Papers.

31. Barber to Pickens, 18 April 1930, Box 1, Pickens Papers.

32. Pickens to Ovington, 28 May 1930, Box 1, Pickens Papers. "I have known for eleven years," Pickens wrote to Joel and Arthur Spingarn, "that Mr. White's attitude was just what it is today, but its origin and cause are to me a profound mystery." Pickens to Joel and Arthur Spingarn, 6 June 1930, Arthur Spingarn Papers.

33. Barber to Pickens, 18 June 1930, Box 1, Pickens Papers.

34. Minutes of the NAACP board meeting, 21 December 1931, Box A-3, NAACP Papers. For more discussion of this internal crisis, see Raymond Wolters's chapter, "Rift in the NAACP" in *Negroes and the Great Depression: The Problem of Economic Recovery* (Westport, Conn.: Greenwood Publishing Corp., 1970); B. Joyce Ross, J. E. *Spingarn and the Rise of the NAACP, 1911–1939* (New York: Antheneum, 1972), 133–34.

35. Copy of the letter, written on 21 December 1931 and signed by Du Bois, Pickens, Wilkins, Bagnall, and Seligmann, is filed in Box 1, Pickens Papers.

36. Minutes of the NAACP board meeting, 21 December 1931, Box A–3, NAACP Papers.

37. Pickens to Du Bois, 23 December 1931, Box 1, Pickens Papers. White sent copies of all the apologies (all dated 22 December) to Arthur Spingarn and (presumably) other NAACP board members, White to Arthur Spingarn, 23 December 1930, Arthur Spingarn Papers. Wilkins was "simply sick over the part [he] took in that awful mess"; Seligmann withdrew "every charge and personal innuendo" made against White; "I have only the excuse," wrote Robert Bagnall, "that I was deeply stirred over the injustice of the Committee's report and did not see it (the statement) as any reflection on anyone's honor." Pickens's apology was essentially the same as that related in his letter to Du Bois.

38. Minutes of the NAACP board meeting, 9 January 1933, Box A–3, NAACP Papers. For Du Bois's break with the NAACP, see his letter to the NAACP board, 26 June 1934, copy in the minutes of the NAACP board meeting, 9 July 1934, Box A-3, NAACP Papers; Rudwick, *W. E. B. Du Bois*, 282, passim.; Broderick, *W. E. B. Du Bois*, 168; Wolters, *Negroes and the Great Depression*, 290–94 passim; see also chap. 8.

39. Du Bois, *Autobiography of W. E. B. Du Bois*, 294.

40. Moon, *Balance of Power*, 112.

41. *New York Times*, 22 March 1930; *World* (New York), 22 March 1930.

42. White to A. M. Rivera, 22 March 1930, Box C–397, NAACP Papers.

43. Rivera to White, 24 March 1930, Box C–397, NAACP Papers.

44. White to Ernest Gruening, 7 April 1930, Box C–397, NAACP Papers.

45. *New York Times*, 26 March 1930.

46. In 1921 the NAACP protested the appointment of Frank Linney, North Carolina Republican state chairman to the post of U.S. attorney for the District of North Carolina. Linney, as candidate for governor in 1916 and 1920, had made a similar lily-white statement about excluding blacks from voting. Despite the NAACP's protest, the Senate confirmed Linney. See Sherman, *Republican Party and Black America*, 15.

47. White to Rivera, 14 April 1930, Box C–397, NAACP Papers.

48. White to Pickens, 2 May 1930, Box C–71, NAACP Papers.

49. *News* (Charlotte, North Carolina), 16 April 1930; *Herald Tribune* (New York), 6 April 1930; *Washington Post*, 26 April 1930, Box C–397, NAACP Papers.

50. H. L. McCrorey to White, 24 March 1930, Box C–397, NAACP Papers.

51. Pickens to White, 3 May 1930, Box C–71, NAACP Papers.

52. R. McCants Andrews to White, 3 April 1930; L. E. Austin to White, 28 April 1930; L. E. Graves to White, 18 April 1930; Benjamin Brawley to White, 29 April 1930, Box C–397, NAACP Papers; Meier and Rudwick, *From Plantation to Ghetto*, 146–47.

53. Schuyler to White, 26 April 1930, Box C–397, NAACP Papers.

54. White, memorandum, 11 April 1930, Box C–397, NAACP Papers.

55. White learned most of his tactics from Johnson during the unsuccessful campaign in 1921–22 for the Dyer federal antilynching bill. See Eugene Levy, "James Weldon Johnson and the Development of the NAACP," in Franklin and Meier, eds., *Black Leaders of the Twentieth Century*, 95–97, Sherman, *Republican Party and Black America*, 193.

56. White to Roy Howard, 16 April 1930; White to Ludwell Denny, 18 April 1930; White to Rollo Ogden, 21 April 1930; White to David Lawrence, 23 April 1930; White to Elliott Thurston, 25 April 1930; White to Walter Lippmann, 26 April 1930, Box C–397, NAACP Papers.

57. White to Herbert Hoover, 12 April 1930, Box C–397, NAACP Papers.

58. *World* (New York), 22 March 1930.

59. Before President Coolidge appointed him, in 1925, to the Fourth Circuit Court, Parker had served as a special assistant to Attorney General Daugherty in 1923 and 1924, prosecuting the so-called war fraud cases of World War I. *New York Times*, 22 March 1930.

60. *Advance* (Elizabeth City, North Carolina), 21 March 1930, Box C–397, NAACP Papers.

61. For another view that Hoover picked Parker as part of a southern strategy linking competent, high-minded Republican whites and blacks, see Donald J. Lisio, *Hoover, Blacks & Lily-Whites: A Study of Southern Strategies* (Chapel Hill: University of North Carolina Press, 1985), chaps. 17, 18.

62. Arthur Capper to White, 29 March 1930, Box C–397, NAACP Papers.

63. See letters to White from Robert Wagner (D-N.Y.), Simeon D. Fess (R-Ohio), James Couzens (R-Mich.) Alben Barkley (D-Ky.), and others, in Parker's file, Box C–397, NAACP Papers.

64. *New York Times*, 12 April 1930; *Herald Tribune* (New York), 12 April 1930.

65. White to Pickens, 24 April 1930, Box C–71, NAACP Papers.

66. *Herald Tribune* (New York), 2 May 1930; *Evening World* (New York), 2 May 1930. With some justification Parker's supporters denied this charge; see the *Washington Post* 29 April, 3 May 1930.

67. *New York Times*, 1 May 1930.

68. *New York Times*, 6 May 1930. Charges that Parker's nomination

stemmed from an administration desire to solidify and expand Republican gains in the South did not begin with disclosure of the Dixon letter. See Heywood Broun's column in the *Telegram* (New York), 17 April 1930; Roy Wilkins's column in the *Call*, (Kansas City) 18 April 1930.

69. *New York Times*, 28 April 1920.

70. *New York Times*, 1 May 1930.

71. U.S., Congress, Senate, *Congressional Record*, 71st Cong., 2nd sess., 6 May 1930, 72, pt. 8: 8435.

72. *New York Times*, 2 May 1930; *Herald Tribune* (New York), 2 May 1930; *New York Times*, 5 May 1930; White to Henry Ashurst, 6 May 1930, Box C–398, NAACP Papers; *New York Times*, 8 May 1930.

73. White, memorandum, 7 May 1930, Box C–398, NAACP Papers.

74. A. Philip Randolph to White, 18 May 1930; Julian D. Rainey to White, 21 May 1930, Box C–398, NAACP Papers; Elmer Carter to White, 12 May 1930, Box C–398, NAACP Papers; *Amsterdam News* (New York), 23 May 1930; Frank R. Crosswaith, *The Commonwealth*, n.d., Box C–398, NAACP Papers. Among others who called the Parker defeat "epochal" were black journalists Alice Dunbar Nelson (*Courier* [Pittsburgh], 3 May 1930), C. A. Franklin (*Call* [Kansas City] 25 April 1930), and Du Bois (*Crisis*, 39 [June 1930], 196).

75. Mark Sullivan, *Herald Tribune* (New York), 8 May 1930.

76. Richard L. Watson, Jr., "The Defeat of Judge Parker; A Study in Pressure Groups and Politics," *Journal of American History* 50 (April 1963): 223.

77. Alpheus T. Mason, *The Supreme Court from Taft to Warren* (1958; reprint ed., New York: Norton, 1969), 74.

78. Hoover blamed Parker's defeat on Senate progressives and "Negro politicians," Lisio, *Hoover, Blacks & Lily-Whites*, 232. "Blacks had little to do with the decision," concluded Harvard Sitkoff, *A New Deal for Blacks: the Emergence of Civil Rights as a National Issue* (New York: Oxford University Press, 1978), 85. Most historians agree with Nancy J. Weiss that "the race issue was one of the factors" responsible for Parker's rejection. See Weiss, *Farewell to the Party of Lincoln: Black Politics in the Age of FDR* (Princeton: Princeton University Press, 1983), 17.

79. White, NAACP press release, 7 May 1930, Box C–398, NAACP Papers.

80. Harry E. Davis to Pickens, 13 October 1930, Box 1, Pickens Papers.

81. Pickens to Davis, 15 October 1930, Box 1, Pickens Papers.

82. *Crisis* 25 (November 1922): 25; Franklin, *From Slavery to Freedom*, 526. Shortridge's active support for the Dyer bill is described in Johnson, *Along This Way*, 370.

83. Wilkins to White, 1 July 1930, Box C–393, NAACP Papers.

84. Ibid.; Allen campaign pamphlet, n.d., Box C–393, NAACP Papers; Pickens, "The Value of the NAACP," *Crisis* 20 (June 1920): 90. Allen had not been "unfair or unfriendly" to the blacks in Kansas, wrote Wilkins, "except in one regard and that was his vote for Parker." *Call* (Kansas City), 1 August 1930.

85. Wilkins to White, 1 July 1930, Box C–393, NAACP Papers; *Star* (Kansas City, Mo.), 28 June 1930.

86. *Crisis* 37 (September 1930): 316.

87. Wilkins to White, 1 July 1930, Box C–393, NAACP Papers. See Wilkins, *Standing Fast*, 98.

88. Pickens to W. L. Hutcherson, 11 July 1930; Pickens to Wilkins, 11 July 1930, Box C–393, NAACP Papers; Wilkins to Pickens, 13 July 1930, Box C–397, NAACP Papers.

89. John H. Grant to White, 14 July 1930; White to Grant, 17 July 1930, Box

C–393, NAACP Papers. Wilkins, in an interview with the writer, corroborated Pickens's account of his Kansas tour. The *Call* (Kansas City), which covered and warmly supported Pickens's Kansas tour, described him as being "regarded by many people as the most effective speaker in the whole Negro race" (1 August 1930).

90. Pickens to White, 29, 30, 31 July 1930, Box C–393, NAACP Papers. "One Allen meeting captured and another routed on two successive days," Pickens wrote to Arthur Spingarn, "ought to be enough for Topeka," 31 July 1930, Arthur Spingarn Papers.

91. NAACP news release, 8 August 1930, Box C–393, NAACP Papers; see also the *Call* (Kansas City), 1, 8 August 1930.

92. White to Pickens, 4 August 1930, Box C–393, NAACP Papers.

93. Pickens, "The Negro Voter and Allen," *Crisis* 37 (October 1930): 357. The *Call* (Kansas City) estimated Allen's Negro support at twenty-seven percent, 8 August 1930.

94. *Gazette* (Emporia, Kansas) 5 November 1930.

95. Ibid.; For more on Henry Allen, Kansas politics, and the 1930 election, see Francis W. Schruben, *Kansas in Turmoil, 1930–1936* (Columbia, University of Missouri Press: 1969), 47, passim.

96. Pickens to White, 9 May 1931, Box C–72, NAACP Papers.

97. *Gazette* (Emporia, Kansas), 7 November 1930; Schruben, *Kansas in Turmoil*, 45–46.

98. In Philadelphia's seven predominantly Negro districts, Grundy received approximately 7,000 out of 35,000 votes cast, NAACP news release, 23 May 1930, Box C–398, NAACP Papers. For the McCullough campaign, see Walter White, "The Test in Ohio," *Crisis* 37 (November 1930): 373; Du Bois, *Crisis* 37 (December 1930): 425. For an analysis of the heavy Negro vote against Baird, see George L. Johnson to White, 11 November 1931; Paul Prayer to White, 4 November 1931, Box C–393, NAACP Papers. See also Moon, *Balance of Power*, 112–13. White, *Man Called White*, 112–13.

99. *Herald* (Newark), 24 October 1931.

100. White to Robert L. Vann, 5 November 1931, Box C–393, NAACP Papers.

101. *Grovey v. Townsend*, 295 U.S. 45 (1935); *Smith v. Allwright*, 321 U.S. 649 (1944); *Elmore v. Rice*, 72 F. Supp. 516 (E.D.S.C. 1947), affirmed 165 F. 2d 387 (C.A. 4th 1947). Parker also wrote an important decision in 1940, finding unconstitutional a racial wage differential for Norfolk, Virginia, public school teachers. See Franklin, *From Slavery to Freedom*, 404.

102. White, *Man Called White*, 114. Judge Parker's friend and neighbor in Charlotte, North Carolina, Harry Golden, editor of the *Carolina Israelite* and civil rights advocate, believed that Parker's defeat was a mistake. Parker's rejection, wrote Golden, "reveals in small part the agony of good men in the emerging South." *The Right Time: The Autobiography of Harry Golden* (New York: G. P. Putnam's Sons, 1969), 292. Parker proved to be an eminent jurist. He served at the Nuremberg War trials, and he was again considered for the Supreme Court before President Eisenhower chose Governor Earl Warren of California. In 1958, while attending a meeting in Washington, D.C., Parker collapsed into the arms of Clement Haynsworth, a colleague on the Fourth Circuit Court, and died soon after. See *New York Times*, 18 March 1958; *Washington Post*, 18 March 1958. When President Richard Nixon chose Haynsworth for the Supreme Court in 1969, a similar group of opponents blocked his nomination. See U.S. Congress, Senate, Judiciary Committee, Hearings on the Nomination of Clement F. Haynsworth, 91st Cong., September 1969.

103. Recalling the Parker defeat, Roy Wilkins wrote: "I was ecstatic. The victory made White a national figure, overshadowing Johnson himself. Earlier it had made a string of important legal victories. . . . And now it began to look quite adept at old-fashioned, brass-knuckle politics." Wilkins, *Standing Fast*, 92.

Chapter 6. Pickens, the Communists, and the Scottsboro Boys, 1926–1933

1. See Wilson Record's two works, *Race and Radicalism: The NAACP and the Communist Party in Conflict* (Ithaca: Cornell University Press, 1964) and *The Negro and the Communist Party* (Chapel Hill: University of North Carolina Press, 1951); Theodore Draper, *The Roots of American Communism* (New York: Viking, 1957); James Oneal and G. A. Werner, *American Communism*, 2d ed. rev. (New York: E. P. Dutton, 1947); Marc Naison, *Communists in Harlem during the Depression* (Urbana: University of Illinois Press, 1983).
2. Rudwick, *W. E. B. Du Bois*, 255.
3. *Crisis* 33 (November 1926): 8.
4. Pickens, "Lynching and Debt-Slavery," ACLU pamphlet, May 1921; copy in Pickens Vertical File. He was not only a charter member but, in the 1930s and 1940s, he was on the National Committee of the ACLU. Roger Baldwin (director of the ACLU) to the writer, 6 December 1969; B. W. Huebsch to Pickens, 6 January 1950, Box 2, Pickens Papers; Ida Epstein to Walter White, 8 May 1930, Box C–398, NAACP Papers.
5. Estimates of the number killed ranged from twenty-five to over 200. For a study of the Elaine, Arkansas, race riots, see Waskow, *From Race Riot to Sit-In*, 121–74.
6. Pickens, "Lynching and Debt-Slavery."
7. Pickens, "The American Congo," *The Nation* 112 (23 March 1921): 426.
8. Pickens, "Lynching and Debt-Slavery."
9. *Daily Worker*, 7 August 1926.
10. Lovett Fort-Whiteman to Pickens, 15 July 1926, Box 1, Pickens Papers.
11. Fort-Whiteman to Pickens, 1 September 1926, Box 1, Pickens Papers.
12. Pickens to Fort-Whiteman, 17 July 1926, Box 1, Pickens Papers.
13. Pickens, "Russia and the Negroes," *The Daily Worker*, 2 August 1926. Pickens would have lost his wager. Some southern whites, concerned with the loss of Negro cheap labor to the North, organized the Mississippi Welfare League in 1919, which took three Negroes on a tour of the South "and sent them back with glowing reports of good treatment, Negro prosperity, and amicable race relations. . . . [But] the attempt to reverse the migration met with scant success." Allan H. Spear, *Black Chicago: The Making of a Negro Ghetto, 1890–1920* (Chicago: University of Chicago Press, 1967), 203.
14. Fort-Whiteman to Pickens, 8 October 1926, Box 1, Pickens Papers.
15. Ibid.
16. Record, *Race and Radicalism*, 40.
17. Minutes of the NAACP board meeting, 11 October 1926, Box A–2; James Weldon Johnson to Pickens, 20 May 1929, Box 1, Pickens Papers; Pickens to Marshall, 28 August 1926, Pickens to Spingarn, 10 November 1926, Pickens to Storey, 13 November 1926, Box C–71, NAACP Papers.
18. *Crisis* 33 (January 1927): 128.
19. Pickens to the NAACP board, 14 February 1927, C–71, NAACP Papers.

20. Pickens, "Bolshevism as Seen by a Colored American," manuscript, 27 January 1927, Box 7, Pickens Papers.

21. For McKay's enthusiastic description of his Russian tour in 1923, see *Crisis*, 27 (December 1923): 61–65 and (January 1924): 115–118. See also Naison, *Communists in Harlem*, 16.

22. Pickens, "Bolshevism as Seen by a Colored American".

23. Manuscript of an address delivered on 21 August 1927, Box 7, Pickens Papers.

24. Record, in *Negro and the Communist Party*, 52, estimates that by 1928, less than two hundred Negroes had joined the Communist party.

25. Pickens was on the Advisory Committee, along with Earl Browder, of the "Hands Off China" Committee, which opposed European and American interference in the Chinese Nationalist Revolution. See Dorothy Borg, *American Policy and the Chinese Revolution, 1925–1928* (New York: Macmillan, 1947). For Pickens's, role in the "Hands Off China" movement, see Browder to Pickens, 3 March 1927; Pickens, manuscripts of "Our China War" and "The War Makers," 1927; Pickens to President Coolidge, 13 May 1927; Pickens, manuscript of a speech for the Hands Off China rally at Union Square, New York, 1927, Box 7, Pickens Papers.

26. See Record, *Race and Radicalism*, 52–56; Cruse, *Crisis of the Negro Intellectual*, 141.

27. Interview with William Patterson, New York, 24 December 1969.

28. Roger Baldwin to James Weldon Johnson, 30 April 1929; Johnson to Pickens, 20 May 1929; Pickens to Johnson, 27 May 1929, Box C–71; minutes of the NAACP board meeting, 13 May 1929, Box A–2, NAACP Papers.

29. Pickens to the NAACP board, n.d., Box C–71, NAACP Papers.

30. Pickens, ANP news release, Series 5, n.d., Box 2, Pickens Papers.

31. Ibid., Series 9.

32. Ibid., Series 11.

33. Pickens, "Fight on Fascism," manuscript, 1939, Box 3, Pickens Papers. William Patterson, in an interview with the writer, corroborated the essentials of Pickens's account.

34. Pickens, ANP release, Series 10, n.d., Box 2, Pickens Papers.

35. See *Daily Worker*, 30 July 1929, 3 October 1933; *Liberator* (St. Louis), 25 April 1931; *New Masses* 4 (March 1929): 26, 5 (October 1929), 28.

36. Interview with Patterson, New York, 24 December 1969.

37. Minutes of the NAACP board meeting, 8 December 1930, Box A–3, NAACP Papers. For a discussion of the NAACP and the Parker appointment, see chap. 5.

38. For a detailed study of the Scottsboro case, see Dan T. Carter, *Scottsboro: A Tragedy of the American South* (Baton Rouge: Louisiana State University Press, 1969). For an account highly critical of the NAACP's role in the case, see Hugh T. Murray, Jr., "The NAACP Versus the Communist Party: The Scottsboro Cases, 1931–1932," *Phylon* 28 (3rd quarter, 1967): 276–87; see also Sitkoff, *New Deal for Blacks*, 148–49.

39. Ibid., 52; *Daily Worker*, 10 April 1931.

40. *Daily Worker*, 16 April 1931.

41. Pickens's letter, written from Kansas City, Missouri, was reprinted in the *Daily Worker*, 24 April 1931.

42. Robert Minor to Pickens, 23 April 1931, Box 8, Pickens Papers.

43. Pickens's column, "Pickens Says," which appeared in the *Amsterdam News*, 29 April 1931.

44. *Daily Worker*, 24 April 1931.
45. Ibid., 29 April 1931.
46. Minor to Pickens, 11 May 1931, Box 8, Pickens Papers; Carter, *Scottsboro*, 70.
47. *New York News*, 4 May 1931.
48. *Daily Worker*, 5 May 1931.
49. Mary W. Ovington to Pickens, 30 April 1931, quoted in the minutes of the NAACP board meeting, 11 May 1931, Box A–3, NAACP Papers.
50. Minutes of the NAACP board meeting, 11 May 1931, Box A–3, NAACP Papers.
51. Barnett to Pickens, 14 September 1931, Box 1, Pickens Papers.
52. Carter, *Scottsboro*, 88–89.
53. Claude Barnett to Pickens, 14 September 1931, Box 1, Pickens Papers.
54. Beginning with the Pink Franklin case, in 1910, the NAACP had resorted to this tactic on several occasions; see Kellogg, *NAACP*, 57, passim.
55. Robert Minor to Pickens, 11 May 1931, Box 1, Pickens Papers.
56. Minor to Pickens, 23 April 1931, Box 1, Pickens Papers.
57. Ibid.
58. White to the NAACP board, 15 May 1931; quoted in Carter, *Scottsboro*, 72.
59. Du Bois to Arthur Spingarn, 11 August 1931, Box C–72, NAACP Papers.
60. Pickens to White, 18, 21 May 1931, C–72, NAACP Papers.
61. Pickens, "The Scottsboro Cases," manuscript, 24 October 1934, Box 7, Pickens Papers.
62. *Courier* (Pittsburgh), 13 June 1931.
63. White, *Man Called White*, 130; Carter, *Scottsboro*, 57, passim.
64. *Daily Worker*, 10 June 1931; *Times* (Chattanooga), 8 June 1931.
65. *Daily Worker*, 10 June 1931.
66. Ibid.
67. Myrdal, *American Dilemma*, 2:782.
68. Pickens, ANP release, 20 August 1931, Box 7, Pickens Papers.
69. Carter, *Scottsboro*, 123–26.
70. Pickens, ANP release, 20 August 1931, Box 7, Pickens Papers.
71. Pickens, letter to the editor of the *Journal and Guide* (Norfolk, Va.), 8 August 1931.
72. See Roy Wilkins to Charles H. Houston, 6 September 1933, Box C–229, NAACP Papers.
73. Minutes of the NAACP board meeting, 4 January 1932, Box A–3, NAACP Papers. For Communist disruptions of NAACP "Scottsboro" meetings, see Pickens to White, 14 June, 5 November 1931, 17 March 1933, Box C–72, NAACP Papers.
74. T. T. McKinney to Robert Bagnall, 5 March 1932, Box C–72, NAACP Papers.
75. Pickens to White, 12 June 1933, Box C–72, NAACP Papers.
76. Pickens to White, 30 October 1934, Box C–72, NAACP Papers.
77. Minutes of the NAACP board meeting, 19 April 1933, Box A–3. For a complete statement of the Association's defense of its actions, see minutes of the NAACP board meeting, 4 January 1932, Box A–3, NAACP Papers.
78. McKinney to Bagnall, 5 March 1932, Box C–72, NAACP Papers.
79. Wilkins to George Schuyler, 15 July 1932, Box C–229, NAACP Papers.
80. Joel Spingarn to Pickens, 9 June 1933, Box 1, Pickens Papers.
81. Record, *Negro and the Communist Party*, 113.

82. Summary of a report on the Second Amenia Conference, the Publicity Committee to W. E. B. Du Bois, 1 September 1933, Box C–229, NAACP Papers. See Wolter's chapter, "The Amenia Conference, 1933," in *Negroes and the Great Depression*.

83. In addition to Pickens's writings previously mentioned, see "Americanism," *Crisis* 19 (April 1920): 332; "The Negro and the Community," *Opportunity* 4 (August 1924): 229; "The Menace of Philanthropy," manuscript, 1931, Box 8, Pickens Papers.

84. Du Bois, "Youth and Age at Amenia," *Crisis* 40 (October 1933): 226.

85. Pickens, "The Scottsboro Cases."

86. Louis L. Redding to Roy Wilkins, 2 September 1933, Box C–229, NAACP Papers.

87. See Rudwick, *W. E. B. Du Bois*, 268–271. For Pickens's dismissal from the field secretaryship, see chap. 7.

88. Summary of a report of the Amenia Conference Publicity Committee.

89. Pickens, "International Labor Defense Tells 2000-Mile Lie!" manuscript, ANP release, 1934, Box 7, Pickens Papers.

90. Pickens, letter to the editor, *Journal and Guide* (Norfolk, Va.) 8 August 1931.

91. Pickens, "The Fight Against Fascism," manuscript, 1939, Box 3, Pickens Papers.

92. Pickens, "New Goals in Negro Education," manuscript, August 1933, Box 8, Pickens Papers.

93. Pickens to Walter White, 28 July 1932, Box C–72, Pickens Papers.

94. Carter, *Scottsboro*, 411, passim; Sitkoff, *New Deal for Blacks*, 229.

95. See chap. 9.

Chapter 7. New Deal or "Old" Deal? 1933–1940

1. Pickens, "A Century of Negro Progress," manuscript of a speech delivered at the Chicago's World Fair, 3 August 1934, Box 8, Pickens Papers. The fair began in 1933.

2. Meier and Rudwick, "Negro Protest at the Chicago World's Fair, 1933–1934. *Journal of the Illinois State Historical Society* 59 (Summer 1966): 161–71.

3. Pickens, "A Century of Progress." For a brief summary, see Leslie H. Fishel, Jr., "The Negro in the New Deal Era," *Wisconsin Magazine of History* 48 (Winter 1964): 111–26. For a more comprehensive study of certain aspects of the relationship between blacks and the New Deal, see Wolters, *Negroes and the Great Depression*; Allen F. Kifer, "The Negro under the New Deal, 1933–1941" (Ph.D. diss., University of Wisconsin, 1961); Richard Sterner, *The Negro's Share: A Study of Income, Consumption, Housing and Public Assistance* (New York: Harper, 1943); Nancy J. Weiss, *Farewell to the Party of Lincoln: Black Politics in the Age of FDR* (Princeton: Princeton University Press, 1983); Sitkoff, *New Deal for Blacks*; John B. Kirby, *Black Americans in the Roosevelt Era: Liberalism and Race* (Knoxville: University of Tennessee Press, 1980).

4. Pickens, "I Told You So," manuscript of an ANP release, September 1933, Box 8, Pickens Papers. Ickes's "obscure" appointee was Clark Foreman, of Georgia, a director of the Julius Rosenwald Fund, which had contributed heavily to Negro school construction in the South. Foreman brought with him Robert C. Weaver, a black economist, who became a leading figure in the New Deal's so-called "Black Cabinet" of Negro advisers to the various government

departments. See Arthur M. Schlesinger, Jr., *The Age of Roosevelt: The Politics of Upheaval* (Houghton Mifflin, Boston, 1960), 436–532; Franklin, *From Slavery to Freedom*, 530–34.

5. See Weiss, *Farewell to the Party of Lincoln*, 51.

6. Pickens, "NRA—Negro Removal Act?" *World Tomorrow* 16 (28 September 1933): 539–40. This view was shared by most black leaders, including Roosevelt's supporters. See Wolters, *Negroes and the Great Depression*, 132–34, 145–46; Kifer, "The Negro under the New Deal," 226–27.

7. Pickens, "NRA—Negro Removal Act?" *World Tomorrow* 16 (28 September 1933).

8. Pickens, "Blue Eagle Medicine Men," ANP release, n.d., Box 8, Pickens Papers.

9. Ibid. For a discussion of the NRA codes, the "Blue Eagle" and Hugh Johnson, see Schlesinger, *The Age of Roosevelt: The Coming of the New Deal* (Boston: Houghton Mifflin, 1959), 103–18. "Johnson, in transforming a government agency into a religious experience," Schlesinger wrote, "had put over all too well a millennial vision of rising wages, spreading work, and six million new jobs by Labor Day."

10. Pickens, "Blue Eagle Medicine Men."

11. Pickens, "I Am with Henry Ford," ANP release, n.d., Box 8, Pickens Papers.

12. See Schlesinger, *Coming of the New Deal*, 486–87.

13. Pickens, "Something for Nothing," ANP release, n.d., Box 8, Pickens Papers.

14. Ibid.

15. See Schlesinger, *Politics of Upheaval*, 111–17.

16. Pickens, "Upton Sinclair and California," ANP release, n.d., Box 9, Pickens Papers.

17. Schlesinger, *Politics of Upheaval*, 116–23.

18. Pickens to Walter White, 14 June 1934, Box C–72, NAACP Papers.

19. Pickens to White, 19 February 1935, Box C–72, Pickens Papers.

20. John P. Murchison to White, 23 October 1934, Box C–73, NAACP Papers. The first project for blacks—Aberdeen Gardens in Newport News, Virginia—was not opened until the winter of 1936. See Paul K. Conkin, *Tomorrow a New World: The New Deal Community Program* (Ithaca, Cornell University Press, 1959), 200–201, passim.

21. John A. Salmond, "The Civilian Conservation Corps and the Negro," *Journal of American History* 52 (June 1965): 75–88.

22. See Robert L. Zangrando, "The NAACP and a Federal Anti-Lynching Bill, 1934–1940," *Journal of Negro History* 50 (April 1965): 106–17.

23. Pickens to White, 28 February 1934, Box C–72, NAACP Papers.

24. Eleanor Roosevelt to White, 2 May 1934, 23 November 1934, Box C–73, NAACP Papers.

25. Zangrando, "Federal Anti-Lynching Bill," 108–9.

26. Pickens to Franklin D. Roosevelt, 28 October 1934, Box 2, Pickens Papers.

27. Pickens to the NAACP home office, 27 November 1934, Box C–72, NAACP Papers.

28. Pickens to the NAACP home office, 25 November 1934, Box C–73, NAACP Papers.

29. Pickens to the NAACP home office, 27 November 1934, Box C–72, NAACP Papers.

30. White's recollection of an interview with Roosevelt, Spring 1935, in *Man Called White*, 169–70.
31. Eleanor Roosevelt to White, 8 May 1935, Box C–73, NAACP Papers.
32. *Defender* (Chicago), 2 May 1936.
33. Harold Ickes to Pickens, 5 August 1936; Pickens to Ickes, 22 August 1936, Box 8, Pickens Papers.
34. Pickens, in *Louisiana Weekly*, 29 February 1936, Pickens Vertical File.
35. Pickens, in *Journal and Guide* (Norfolk), 13 April 1935. For another reference to *Grovey v. Townshend*, see chap. 5. For a discussion of *Norris v. Alabama*, see Carter, *Scottsboro*, 319–24.
36. Pickens, in *Louisiana Weekly*, 29 February 1936.
37. Pickens, in supporting Henry Ford's opposition to NRA codes, had anticipated the Court's ruling against NRA. See Pickens, "I Am with Henry Ford."
38. See Schlesinger, *Politics of Upheaval*, 287. For Roosevelt's plan, after his reelection in 1936, to liberalize the Supreme Court, see William E. Leuchtenburg, *Franklin D. Roosevelt and the New Deal, 1932–1940* (New York: Harper, Torchbook, 1963), 231–36.
39. Pickens, in *Louisiana Weekly*, 29 February 1936.
40. John P. Davis, "Black Inventory of the New Deal," *Crisis* 42 (May 1935): 141–42; also see the summary of Davis's report to the NAACP, "TVA Projects Called of Little Benefit to Negroes," NAACP news release, 4 June 1935, Box C–416, NAACP Papers.
41. Those black papers supporting Roosevelt were the *Courier* (Pittsburgh), the *Afro-American* (Baltimore), the *Journal and Guide* (Norfolk), the *Amsterdam News*, and the *Independent* (Philadelphia); the *Defender* (Chicago), Argus (St. Louis), and the *Call* (Kansas City) opposed him. James H. Brewer, "Robert Lee Vann, Democrat or Republican: An Exponent of Loose-Leaf Politics," *Negro History Bulletin* 21 (February 1958): 103.
42. White, "An Estimate of the 1936 Vote," *Crisis* 43 (February 1936): 46.
43. Pickens, "National Democratic Party Intolerable," ANP release, Spring 1936, Box 2, Pickens Papers.
44. Pickens, "National Democratic Administration and the Negro," ANP release, Spring 1936, Box 2, Pickens Papers.
45. Robert Vann to White, 1 July 1936, copy in Box 2, Pickens Papers.
46. Brewer, "Robert Lee Vann, Democrat or Republican," 102; John Hope Franklin, *From Slavery to Freedom*, 527. Vann switched back again in 1940 and supported Willkie; Kirby, *Black Americans in the Roosevelt Era*, 138.
47. Pickens, Robert L. Vann's 'Soothing Syrup,'" ANP release, n.d., Box 8, Pickens Papers.
48. Vann to Pickens, 22 January 1936; Pickens to Vann, n.d., Box 2, Pickens Papers.
49. Vann to White, 1 July 1936, Box 2, Pickens Papers.
50. When Robert Bagnall left the NAACP in 1933, his post as director of branches was not filled. The Association had two field secretaries at the time—Pickens and Daisy Lampkin. In September 1935, "in order to avoid the confusion of having two field secretaries," Pickens was given the title director of branches. His duties and salary remained unchanged. Minutes of the NAACP board meeting, 9 September 1935, Box A–3, NAACP Papers.
51. White to Vann, 8 July 1936, copy in Box 2, Pickens Papers.
52. Minutes of the NAACP board meeting, 11 October 1937, Box A–3, NAACP Papers.

53. White to Pickens, 8 July 1936, Box 2, Pickens Papers.
54. Pickens to White, 10 July 1936, Box 2, Pickens Papers.
55. Pickens, in the *Tribune* (Washington), 14 July 1936, copy in Pickens Vertical File.
56. See James A. Harrell, "Negro Leadership in the Election Year, 1936," *Journal of Southern History* 34 (November 1968): 546–64.
57. Moon, *Balance of Power*, 18. See Weiss, *Farewell*, 168, 178–80, 205.
58. "Editorial," *Crisis* 43 (December 1936): 369.
59. Pickens, "Reflection on the Election," *Argus* (St. Louis), 13 November 1936, Pickens Vertical File.
60. Elvena Miller, "Making Democracy Work," *Crisis* 44 (September 1937): 276.
61. Pickens, "Smashing Tradition in West Virginia," *Crisis* 44 (May 1937): 141.
62. Pickens to White, 4 April 1938, Box C–73, NAACP Papers.
63. Pickens to the NAACP office, 1 November 1937, Box C–73, NAACP Papers.
64. Pickens to Roy Wilkins, 20 February, 23 February 1937, Box C–73, NAACP Papers; Pickens, "Smashing Tradition," 141.
65. Pickens to the NAACP home office, 9 May 1937, Box C–73, NAACP Papers. The speech originally appeared as "Unthanked Workers for Democracy," *World Tomorrow* 9 (April 1926): 119.
66. See Lisio, *Hoover, Blacks & Lily-Whites*, 266.
67. Pickens to White, 7 June 1937, July 19, 1937, Box C–73, NAACP Papers.
68. See S. J. Lake to Pickens, 11 May 1939; E. K. Burlew to Pickens, 25 May 1939, W. J. Trent to Thurgood Marshall, 1 June 1939; Harold Ickes to Pickens, 15 June 1939; W. B. Cook to Frank Maynars, 25 May 1939; Lake to Construction Engineer, Bureau of Reclamation, 26 May 1939, Box C–304, NAACP Papers; "Editorial," *Crisis* 47 (November 1940): 343.
69. Pickens to White, 4 January 1938, Box C–73, NAACP Papers.
70. Wilkins to Pickens, 29 May 1937, Box C–73; minutes of the NAACP meeting, 12 April 1937, Box A–3, NAACP Papers; Tracey E. Griffin to Elvena Miller, director, Seattle Public Forums, 6 April 1938, copy in Box C–73, NAACP Papers.
71. Elvena Miller, "Making Democracy Work," 276.
72. Pickens to White, 4 April 1938, Box C–73, NAACP Papers.
73. Moon, *Balance of Power*, 32.
74. "Editorial," *Crisis* 47 (November 1940): 343.
75. See Weiss, *Farewell to the Party of Lincoln*, 179–81, 267, 287, 299.
76. Minutes of the NAACP meeting, 13 March 1939, Box A–3, NAACP Papers.
77. "Editorial," *Crisis* 47 (November 1940): 343.
78. Thomas E. Dewey to Pickens, 26 July 1940, Box 2; Emmett J. Scott to Pickens, 23 August 1940; Pickens to Claude Barnett, 16 September 1940, Pickens to Raymond Buell, 30 October 1940, Box 3, Pickens Papers.
79. Pickens to White, 10 September 1940, Box 384, NAACP Papers.
80. Leuchtenburg, *Roosevelt and the New Deal*, 319–21. Pickens was an early advocate of intervention against Germany. See chap. 8.
81. *Afro-American* (Baltimore), 11 September 1940; Pickens to White, 20 September 1940, Box 384, NAACP Papers.
82. Pickens, ANP release, 11 September 1940; Pickens to White, 20 September 1940, Box 384, NAACP Papers.

83. Colored Citizens Committee for Willkie advertisement in the *Tribune* (Washington), 28 September 1940, Box 384, NAACP Papers.
84. White to Pickens, 12 September 1940, Box 384, NAACP Papers.
85. Roy Garvin to White, 27 September 1940, Box 384, NAACP Papers.
86. William H. Hastie to Arthur Spingarn, 23 September 1940, Box 384, NAACP Papers.
87. Minutes of the NAACP board meeting, 14 December 1936, Box A–3, NAACP Papers.
88. Minutes of the NAACP board meeting, 11 October 1937, Box A–3, NAACP Papers.
89. Pickens to the NAACP board, 25 October 1937, Box 2, Pickens Papers.
90. Statement of the Committee on Administration's ruling of 24 September in the minutes of the NAACP board meeting, 14 October 1940, Box A–3, NAACP Papers.
91. Pickens to L. Pearl Mitchell, 30 September 1940, Box 384; Pickens to White, 23 May 1941, Box 247, NAACP Papers.
92. NAACP news release, 2 October 1940, Box 384, NAACP Papers.
93. Pickens to John Martin, 26 September 1940, Box 3, Pickens Papers.
94. Mitchell to White and Wilkins, 11 October 1940, Box 384, NAACP Papers.
95. Grant Reynolds to Pickens, 30 September 1940, Box 384, NAACP Papers.
96. Pickens to Reynolds, 2 October 1940, Box 384, NAACP Papers.
97. Mitchell to White and Wilkins, 11 October 1940, Box 384, NAACP Papers.
98. *Tribune* (Washington), 3 October 1940; *New York News*, 31 August 1940; see Wilkins's critical editorial on Willkie, *Crisis* 47 (September 1940): 279.

Chapter 8. A War on Two Fronts, 1934–1942

1. Erna Kalisch to Pickens, 12 April 1933; Arnold Kalisch to Pickens, 7 January 1937. Pickens, who was fluent in German, had been a Germanophile, having visited there four times—in 1913, 1927, 1929, and 1932. "The Germans are singularly without color prejudice," he had written in 1929, "and know how to do business with a fellow of any race." (ANP release, Series 12, 1929, Box 2, Pickens Papers.) As late as July 1932, he believed that "All-told, the Germans are just about the most civilized and dependable people I've met anywhere yet." (Pickens to White, 28 July 1932, Box 8, Pickens Papers). Even after Hitler ("this monstrous thing in Germany") came to power, Pickens found it hard to accept "that the majority of the German people are, heart and soul, behind Hitler's plans." (Pickens, "Hitler's Challenge to Human Brotherhood," text of a radio address, delivered 16 September 1934, New York, Box 8, Pickens Papers).
2. Pickens, "Hitler's Challenge to Human Brotherhood," text of a radio address, delivered 16 September 1934, New York, Box 8, Pickens Papers.
3. For black opposition to intervention in 1940, see Sitkoff, *New Deal for Blacks*, 301.
4. Robert A. Rosenstone, "The Men of the Abraham Lincoln Battalion," *Journal of American History* 54 (September 1967): 334.
5. Pickens, "What I Saw in Spain," *Crisis* 45 (October 1938): 321.
6. Pickens, "Those British Are No Sissies," ANP release, n.d., Box 3, Pickens Papers.

7. See Myrdal, *American Dilemma* 755, passim; Lester M. Jones, "The Editorial Policy of Negro Newspapers of 1977–1918 as Compared with that of 1942–1942," *Journal of Negro History* 29 (January 1944): 24–31; Richard M. Dalfiume, *Desegregation of the U.S. Armed Forces: Fighting on Two Fronts, 1939–1953* (Columbia: University of Missouri Press, 1969), 111–13.

8. "Views and Reviews," *Courier* (Pittsburgh), 26 October 1940.

9. Metz T. P. Lochard, "Negroes and Defense," *Nation* 152 (4 January 1941): 14–16.

10. James L. H. Peck, "When Do We Fly?" *Crisis* 47 (December 1940): 376. For many black leaders' ambivalent support for the war effort, even after Pearl Harbor, see Phillip McGuire, "Desegregation of the Armed Forces: Black Leadership, Protest and World War II," *Journal of Negro History* 88 (Spring 1983): 153.

11. *Crisis* 45 (May 1938): 145.

12. "Air Pilots," *Crisis* 46 (August 1939): 247.

13. "Lynching and Liberty," *Crisis* 47 (July 1940): 209.

14. White to Pickens, 9 April 1935, Box 2, Pickens Papers.

15. Ibid.

16. Pickens to White, 12 April 1935, Box 2, Pickens Papers.

17. Pickens to Mary Ovington, 15 April 1935; Pickens to Roy Wilkins, 20 December 1939, Box 2, Pickens Papers.

18. Daisy Lampkin to Pickens, 8 February 1936, Box 2, Pickens Papers.

19. J. A. Gregg to Joel E. Spingarn, 9 March 1936, copy in Box 2, Pickens Papers.

20. Ovington to Pickens, 18 February 1936, Box 2, Pickens Papers.

21. Archibald S. Pinkett to Pickens, 21 June 1937; Martha Gruening to Pickens, 15 September 1936; Carl Murphy to Pickens, 27 October 1937; Sidney Redmond to Pickens, 18 July 1938, Box 2, Pickens Papers.

22. Minutes of the NAACP board meeting, 11 December 1939, Box A–3, NAACP Papers; Pickens to Wilkins, 20 December 1939, Box 2, Pickens Papers.

23. Sidney Redmond to the NAACP board, 4 December 1939, Box 384, NAACP Papers.

24. Minutes of the NAACP meeting, 8 September 1941, Box A–4, NAACP papers; interview with Wilkins, December 1969.

25. Record of the business session of the NAACP annual meeting in Philadelphia, 21 June 1940, Box X–21, NAACP Papers.

26. Ibid. Board Director Isadore Martin held the same view. Martin to Pickens, 4 November 1939, Box 3, Pickens Papers. See Record, *Race and Radicalism*, 97.

27. Record of the business session, NAACP annual meeting, 21 June 1940, Box X–21, NAACP Papers.

28. Ibid. Emphasis added.

29. Interview with Wilkins; minutes of the NAACP board meeting, 8 September 1941, Box A–4, NAACP Papers.

30. Interview with Wilkins; John Haynes Holmes to Pickens, 18 December 1940; Thomas L. Griffith, Jr. to the Spingarn Award Committee, 10 October 1940; Pickens to Weaver, 19 November 1940, Box 3, Pickens Papers; Archie Weaver to the NAACP board; copy in the minutes of the board meeting, 8 September 1941, Box A–4, NAACP Papers; George Schuyler in the *Courier* (Pittsburgh); 15 January 1940.

31. Pickens to Weaver, 19 November 1940, Box 3, Pickens Papers.

32. Helen Boardman, "The U.S. Treasury Takes a Step," *Opportunity* 19 (August 1941): 238–39.

33. Minutes of the NAACP board meeting, 12 May 1941, Box A–4; NAACP news release, 16 May 1941, Box 247, NAACP Papers; *New York Times*, 13 May 1941.

34. 10 May 1941, copy in Box 247, NAACP Papers.

35. *Call and Post* (Cleveland), 24 May 1941; copy in Box 247, NAACP Papers.

36. White to Pickens, 14 April 1942, Box 247, NAACP Papers.

37. Pickens to the NAACP board, 13 April 1942, Box 8, Pickens Papers.

38. White, "It's Our Country, Too," *Saturday Evening Post*, 213 (14 December 1940): 27, 68.

39. *Crisis* 49 (January 1942): 36.

40. Minutes of the NAACP board meeting, 8 December 1941, Box A–4, NAACP Papers.

41. Minutes of the NAACP board meeting, 14 November 1941, Box A–4, NAACP Papers. See Sitkoff, *New Deal for Blacks*, 324–25.

42. See chapter 2.

43. Pickens, in "Views and Reviews," *Courier* (Pittsburgh), 6 September 1943.

44. Pickens to Herbert Hoover, 2 April 1930, Box C–71, NAACP Papers.

45. Although there was improvement at Negro military camps, conditions were far from satisfactory. See Dalfiume, *Desegregation of the U.S. Armed Forces*, 67, 84.

46. Pickens, "Pursuit Squadron," *Amsterdam News* (New York), 31 January 1942. Emphasis added.

47. Minutes of the NAACP board meeting, 9 February 1942, Box A–4, NAACP Papers.

48. Ovington to Pickens, 25 February 1942, Box 8, Pickens Papers.

49. William E. Taylor to Pickens, 26 February 1942, Box 8, Pickens Papers.

50. Frederick Patterson to Pickens, 3 March 1942, Box 8, Pickens Papers.

51. Patterson, letter to the editor, *Courier* (Pittsburgh), 21 March 1942.

52. Prattis, "The Horizon," *Courier* (Pittsburgh), 7 March 1942.

53. C. F. Richardson, "The Mirror," *Defender* (Houston), 28 February 1942, copy in Box 247, NAACP Papers.

54. "National Grapevine," *Defender* (Chicago), 21 March 1941.

55. Text of Pickens's statement to the board, 13 April 1942, Box 8, Pickens Papers.

56. Minutes of the NAACP board meeting, 13 April 1942, Box A–4, NAACP Papers.

57. Pickens to Arthur Spingarn, 14 April 1942; Spingarn to Pickens, 16 April 1942, Box 247, NAACP Papers.

58. Minutes of the NAACP board meeting, 11 May 1942, Box A–4, NAACP Papers.

59. Pickens to White, 27 May 1942, copy in the minutes of the NAACP board meeting, 8 June 1942, Box A–4, NAACP Papers.

60. Dabney, "The Negroes and the War," *Times-Dispatch* (Richmond, Va.), 26 April, 2 May 1942; "Nearer and Nearer the Precipice," *Atlantic Monthly* 171 (January 1943): 100.

61. For the black press's critical response to Dabney's editorials, see Dalfiume, *Desegregation of the U.S. Armed Forces*, 125. Pickens's letter to Dabney appeared in the *Times-Dispatch* (Richmond, Va.), 17 May 1942.

62. See Dalfiume, *Desegregation of the U.S. Armed Forces*, 110–111; Ottley, *New World A-Coming*, 322–42.

63. "Pickens Should Name the Traitors," *Journal and Guide* (Norfolk), 23 May 1942; copy in Box 247, NAACP Papers.
64. T. J. Sellers, "The Passing of Dean Pickens," *Afro-American* (Baltimore), 6 June 1942.
65. Rudwick, *W.E.B. Du Bois*, 282; Broderick, *W.E.B. Du Bois*, 168; Wolters, *Negroes and the Great Depression*, 236–43.
66. Du Bois to the NAACP board, 26 June 1934; copy in the minutes of the board meeting, 9 July 1934, Box A–3, NAACP Papers; see Rudwick, *W.E.B. Du Bois*, 278.
67. Pickens to Spingarn, 12 April 1934; Pickens to Du Bois, 16 June 1934, copies in Box C–72, NAACP Papers.
68. Pickens to White, 17 June 1934, Box C–72, NAACP Papers.
69. Minutes of the NAACP board meeting, 8 July 1934, Box A–3, NAACP Papers.
70. Minutes of the NAACP board meeting, 8 June 1942, Box A–4, NAACP Papers.
71. White to Pickens, 15 June 1942, Box 247, NAACP Papers.
72. Pickens to White, 19, 20 June 1942, Box 247, NAACP Papers.
73. Pickens to Holmes, 5 March 1942, Box 2, Pickens Papers.
74. "Pickens Should Name the Traitors."
75. White to Pickens, 21 May 1941, Box 247, NAACP Papers.
76. *Afro-American* (Baltimore), 6 June 1942.
77. Isadore Martin to Pickens, 18 April 1942, Box 8, Pickens Papers; *Daily Worker*, 28 June 1942. Roy Wilkins had reported to the board that "the overwhelming sentiment among colored people interested in the National Defense program" was to accept segregated facilities for training Negro officers, rather than the alternative of having no Negro officers at all. Minutes of the NAACP board meeting, 9 December 1940, Box A–4, NAACP Papers.
78. White, *Man Called White*, 193; Herbert Garfinkel, *When Negroes March: The March on Washington Movement in the Organizational Politics for FEPC* (Glencoe, Ill.: Free Press, 1959), 65–67; Dalfiume, *Desegregation of the U.S. Armed Forces*, 118–21; Sitkoff, *New Deal for Blacks*, 322; Kirby, *Black Americans in the Roosevelt Era*, 74.

Chapter 9. The Last Battle, 1943–1954

1. Pickens, "The American Negro Participates in War Finance," *Opportunity* 23 (Winter 1945): 25.
2. Pickens to Claude Barnett, 10 May 1949, Box 3, Pickens Papers.
3. Pickens to Holmes, 5 March 1942, Box 3, Pickens Papers. For works that make brief references to Pickens's encounter with the Dies committee, see Goodman, *Committee*, 140–44; Ogden, *Dies Committee*, 274–75; Gellerman, *Martin Dies*, 254; Sitkoff, *New Deal for Blacks*, 119–20.
4. Quoted in Ogden, *Dies Committee*, 269.
5. U.S., Congress, Senate, *Congressional Record*, 78th Cong., 1st sess., 1 February 1943, 89, pt. 1: 475–83; hereafter cited as *C.R.*
6. Goodman, *Committee*, 140; Ogden, *Dies Committee*, 274; *The New York Times*, 3 February 1943; "Victims of Mr. Dies," *New Republic* 107 (12 October 1943): 468–69.
7. *C.R.*, 1 February 1943, 484.
8. Ibid., 486.

9. Ibid., 5 February 1943, 646–47; Pickens, "Against War," copy of an address delivered in New York on 29 September 1933, Box 9, Pickens Papers.
10. C.R., 5 February 1943, 647; H.R. 1648.
11. Ibid.
12. Ibid., 648.
13. Ibid., 656. *The New York Times*, 6 February 1943, Goodman, *The Committee*, 141, and Ogden, *Dies Committee*, 275, reported incorrectly that the House defeated Hendricks's original amendment by a vote of 146:153. That vote was on a motion to table the amendment. The House never voted on the original amendment to cut off Treasury funds to all of the 39 accused of subversion. See C.R., 656.
14. Pickens to Houghteling, 15 May 1946, Box 3, Pickens Papers; C.R., 8 February 1943, 703.
15. Ibid., 702.
16. Ibid.
17. C.R., 700–701.
18. C.R., 8 February 1943, 702.
19. Ibid., 705.
20. Ibid., 707.
21. Ibid., 714.
22. Ibid., 9 February 1943, 734; H. Res. 105.
23. Ibid., 737.
24. Ibid.
25. Ibid.
26. Ibid.
27. Ibid., 742.
28. Pickens to Charles W. Adams, 4 July 1944, Box 6, Pickens Papers; interview with his daughter, Harriet Ida Pickens, July 1968.
29. *Call* (Oklahoma), 12 February 1943; copy in Box 6, Pickens Papers.
30. Typed statement, n.d., Box 9, Pickens Papers. See Lamont, *Trial of Elizabeth Gurley Flynn*, appendix.
31. Typed statement, n.d., Box 9, Pickens Papers.
32. See Lovett, *All Our Years*, 297–309; Goodman, *Committee*, 36, 146–51. The other members of the five-man committee were Democrats Clinton P. Anderson (N.Mex.) and Albert Gore (Tenn.) and Republicans Frank B. Keefe (Wis.) and D. Lane Powers (N.J.).
33. *Times-Dispatch* (Richmond, Va.), 6 February 1943.
34. *New York Times*, 13 February 1943.
35. R. R. Wright, Jr. to Judge John H. Kerr, 16 March 1943, copy in Box 6, Pickens Papers. For Pickens's clash with Wright, see pp. 93–94.
36. Minutes of the NAACP board meeting, 8 February 1943, Box A–4, NAACP Papers.
37. C.R., 10 February 1943, 844.
38. Pickens to Adams, 4 July 1944, Box 6, Pickens Papers.
39. Pickens to Houghteling, 15 May 1946, Box 6, Pickens Papers.
40. Pickens, "The American Negro Participates in War Finance," *Opportunity* 23 (Winter 1945): 24–25.
41. Pickens, "Position Description: Director of the Interracial Section, Savings Bonds Division, United States Treasury Department," manuscript, n.d., Box 3, Pickens Papers.
42. Martha Goldman, "Report of the Interracial Section for 1943," n.d., a copy in Box 6, Pickens Papers.

43. Pickens, "Some Notes from the War Finance Record," manuscript, n.d., Box 9, Pickens Papers.
44. Pickens, "American Negro Participates in War Finance."
45. Ibid.
46. Ibid.
47. See Ottley, *New World A-Coming*, 306–42; Dalfiume, *Desegregation of the U.S. Armed Forces*, 110–11.
48. Pickens, "The American Negro and His Country in World War," manuscript, 20 May 1944, Box 6, Pickens Papers.
49. See Guzman, *Negro Year Book*, 185–86; Kathryn Williams and Martha Goldman (Pickens's secretaries in the Interracial Division) to the writer, November, 1969; interview with Pickens's colleague, Harold Master, Washington, D.C., August, 1969; interview with Pickens's successor as head of the Interracial Division, Lemuel Foster, New York, December 1969.
50. Pickens, "Position Description." Also see Pickens, "Dollars and Sense," *Opportunity* 25 (Winter 1947): 12–13, 46.
51. Houghteling to Pickens, 29 October 1946, Box 6, Pickens Papers.
52. Vernon L. Clark to Pickens, 8 September 1950, Box 8, Pickens Papers.
53. Pickens, "Position Description," Pickens to Du Bois, 31 August 1950, Box 3, Pickens Papers.
54. Pickens, "American Negro and the Country in World War."
55. Pickens to White, 22 April 1932, Box C–72, NAACP Papers.
56. Pickens to George Schuyler, (?) July 1951, Box 4, Pickens Papers.
57. Pickens to Charles Adams, 6 March 1944, Box 3, Pickens Papers.
58. Schuyler, "The Phantom American Negro," *Reader's Digest* 59 (July 1951): 61–63; Pickens to Schuyler, (?) July 1951, Box 4, Pickens Papers.
59. Pickens to Franklin D. Roosevelt, 9 November 1944; Pickens to Houghteling, 1 March 1945, Box 6, Pickens Papers.
60. Guzman, "The Social Contributions of the Negro Woman Since 1940," *Negro History Bulletin* 11 (January 1948): 88.
61. Pickens to Houghteling, 13 August 1945, Box 6, Pickens Papers.
62. Pickens to Claude Barnett, 10 May 1949; Pickens to Baker and Taylor Book Dealers, 3 June 1949; Jonathan Leff to Pickens, 28 June 1951, Box 3, Pickens Papers.
63. J. Percy Bond to Pickens, 27 September 1951; A. D. Beittel to Pickens, 16 October 1951, Box 3; Benjamin Baron to Pickens, 21 February 1953, Box 4, Pickens Papers.
64. *New York Times*, 7 April 1954; *Defender* (Chicago), 10 April 1954.
65. *Courier* (Pittsburgh), 17 April 1954.
66. A. Philip Randolph to the writer, 30 December 1969.
67. *Courier* (Pittsburgh), 15 January 1940.
68. Pickens, "In Memorium: James Weldon Johnson," *Crisis* 45 (September 1938): 294.
69. William Brewer, *Journal of Negro History* 39 (July 1954): 243.
70. Ibid.; A. Philip Randolph to the writer, 30 December 1969; Walter White, "Along the NAACP Battlefront," *Crisis* 61 (May 1954): 293; Holmes quoted in *Amsterdam-Star News*, 8 May 1954.
71. Washington, *Man Farthest Down*, 386. This aspect of Washington's thought is often ignored. Yet in his most famous accommodationist speech—at the Atlanta Exposition in 1895—he told his white audience:

> Nearly sixteen millions of [black] hands will aid you pulling the load upwards, or they will pull against you the load downwards. We shall constitute one-third and much more of the ignorance and

crime of the South, or one-third of its intelligence and progress; we shall contribute one-third to the business and industrial prosperity of the South, or we shall prove a veritable body of death, **stagnating, depressing, retarding every effort to advance the body politic.**

72. Pickens, "The Negro's Contribution to Democracy," manuscript, 1926, Box 4, Pickens Papers. Similarly, Washington had told a white audience in Chicago in 1898 that, unless racial prejudice was conquered, "we shall have a cancer gnawing at the heart of this republic that shall some day prove to be as dangerous as an attack from an army without or within." Quoted in Meier, *Negro Thought in America,* 107.

73. Pickens, "Educating Negroes for Democracy," *Opportunity* 17 (June 1939): 164–65.

WORKS CITED

Primary Sources

Manuscript Collections

National Association for the Advancement of Colored People Papers. Manuscript Division, Library of Congress, Washington, D.C.

Pickens, William. Papers. Schomburg Center for Research in Black Culture, New York Public Library, New York City.

Spingarn, Arthur B. Papers. Manuscript Division, Library of Congress, Washington, D.C.

Spingarn, Joel E. Papers. The Moorland-Spingarn Collection, Howard University, Washington, D.C.

Washington, Booker T. Papers. Manuscript Division, Library of Congress, Washington, D.C.

Published Works by William Pickens

Books and Pamphlets

Negro Evolution. Talladega, Ala.: Talladega College Press, 1900. Pamphlet.

The Heir of Slaves: An Autobiography. Boston: Pilgrim Press, 1911.

The New Negro: His Political, Civil and Mental Status and Related Essays. New York: The Neale Publishing Co., 1916.

The Negro in Light of the Great War. Baltimore: Morgan College Press, 1918. Pamphlet.

Lynching and Debt Slavery. New York: American Civil Liberties Union Publication, 1921. Pamphlet.

Bursting Bonds. Boston: Jordan and More Press, 1923.

Articles

"Hayti." *Yale Literary Magazine* 68 (April 1903): 232–38.

"What Talladega Is Doing for the Negro." *Missionary Review of the World* 28 (June 1905): 436–37.

"Southern Negro in a Northern University." *Voice of the Negro* 2 (April 1905): 234–36.

"Social Equality." *Voice of the Negro* 3 (January 1906): 25–27.

"Choose!" *Voice of the Negro* 3 (June 1906): 404–7.

"Negro Public Education in Alabama." *Voice of the Negro* 3 (September 1906): 641–44.

"The Educational Conditions of the Negro in Cities." *Voice of the Negro* 3 (October 1906): 427–30.

"Utica." *Independent* 72 (22 February 1912): 404–8.

"The Status of the Free Negro from 1860 to 1870." *Occasional Papers of the American Negro Academy* 18 (1916): 62–70.

"Americanism." *Crisis* 19 (April 1920): 332.

"The Value of the NAACP." *Crisis* 20 (June 1920): 90.

"The American Congo." *Nation* 112 (23 March 1921): 425–26.

"Africa for the Americans: The Garvey Movement." *Nation* 113 (28 December 1921): 750–51.

"Things No Body Believes: A Lesson in Religion." *Messenger* 5 (February 1923): 419–20.

"Political Parties and the Negro." *Messenger* 5 (March 1923): 625.

"Intelligent Christianity: Not the Fear of Hell." *Messenger* 5 (April 1923): 1790–99.

"The Emperor of Africa: The Psychology of Garveyism." *Forum* 70 (23 August 1923): 668–69, 1790–99.

"The Negro and the Community." *Opportunity* 4 (August 1924): 229–31.

"Progressive Political Action." *Crisis* 28 (September 1924): 211.

"Unthanked Workers for Democracy." *World Tomorrow* 9 (April 1926): 119–20.

"The Negro Vote and Allen." *Crisis* 37 (October 1930): 357.

"NRA—Negro Removal Act?" *World Tomorrow* 16 (28 September 1933): 539–40.

"Smashing Tradition in West Virginia." *Crisis* 44 (May 1937): 141–42.

"In Memorium: James Weldon Johnson." *Crisis* 45 (September 1938): 294.

"What I Saw in Spain." *Crisis* 45 (October 1938): 321–23.

"Educating Negroes for Democracy." *Opportunity* 17 (June 1939): 164–65.

"The American Negro Participates in War Finance." *Opportunity* 23 (Winter 1945): 124–25.

"Dollars and Sense." *Opportunity* 25 (Winter 1947): 12–13, 46.

Interviews with the Author

Foster, Lemuel. 16 December 1969, New York City.
Master, Harold. 10 July 1969, Washington, D.C.
Moon, Henry Lee. 18 December 1969, New York City.
Patterson, William. 3 December 1969, New York City.
Pickens, Harriet Ida. 21 July 1968, New York City.
Wilkins, Roy. 18 December 1969, New York City.

Personal Communication with the Author

Baldwin, Roger. Telephone conversation, 11 December 1969.
Bunche, Ralph. Telephone conversation, 11 December 1969.

Dawson, William L. Telephone conversation, 27 November 1969.
Goldman, Martha. Telephone conversation, 3 December 1969.
Gruening, Ernest. Letter, 17 November 1969.
Laidler, Harry. Telephone conversation, 5 December 1969.
Randolph, A. Philip. Telephone conversation, 30 December 1969.
Williams, Kathryn. Letter, 21 November 1969.

Newspapers and Periodicals

Baltimore *Afro-American (-Ledger)*. 1903–10; 1928–30.
Boston *Guardian*. 1902–10.
Chicago *Defender*. 1928–31.
Crisis. 1910–54.
Emporia (Kans.) *Gazette*. 1930.
Kansas City (Mo.) *Call*. 1928–31.
The Messenger. 1920–24.
Nation. 1900–54.
New Republic. 1924–54.
New York *Amsterdam (-Star) News*. 1928–54.
New York *Daily Worker*. 1920–40.
New York Times. 1900–1954.
Norfolk (Va.) *Journal and Guide*. 1928–31.
Opportunity. 1920–47.
Pittsburgh Courier. 1923–54.
Voice of the Negro. 1904–7 (*Voice*. 1906–1907).
Washington Post. 1928–50.

Secondary Works

Books

Allswang, John M. *A House for All Peoples: Ethnic Politics in Chicago, 1890–1936*. Lexington: University of Kentucky Press, 1971.
Aptheker, Herbert, ed. *A Documentary History of the Negro People in the United States*. New York: Citadel Press, 1951.
Balch, Emily Greene, ed. *Occupied Haiti*. New York: The Writers Publishing Co., 1927.
Bardolph, Richard. *The Negro Vanguard*. New York: Vintage Books, 1961.
Beaver, Daniel R. *Newton D. Baker and the American War Effort, 1917–1919*. Lincoln: University of Nebraska Press, 1966.
Blaustein, Albert P., and Robert Zangrando, eds. *Civil Rights and the American Negro: A Documentary History*. New York: Washington Square Press, 1968.
Borg, Dorothy. *American Policy and the Chinese Revolution, 1925–1928*. New York: Macmillan Publishing Co., 1947.
Broderick, Frances L. *W. E .B. Du Bois: Negro Leader in a Time of Crisis*. Stanford: Stanford University Press, 1959.

Brooks, Maxwell P. *The Negro Press Re-Examined: Political Content of Leading Negro Newspapers.* Boston: Christopher Publishing House, 1959.

Burner, David. *The Politics of Provincialism: The Democratic Party in Transition, 1918–1932.* New York: Alfred A. Knopf, 1968.

Carter, Dan T. *Scottsboro: A Tragedy of the American South.* Baton Rouge: Louisiana State University Press, 1969.

Clarke, John H., ed. *Marcus Garvey and the Vision of Africa.* New York: Vintage, 1974.

Conkin, Paul K. *Tomorrow a New World: The New Deal Community Program.* Ithaca: Cornell University Press, 1959.

Cronon, Edmund David. *Black Moses: The Story of Marcus Garvey and the Universal Negro Improvement Association.* 1955. Reprint. Madison: University of Wisconsin Press, 1968.

Cruse, Harold. *The Crisis of the Negro Intellectual.* New York: William Morrow & Co., 1967.

Dalfiume, Richard M. *Desegregation of the U.S. Armed Forces: Fighting on Two Fronts, 1939–1953.* Columbia: University of Missouri Press, 1969.

Detweiler, Frederick G. *The Negro Press in the United States.* Chicago: University of Chicago Press, 1922.

Draper, Theodore. *The Roots of American Communism.* New York: The Viking Press, 1957.

Du Bois, W. E. B. *The Autobiography of W. E. B. Du Bois.* New York: International Publishers, 1968.

Fox, Stephen R. *The Guardian of Boston: William Monroe Trotter.* New York: Atheneum Publishers, 1970.

Franklin, John Hope. *From Slavery to Freedom: A History of Negro Americans.* 3d ed., rev. New York: Alfred A. Knopf, 1967.

Franklin, John Hope, and August Meier, eds. *Black Leaders of the Twentieth Century.* Urbana: University of Illinois Press, 1982.

Garfinkel, Herbert. *When Negroes March: The March on Washington Movement in the Organizational Politics for FEPC.* Glencoe, Ill.: The Free Press, 1959.

Gellerman, William. *Martin Dies.* New York: John Day, 1954.

Glazer, Nathan. *The Social Basis of American Communism.* New York: Harcourt, Brace & World, 1961.

Golden, Harry. *The Right Time: The Autobiography of Harry Golden.* New York: G. P. Putnam's Sons, 1969.

Goodman, Walter. *The Committee: The Extraordinary Career of the House Committee on Un-American Activities.* New York: Farrar, Straus & Giroux, 1968.

Guzman, Jessie P., ed. *Negro Year Book: A Review of Events Affecting Negro Life, 1941–1946.* Tuskegee: Tuskegee Institute Press, 1947.

Harlan, Louis R. *Booker T. Washington: The Wizard of Tuskegee, 1901–1915.* New York: Oxford University Press, 1983.

Hicks, John D. *The Republican Ascendency, 1921–1933.* 1960. Reprint. New York: Harper & Row, 1963.

Hughes, Langston. *Fight for Freedom: The Story of the NAACP.* New York: W. W. Norton & Company, 1962.

Jackson, Kenneth. *The Ku Klux Klan in the City, 1915–1930.* New York: Oxford University Press, 1967.

Jacques-Garvey, Amy, ed. *Philosophy and Opinions of Marcus Garvey.* 1923. Reprint. New York: Atheneum Publishers, 1969.

Johnson, James Weldon. *Along This Way.* New York: The Viking Press, 1933.

Kellogg, Charles Flint. *NAACP: A History of the National Association for the Advancement of Colored Peoples, 1901–1920.* Baltimore: Johns Hopkins Press, 1967.

Kirby, John B. *Black Americans in the Roosevelt Era: Liberalism and Race.* Knoxville: University of Tennessee Press, 1983.

Lamont, Corliss, ed. *The Trial of Elizabeth Gurley Flynn.* New York: Horizon Press, 1968.

Leuchtenburg, William E. *Franklin D. Roosevelt and the New Deal, 1932–1940.* New York: Harper, Torchbook, 1963.

Lisio, Donald J. *Hoover, Blacks & Lily-Whites: A Study of Southern Strategies.* Chapel Hill: University of North Carolina Press, 1985.

Lovett, Robert Morss. *All Our Years.* New York: The Viking Press, 1948.

Mac Kay, Kenneth C. *The Progressive Movement of 1924.* New Columbia University Press, 1947.

Marable, Manning. *W. E. B. Du Bois: Black Radical Democrat.* Boston: Twayne Publishers, 1986.

Martin, Tony. *Race First: The Ideological and Organizational Struggles of Marcus Garvey and the Universal Negro Improvement Association.* Westport, Conn.: Greenwood Press, 1976.

Mason, Alpheus T. *The Supreme Court from Taft to Warren.* 1958. Reprint. New York: W. W. Norton & Company, 1964.

Meier, August. *Negro Thought in America, 1880–1915: Racial Ideologies in the Age of Booker T. Washington.* 1963. Reprint. Ann Arbor: University of Michigan, 1966.

Meier, August, and Elliott Rudwick, eds. *Along the Color Line: Explorations in the Black Experience.* Urbana: University of Illinois Press, 1976.

Meier, August, and Elliott Rudwick. *From Plantation to Ghetto: An Interpretative History of American Negroes* 1966. Reprint. New York: American Century Series Paperback, 1968.

Millspaugh, Arthur C. *Haiti under American Control, 1915–1930.* Boston: World Peace Foundation, 1931.

Montague, Ludwell Lee. *Haiti and the United States, 1714–1938.* 2d ed. New York: Russell & Russell Publishers, 1966.

Moon, Henry Lee. *Balance of Power: The Negro Vote.* Garden City: Doubleday & Company, 1949.

Myrdal, Gunnar. *An American Dilemma: The Negro Problem and Modern Democracy.* New York: Harper & Row, Publishers, 1944.

Naison, Marc. *Communists in Harlem during the Depression.* Urbana: University of Illinois Press, 1983.

Nalty, Bernard C. *Strength for the Fight: A History of Black Americans in the Military.* New York: The Free Press, 1986.

Nye, Russell B. *Midwestern Progressive Politics: An Historical Study of Its*

Origins and Developments, 1870–1958. 1959. Reprint. New York: Harper & Row Publishers, 1965.

Oak, Vishnu V. *The Negro Newspaper.* Yellow Springs, Ohio: Antioch Press, 1948.

Ogden, August Raymond. *The Dies Committee: A Study of the Special Committee for the Investigation of Un-American Activities, 1939–1944.* Washington: Catholic University of America Press, 1945.

Oneal, James, and G. A. Werner, *American Communism.* 2d ed. rev. New York: E. P. Dutton & Co., 1947.

Osofsky, Gilbert. *Harlem: The Making of a Ghetto.* 1963. Reprint. New York: Harper & Row Publishers, 1968.

Ottley, Roi. *The Lonely Warrior: The Life and Times of Robert S. Abbott.* Chicago: Henry Regnery, 1955.

———. *New World A-Coming: Inside Black America.* Boston: Houghton Mifflin Company, 1943.

Quarles, Benjamin. *The Negro in the Making of America.* New York: Macmillan-Collier Publishing Co., 1964.

Record, Wilson. *The Negro and the Communist Party.* Chapel Hill: University of North Carolina Press, 1957.

———. *Race and Radicalism: The NAACP and the Communist Party in Conflict.* Ithaca: Cornell University Press, 1964.

Ross, B. Joyce J. E. *Spingarn and the Rise of the NAACP, 1911–1939.* New York: Atheneum Publishers, 1972.

Rudwick, Elliott. *W. E. B. Du Bois: Propagandist of the Negro Protest.* 1960. Reprint. New York: Atheneum Publishers, 1968.

St. James, Warren D. *The National Association for the Advancement of Colored People: A Case Study in Pressure Groups.* New York: Exposition Press, 1958.

Schlesinger, Arthur M., Jr. *The Age of Roosevelt: The Coming of the New Deal.* Boston: Houghton Mifflin Company, 1959.

———. *The Age of Roosevelt: The Politics of Upheaval.* Boston: Houghton Mifflin Company, 1960.

Schruben, Francis W. *Kansas in Turmoil, 1930–1936.* Columbia: University of Missouri Press, 1969.

Schuyler, George S. *Black and Conservative: The Autobiography of George S. Schuyler.* New Rochelle, N.Y.: Arlington House, 1966.

Scott, Emmett J. *The American Negro in the World War.* Chicago: Homewood Press, 1919.

Shannon, David A. *The Socialist Party of America.* 1955. Reprint. Chicago: University of Chicago Press, 1967.

Sherman, Richard B. *The Republican Party and Black America: From McKinley to Hoover, 1896–1933.* Charlottesville: University of Virginia Press, 1973.

Sitkoff, Harvard. *A New Deal for Blacks: The Emergence of Civil Rights as a National Issue.* New York: Oxford University Press, 1978.

Spear, Allan H. *Black Chicago: The Making of the Negro Ghetto, 1890–1920.* Chicago: University of Chicago Press, 1967.

Spencer, Samuel R., Jr. *Booker T. Washington and the Negro's Place in American Life.* Boston: Little, Brown and Company, 1955.

Stein, Judith. *The World of Marcus Garvey: Race and Class in Modern Society.* Baton Rouge: Louisiana State University Press, 1986.

Sterner, Richard. *The Negro's Share: A Study of Income, Consumption, Housing and Public Assistance.* New York: Harper & Brothers, 1943.

Washington, Booker T. *The Man Farthest Down: A Record of Observation and Study in Europe.* Garden City, N.Y.: Doubleday, Page, 1912.

———. *Up From Slavery: An Autobiography.* London: Alexander Moring, 1902.

Waskow, Arthur I. *From Race Riot to Sit-In: 1919 and the 1960s.* 1966. Reprint. Garden City, N.Y.: Doubleday, 1967.

Weiss, Nancy J. *Farewell to the Party of Lincoln: Black Politics in the Age of FDR.* Princeton: Princeton University Press, 1983.

White, Walter. *A Man Called White.* New York: The Viking Press, 1948.

———. *How Far the Promised Land?* New York: The Viking Press, 1956.

Wilkins, Roy. *Standing Fast: The Autobiography of Roy Wilkins.* New York: The Viking Press, 1981.

Wolters, Raymond. *Negroes and the Great Depression: The Problem of Economic Recovery.* Westport, Conn.: Greenwood Press, 1970.

———. *The New Negro on Campus: Black College Rebellions of the 1920s.* Princeton: Princeton University Press, 1975.

Woodward, C. Vann. *The Strange Career of Jim Crow.* 2d ed. rev. 1955. Reprint. New York: Oxford University Press, 1966.

Articles

Bassett, E. D. C. "Should Haiti Be Annexed to the United States?" *Voice of the Negro* 1 (May 1904): 191–98.

Blair, John L. "A Time of Parting: The Negro During the Coolidge Years." *Journal of American Studies* 3 (December 1969): 177–99.

Boardman, Helen. "The U.S. Treasury Takes a Step." *Opportunity* 19 (August 1941): 238–39.

Brewer, James H. "Robert Lee Vann, Democrat or Republican: An Exponent of Loose-leaf Politics." *Negro History Bulletin* 21 (February 1958): 100–103.

Crowe, Charles. "Racial Massacre in Atlanta, September 22, 1906." *Journal of Negro History* 54 (April 1969): 150–68.

Dabney, Virginius. "Nearer and Nearer the Precipice." *Atlantic Monthly* 171 (January 1943): 94–100.

Fishel, Lesslie H., Jr. "The Negro in the New Deal Era." *Wisconsin Magazine of History* 48 (Winter 1964): 111–26.

Guzman, Jessie P. "The Social Contribution of the Negro Woman Since 1940." *Negro History Bulletin* (January 1948): 86–90.

Harrell, James A. "Negro Leadership in the Election Year, 1936." *Journal of Southern History* 34 (November 1968): 546–64.

Kifer, Allen F. "The Negro Under the New Deal, 1933–1941." Ph.D. dissertation, University of Wisconsin, 1961.

Littell, Robert. "La Follette for President!" *New Republic* 39 (16 July 1924): 201–2.

Lochard, Metz T. P. "Negroes and Defense." *Nation* 152 (4 January 1941): 14–16.

McGuire, Phillip. "Desegregation of the Armed Forces: Black Leadership, Protest and World War II." *Journal of Negro History* 88 (Spring 1983): 147–58.

———. "Judge Hastie, World War II and Army Racism." *Journal of Negro History* 62 (October 1977): 351–62.

Meier, August, and Elliott Rudwick. "Negro Protest at the Chicago World's Fair, 1933–1934." *Journal of the Illinois State Historical Society* 59 (Summer 1966): 161–71.

Murray, Hugh T., Jr. "The NAACP Versus the Communist Party: The Scottsboro Cases, 1931–32." *Phylon* 28 (3rd quarter 1967): 276–87.

O'Dell, Samuel. "Blacks, the Democratic Party and the Presidential Election of 1928: A Mild Rejoinder." *Phylon* 48 (March 1987): 1–11.

Ovington, Mary. "The NAACP." *Journal of Negro History* 9 (April 1924): 107–16.

Record, Wilson. "Negro Intellectual Leadership in the National Association for the Advancement of Colored People, 1910–1940." *Phylon* 17 (4th quarter 1956): 375–89.

Rosenstone, Robert A. "The Men of the Abraham Lincoln Battalion." *Journal of American History* 52 (June 1965): 327–38.

Salmond, John A. "The Civil Conservation Corps and the Negro." *Journal of American History* 52 (June 1965): 75–88.

Schuyler, George S. "The Phantom American Negro." *Reader's Digest* 59 (July 1951): 61–63.

Sherman, Richard B. "The Harding Administration and the Negro: An Opportunity Lost." *Journal of Negro History* 49 (July 1964): 151–68.

Tillman, Nathaniel P., Jr. "Walter Francis White: A Study in Interest Group Leadership." Ph.D. dissertation, University of Wisconsin, 1961.

Tinsley, James A. "Roosevelt, Foraker and the Brownsville Affray." *Journal of Negro History* 41 (January 1956): 43–65.

Villard, Oswald G. "An Honest Convention." *Nation* 119 (16 July 1924): 63.

Watson, Richard L., Jr. "The Defeat of Judge Parker: A Study of Pressure Groups and Politics." *Journal of American History* 50 (April 1963): 213–34.

White, Walter. "It's Our Country, Too." *Saturday Evening Post* 213 (14 December 1940): 27–29.

Zangrando, Robert L. "The NAACP and a Federal Anti-Lynching Bill, 1934–1940." *Journal of Negro History* 50 (April 1965): 106–17.

INDEX

Accommodationist speech, Washington's, 231–32 n.71
"Africa for Africans," 64–66
Afro-American, 176, 180
Afro-American Ledger, 26
Allen, Senator Henry: battle of NAACP against, 106–9
Amenia Conference, 38–40
Amenia Conference, Second, 129, 130–33
American Missionary Association (AMA), 21, 22, 31, 201 n.27
American Negro Academy, 204 n.18
American Negro Labor Congress, 113
Andrews, G. W., 18, 21
Antilynching legislation, 144–45
Antimiscegenation laws, 44
Associated Negro Press (ANP), 10, 55–56
Atlanta "riot," 27
Attacks against Negroes, 36
Avery, Flora Olmstead, 58, 207 n.26

Bagnall, Robert, 96
Baker, Newton D. (secretary of war), 46–47
Bethune, Mary McLeod, 182
Black delegation to Brussels Conference, 116
Black economic progress, 136
Black militants, position of, 41–42
Black press: view on Pickens's shift to Treasury Department, 168–69
Black soldiers: postwar treatment of, 50; separate facilities for, 46–47; training of, 46–47; treatment of, 46
Black Star shipping line, 62, 67
Black support for Republican party, 75–76, 78, 79, 86, 88, 212–13 n.53
Blacks: as executive officers in NAACP, 57
Blue Eagle insignia, 139–40

Boston *Guardian*, 16, 17
"Boston Riot," 17
Bouchet, Edward Alexander, 24
Boulder Dam incident, 145
Break, final: of Pickens with NAACP, 171–72
Brownsville "affray," 27
Brussels Conference: black delegation to, 116

Camp Hill Riot, 128
Campaign, Supreme Court: of J. J. Parker, 98–105
Candidacy of Wendell Willkie, 154–55
Cannon, Dr. George E., 86
Central Committee of Negro College Men, 47
Chicago World's Fair, 135–36
Churchmen, Negro: feud with, 94–95
Civil rights for Negroes, 26
Committee of Eight, 69–70
Committee of Forty, 30, 31
Committee of One Hundred, 31
Communism: attempt to convert Pickens to, 115–18; attitudes concerning, 132, 133; as enemy of blacks, 112
Communist change in attitude toward blacks, 119, 121
Communist party: recruitment of blacks into, 112–13
Communist sympathies: Pickens attacked for, 181–91
Communists: and the NAACP, 121–22; and the Scottsboro case, 122–29
Conference for Progressive Political Action (CPPA), 75, 79
Conflict between Pickens and NAACP main office, 95
Congregational Church, 21

241

Congress: actions by against subversives, 183–91
Contributions to NAACP, 197
Coolidge, Calvin: position of toward Negroes, 77–78
Cooper, James W., 30
CPPA, political platform of, 81–82
Criticism of Franklin D. Roosevelt, 135
Crosswaith, Frank, 161–62

Dabney, Virginius, 190; letter to from Pickens, 175–77
Daily Worker, 122, 123, 127
Dawson, William L.: support for Pickens by, 186
Deanship of Morgan College, 38
Debate against Pickens, 181–91
Defense of Pickens by Treasury Department, 191
Demands of Negroes as outlined by Pickens, 49
Democracy for the Negro race, 49
Democratic party: criticism of by Pickens, 147
Dies Committee, 190, 191
Dies, Martin (representative): and efforts against subversives, 181–87
Discrimination: among workers at Grand Coulee Dam, 151–52
Dismissal from Talladega College, 33, 34
Dogan, M. W., 37, 38; eyewitness account of on the Houston riot, 45–46
Domingo, W. A., 72
Du Bois, W. E. B., 18, 38–39; attempt by to purge White, 89; attitude concerning the war effort, 48–50; break with NAACP, 177; and the Communist party, 113; evaluation of Garvey by, 62–63; issue of "two-ness" of Negro, 44

Economic benefits of New Deal for blacks, 153
Economic concerns of blacks, 130–31
Economic progress of blacks, 136
Economic reform: Pickens's plan for, 140–41
Economic repression: as cause for race clash, 114
Economics: issue of, 28

Education: issue of, 28
Elaine, Arkansas: Negro violence in, 114
EPIC Plan (End Poverty in California), 141
Equality for Negroes, 134

Federal Forum Project pilot program, 150–51
Fess, Simeon D., 104
Feud with Negro churchmen, 94–95
Forbes, George Washington, 17, 18
Ford, Henry, 140
Fort Des Moines, 47
Fort Huachuca, Arizona, 171
Fort-Whiteman, Lovett, 115–16
Fourth Pan-African Congress, 118–19
Franklin D. Roosevelt, criticism of, 135

Garvey, Marcus, 52, 61, 62; appeal to Negroes, 72–73; attack against Pickens, 69, 70; conviction of, 70, 73; evaluation of by W. E. B. Du Bois, 62–63; issues raised against, 65–66; reasons for failure of, 73, 74; relations with Ku Klux Klan, 67–68; setbacks against, 67
Garvey movement: West Indian role in, 71
German fascism: threat to world peace by, 160
Goodwill of white America, 43, 44
Grand Coulee Dam: discrimination among workers at, 151–52
Graves, Harold N. (director of Treasury's Savings Division), 184

Haiti, 16, 77
Haitian misrule, 16, 18
Harding, Warren G.: and the Negro vote, 77–78
Hayti. See Haiti
Hendricks, Joe: and Treasury Department appropriations bill, 183, 184–85, 230 n.13
Hitler, Adolf: Negro role in fight against, 160–62
Hoover, Herbert: and nomination of Parker, 98–105; support of as presidential candidate, 87, 88
Houghteling, James, 168, 184, 193

Houston riot, 45–46
Hunter, Nell, 192
Hunton, Addie W., 60, 208 n.37

Ickes, Harold, 138, 145, 190
Image of the Negro, 41
International Labor Defense (ILD), 122–26
Interracial Division: Pickens as director of, 192–93
Interrelated destiny of two races: Washington's theme of, 198
Intervention into Europe: advocacy of, 159, 160
Intervention in war: Negro support for, 162

"Jim Crow," 36–37
Jim Crow training camp, 47
Johnson, James Weldon, 79, 80

Kansas: test of NAACP political power in, 106–9
Kerr, John H.: defense of Pickens by, 189–90
Ku Klux Klan, 67, 68; and the Negro, 80

La Follette, Robert (senator), as presidential candidate, 75, 81, 83–85
Labor unions and the Negro, 44
Lampkin, Daisy, 163
Leave of absence from NAACP, 174–75
Lifestyle of Pickens and his family, 58–59
Linney, Frank, 216 n.46
Little Rock, Arkansas, 20
Lochard, Metz, 162
Louisville segregation ordinance, 31
Lovett, Robert Morss, 190
Lowry, Henry: lynching of, 114–15
Lynching, 143–44

Marshall, Texas, 35
Metcalf, J. M. P., 21, 31, 32
Military service for Negroes, 44–45
Morgan College, 35, 37, 38, 52; Pickens as first black vice president of, 53
Murphy, J. M., 26
Myrdal, Gunnar, 9, 51, 112, 127–28

National Association for the Advancement of Colored People (NAACP), 31; battle of against Senator Henry Allen, 106–9; blacks as executive officers in, 57; campaign against Parker, 98–105; changes in structure, 57, 59; and Communists, 121–22; contributions to, 197; dismissal of Pickens, 172–73; expansion of to include Pickens, 54–55; final break of Pickens with, 171–72; growth of, 56–57; leadership clash between Pickens and, 163–67; Pickens's relationship with, 90–92; Pickens's work for, 31; political activity of, 77; political activity of employees, 155–58; representation at Brussels Conference, 116; role of in defeat of John J. Parker, 98–105; and Scottsboro case, 122–29; "two-front" policy of, 170; W. E. B. DuBois and break with, 177; withdrawal of from Scottsboro case, 128–29; Youth Council, 164–67
National Conference of Charities and Corrections, 32
National Negro Committee (NNC), 30
National Recovery Act (NRA), 138–39
National Urban League, 53
Navy Women's Auxiliary (WAVES), 196
Negro churches: Pickens's attitude toward, 92–94
Negroes: contribution of to war effort, 50; equality of, 134; and labor, 130–31; new image of, 41; and organized labor, 44; role of in fight against Hitler, 160–62; self-government of, 136–37; status of in armed forces, 170–71; support of for intervention in war, 162; and support of war effort, 170; and violence in Elaine, Arkansas, 114; and vote in presidential election, 83–85
"Negro Evolution," 22–23
Negro Political Union, 75
"Negro Removal Act," 138–39
New Deal: change for blacks as a result of, 153; economic benefits of for blacks, 153; legislation and blacks, 138; Pickens's attitude toward, 137–39; Pickens's involvement with, 150–51

The New Negro, 35, 40, 204–5 n.28
New York World's Fair: and treatment of blacks, 153–54
Niagara Movement, 25, 26, 27
Niagarans, 28

Ovington, Mary, 163

Parker, John J., 218 n.102; appointment to Supreme Court, 89; Senate debate on confirmation, 102–4; debate over appointment of, 98–105
Partisan political activity, 156–58
Phi Beta Kappa, 24
Pickens and White: break in relations with, 162–63, 164; conflict between, 90–91, 96–97
Pickens, William: allegations against as Communist, 181–91; as assistant field secretary of NAACP, 54–56; attitude of toward Negro churches, 92–94; attitude of toward New Deal, 137–38; change in attitude of about race question, 194–95; clash with Robert Vann, 147–49; clashes with NAACP, 58–59; criticism of Democratic party, 147; demands outlined for Negroes, 49; as director of Interracial Division, 192–93; dismissal from NAACP, 172–78; dissatisfaction with NAACP, 59; efforts to convert to Communism, 115–18; as first black vice president of Morgan College, 53; involvement with NAACP, 31; reaction against Garvey, 68–69; retirement activities, 196–97; retirement from Treasury Department, 193–94; as student, 20–21; theology of, 93–94; view of Soviet Union, 117–18
Pickens, Harriet Ida, 208 n.35
Picket line: interracial, 32
Political activity: by NAACP employees, 155–58; of NAACP, 77
Political platform of CPPA, 81–82
Politics: issue of, 28
Postwar period: new options in, 51
Postwar treatment of black soldiers, 50
Presidential convention of CPPA, 79–81

Public education: for blacks, 29; for whites, 29

Quality of education, 29

Race leadership, 9
Race question: America's mission in, 40–41; change in attitude of Pickens on, 194–95; solutions to, 42
Race relations: progress in, 25
Racial separatism, 62
Radicals, 15, 27
Relations with white administration at Talladega College, 32
Republican party: black support for, 53, 75–76, 78, 79, 86, 88, 212–13 n.53
Roberts, Owen J.: as Supreme Court Justice, 110
Roosevelt administration: and blacks, 135
Roosevelt, Franklin D.: attitude of NAACP toward, 142–43; criticism of, 135; Pickens's support for, 195–96; support for from Walter White, 147
Roosevelt, Theodore: and black voters, 75

Sabath, Adolph J.: and his resolution, 187
Savings Bonds Division's Negro section, 168
Schuyler, George, 161, 195, 197
Scottsboro case, 112, 122–29; withdrawal of NAACP from, 128–29
Second Amenia Conference, 129, 130–33
Second World Congress against Imperialism, 120–21
Secretarial help: conflict with NAACP over, 95–96
Segregated camps: support for Pickens's position on, 172–73
Segregated training camps, 170–71
Segregation ordinance, Louisville, 31
Selective Service Act of 1917, 45
Selective Service Act of 1940, 170
Self-government, Negro, 136–37
Sellers, T. J., 176, 180
Shillady, John R., 56, 57

Sinclair, Upton, 141–42
Slaves, runaway, 40, 43
Smith, Al, 87, 213 n.64
Smith, Wilford H., 17
Social equality: issue of, 28
Socialist party: attitude toward, 86–87
Soldier, Negro: status of, 48
South: change in attitude toward, 195; public education in, 29
Soviet Union: black visitation to, 115; Pickens's view of, 117–18
Spencer, John O. (president of Morgan College), 38, 50
Spingarn, Joel, 31, 38, 46, 174
Status of Negro soldier, 48
Student life of Pickens, 20–21
Student strike at Talladega College, 32–33
Subversives: fight against, 182–87
Support for Franklin D. Roosevelt, 195–96
Support for Pickens, 190, 191
Support for Pickens's position on segregated camps, 172–73
Supreme Court, 146
Supreme Court: confirmation of J. J. Parker to, 98–105

Talladega College, 15, 21; Pickens's dismissal from, 33, 34; student strike at, 32–33; white faculty at, 32
Teaching career, 24–25
Ten Eyck Prize, 16, 24
Tennessee Valley Authority, 146–47
Theology of Pickens, 93–94
Trade unionism, 44
Training camps for black soldiers, 46–47, 170–71
Treasury Department: attempted dismissal from, 181–91; Pickens's shift to view of black press on, 168–69; role of Pickens in, 168–70, 171
Treatment of blacks at New York World's Fair, 153–54
Trotter, William Monroe, 16, 17
Tuskegee Institute, 15, 16
"Two-front" policy of the NAACP, 170
"Two-ness" of the Negro, 44

Universal Negro Improvement Association (UNIA), 61, 62; analysis of, 64–66; decline of, 67

Vann, Robert: and clash with Pickens, 147–48
Violence between black soldiers and whites, 45
Vocational education, 29
Vocational training: rejection of Washington's position on, 43
Voice of the Negro, 27–28

Wagner-Costigan Bill, 143, 144, 145
Walker, Mme C. J., 53–54
War effort: Negro contribution to, 50; Negro support of, 170
Washington, Booker T., 15; accommodationist speech, 231–32 n.71; actions by, against Pickens, 37; changes in leadership of, 26; criticism of, 27–28, 31; Pickens's view of, 34; rejection of on issue of vocational training, 43; theme of interrelated destiny of two races, 198
Washingtonians, 28
West Indian role in Garvey movement, 71, 72
White and Pickens: break in relations with, 162–63, 164; conflict between, 90–91, 96–97
White faculty: at Talladega College, 32
White, Walter, 89–91, 110–11, 122, 125; removal of Pickens from NAACP by, 178–79; support for Roosevelt, 147
Wiley College, 35
William Pickens Papers, 10
Willkie, Wendell: candidacy of, 154–55
World peace: threat to by German fascism, 160
World's Fair, Chicago, 135–36
Wright, R. R., Jr., 190–91

Yale University, 16, 23–24
Young Turks at Amenia, 130–33
Youth Council, NAACP, 164–67